The Electronic Traveller

Exploring Alternative Online Systems

Elizabeth Powell Crowe

Windcrest®/McGraw-Hill

New York San Francisco Washington, D.C. Auckland Bogotá
Caracas Lisbon London Madrid Mexico City Milan
Montreal New Delhi San Juan Singapore
Sydney Tokyo Toronto

FIRST EDITION
FIRST PRINTING

Library of Congress Cataloging-in-Publication Data

Crowe, Elizabeth Powell.
    The electronic traveller: exploring alternative online systems/ by Elizabeth Powell Crowe.
        p.   cm.
    Includes index.
    ISBN 0-8306-4498-9 (p)
    1. Wide area networks (Computer networks) I. Title.
TK5105.87.C76   1993
004.6'7—dc20   92-43952
                                                        CIP

Acquisitions editor: Brad Schepp
Editorial team: Robert E. Ostrander, Executive Editor
                David M. McCandless, Book Editor
Production team: Katherine G. Brown, Director
                  Susan E. Hansford, Typesetting
                  Sandy Hanson, Typesetting
                  Ollie Harmon, Typesetting
                  Wendy L. Small, Layout
                  Linda L. King, Proofreading
                  Jodi L. Tyler, Indexer
Design team: Jaclyn J. Boone, Designer
             Brian Allison, Associate Designer   WC1
Cover Design and Illlustration: Sandra Blair Design, Harrisburg, Pa.   4457

To the memory of my father, **Dedication**
James Toxie Powell, Jr.
1926–1992

Soli Deo Gloria

Contents

Part three: Villages of the electronic underground

Appendices

Acknowledgments

Many kind people across the internets gave their time to help with this book.

The greatest debt is owed to Judy Heim, who thought up the project in the first place and held my hand through the worst of it.

To all those who agreed to be interviewed, thank you.

And special thanks to these people and their colleagues who helped in the background:

Mike Chambliss, Cyrus Cathey, Jillaine at the Institute for Global Communications, Robert Adams, Reva Basch, David Brookshire, Tom Czarnik, J. DeBert, Jeff Ehmen, Ian Feldman, David Feustel, Carol Johnson, Karen Storek Lange, Steve LaLiberte, Tony Lockwood, Matisse Enzer, Jim McCullars and the data processing department at UAH, Bob Reiger, Donald S. Retallack, Ph.D., Kathy Ryan, Dave Smythe, Spartan, Morgan Schweers, Scott Yanoff, and Debra Pederson Young.

Any errors in the book are mine alone; I am grateful to all of these people for sharing their views, experiences, and facts of life in the electronic underground.

Acknowledgment is due also to Brad Schepp and Lisa Black at TAB Books for their fortitude and understanding.

Finally, countless lauds also to my family and friends, who were so supportive, patient, and kind.

Introduction
Let's wander down the wire . . . uh, road

A new *terra incognita* has been found. It's somewhat like the Western Hemisphere was in the 1600s: The maps are few, and frequently inaccurate. The maps' perspective may be wrong, and there are regions marked "This way lie monsters." Yet fun, adventure, and even profit can befall those who travel there. A big difference is that no one has (yet!) perished exploring this new region.

That's because it's all virtual. It exists mainly in the minds of the participants, though it definitely has its physical components.

Before the age of every telephone wire's becoming a road to travel, you could think of your community as people living near you, a smaller unit of your larger landscape. But now, in the sense of friendly association and fellowship, your community need not include only those whom you see physically. In fact, it might include people who will never be in the same room with you, and you may come to know some of them better than you know your blood cousins.

You can work with people you have never seen, shop in stores you will never walk into. You can read articles from publications you will never hold in your hand, and submit to those publications, as well. You can use a program on a computer miles away, or you can live the life of another, even imaginary, creature. You can retrieve programs, data files and information you could not gather on your own. Indeed, you might even meet someone through words and later meet in person, perhaps even marry. It's happened.

The phenomenon of communities online has been called the virtual society, the online world, cyberspace, as well as many other names. Although it's hard to label, it's real, growing, and affecting your life whether you participate in it or not. I call it the Electronic Underground because it is so large, and active, and densely populated, yet rarely gets much attention. It should, though. Scientific research, political feedback, and other important but everyday activities are moving online.

In the Electronic Underground, you can play games, carry on conversations, read articles, shop in various stores or buy directly from the manufacturer, play a role, look at pictures, conduct business, and do almost anything else you'd do on a trip, only you don't have to leave your office or house.

It's a fascinating and compelling place because so much of it exists only as thought. Written, sent, and received electronically, these messages may be. Yet, in some sense, it's a very personal way to communicate.

It's a way to be who you wish you were, or even who you know you really are but have trouble conveying that to others face to face (or, in Electronic Underground jargon, F2F).

It's a way to accomplish what might be physically or financially impossible: collaborate with a colleague across the ocean, research the card catalog of a library 1000 miles away, or converse with someone for weeks before she finds out you were born blind, by which time she's used to treating you as "normal" (which, of course, you are).

It's a way to send your careful, considered, and erudite opinions to thousands of people across the world. And to send your worst moments, too.

I must pause here to give some special credit. The idea was originally given to me by Judy Heim. In her *PC World* columns on computers, modems, and how to get the most out of them, she noticed that several choices face the person who would like to sign on to some service or BBS. First of those choices, of course, is whether to visit a mom-and-pop bulletin board or one of the nationally advertised online services.

So you try one or the other and find a definite sense of place. Or maybe a place with nonsense. Anyway, you begin to wonder about some cryptic references to various "nets": Inter, Use, Fido, Smart—the prefixes to net seem to go on and on. What are they? Where are they? *Why* are they?

Well, in the course of this book, I'll visit some of them to find out. I'll go from the Internet (sort of the Rome of this new civilization) to some of the places that are perhaps cozier and perhaps wilder. And even see some places in between. And while I'm conducting this Grand Tour, you might find a place or two you want to visit with your own modem.

Fellow travellers

You will have your own experiences on these back roads, but one experience is universal: You're going to meet new people. Be aware, however, that the modem can bring out or hide a personality; it's often between the lines that the real message hides. But whether their personae are real or imagined, the people you meet will be as interesting as any who travelled with Geoffery Chaucer.

As on any road, the police are here. Alert to the possibility of using the power of connected computers for anything from vandalism to grand larceny to international pornography, several government agencies are watching (and sometimes sparring with) the anarchists here. Just as in any public place, everything is out in the open, and some of it turns out to be illegal.

Professors, teachers, and students are here. The corporate moguls hold conferences with end users, taking away a clear picture of what those users *really* think of their products. The lawyers are here, and the criminals are here. Artists, photographers, musicians and programmers, all travel these virtual highways. You can as well.

But should you decide to ride the wires, where should you go? What should you see? Is there more to the online world than the drawings on Prodigy? And is it something you'll be glad you did?

I wrote this book to answer some of those questions. We'll look at where we'll go in the Overview section. Right now, let's look at logistics.

The things you can do online are still limited to sight, sound, and imagination. Yet those do create a sense of community that is fascinating. I hope you will not get quite addicted to online communities, although it has happened: people have been fired for reading so much online mail and news that they are forgetting to do their jobs. A very popular signature to electronic messages is "It's only a hobby, only a hobby, only . . . ."

Hitching up

Lots of us who travel in the Electronic Underground have a mental image of the online services and boards as three-dimensional places. We think of running the different programs as going into different rooms or as looking in different mailboxes. In our imaginations, some of us see the boards, the forums, the newsfeeds as distinct "places" as different as the house, the park and the office.

In his novels, William Gibson describes what he calls *cyberspace*, and that has become a nickname for the Electronic Underground. In the novels, characters experience places and people without physical contact but instead by receiving signals through a brain implant. This fictional computer transmits sights, sounds, smells, tastes, and textures by fictional software and integrates with the "wetware" (human being) to create a virtual reality. When Gibson's characters break the connection, they experience an alienation from having to deal with plain old reality.

Technology hasn't quite gotten that far yet.

So, lacking Gibson's fictional systems, we will use plain old everyday modems and communications programs. You could think of the modem as the coach and the programs as the horses. First, let's look at the coach. Modems, to the average user, are boxes that sit on the computer or cards that insert into the expansion slots. They translate data to and from sound signals that can go over telephone lines. The speed and variety of modems available today are dizzying to me because I started out with a little old 300-baud Hayes SmartModem 10 years ago. Entire volumes, from textbooks to consumer tomes, purport to tell you what modem is best to buy, so I won't try to get detailed here. Just let me recommend these features:

- Get at *least* a 2400-baud modem, or even one with 14,400 baud if you can afford it. Baud is a measure of how fast the data travels to and from your computer. Many systems won't let you log on anymore at 300 and 1200 baud, which used to be the norm. Another reason for high speed is to minimize your time online: various places you'll go either charge by the hour or have a daily time limit. In early 1993, you can buy a 2400-baud modem for under $100; a 14.4 can set you back $250.
- The highest speed modems use "compression" to make the data go through faster. The methods to do this vary, and the two modems communicating *must* use the same method or nothing constructive happens. The most-often used compression method is V.32, with the very close runner up being MNP. Some modems do both. Buy a modem with at least one of the two most popular standards, or a "dual standard" modem if you can afford it.

- If possible, buy a modem with a communications program bundled with it. This way, you know that your compression method and protocol (two of your horses) will match the capabilities of your modem (coach).
- If you discover a system with especially neat sound effects, or you are into the newest electronic music composition systems, you might want to invest in a sound board. Other than that, your carriage will be complete.

Now, let's look at the horses.

An average communications program is really a suite of software to help you do what you want. The main functions are to let you tell the modem when to pick up the phone, what to dial, how fast to send the data, and when to hang up. Some also let you write small programs called *scripts* to sign onto a favorite place, do what you usually do there, and sign off—all while you go have a cup of coffee or even grab a few ZZZs.

When you decide to upload or download (send or receive) something, you tell the main communications program which "protocol" (a program to transfer data) to use. There are dozens out there with names like xmodem, ymodem, zmodem, kermit, hslink, to name a very few. Your communications program will come bundled with some combination of different protocols; some communications programs allow you to pick up the newest protocol and add it to the list of your available protocols. Like compression standards, the same protocol must be used at both ends of the link-up, or nothing beneficial happens.

Also worthwhile to have along are file compression programs (StuffIt for Macs and PKZIP for DOS are two popular ones.) These make the file to be uploaded or downloaded smaller, making your online time shorter. "Mail readers" are programs that compress a lot of messages you want to read, send them to you, and let you uncompress and read them off line later. Sometimes they come with a communications program; more often you'll download a few shareware mail readers, and register as a user of the one you like best.

"Front End Software" is a program that knows the commands and available features of one specific online service or board. It dials up the service for you and then allows you to choose what you want to do from menus. The actual character string that makes up the command is typed by the program. The idea is to make the service or board easier to use. Many front ends do; unfortunately, a few of them just get in the way.

When you enter some systems, you will sometimes use the horses you find there to get you around; then you will use your own horse to come home. These programs are called *doors*, and you find them when you log on to a system. These programs let you play games, pick the messages you want to read offline, and so on. When you enter a door, the remote system's software steps aside while you do what you want, then steps back in when you're through. Try not to log off a system while in a door; it makes life very hard on the sysop (system's operator).

Using these programs, you can do many things in the Electronic Underground. Some places we'll visit will have online shopping; or a program to let you type messages back and forth with other people who are logged on at the same time you are (called "chat" or "conferencing" or "CB"); or vast message groups (usually called a "forum," sometimes a "conference," sometimes something else) with conversations among many people on the same subjects (called "threads"). The possibilities are limited only by the sysop's imagination; however, many of the things you do in the Electronic Underground have labels.

In 1990, at a seminar on mailing (the old-fashioned way), a local postmaster opened the seminar by saying "Personal messages rarely travel through USPS anymore. It's become a business communication system: advertising, orders, billing, and payments are the main bulk of USPS traffic now. Oh, you get your wedding invitations and so on, but personal letters? Not very often."

E-mail

One might assume that means that people are not writing personal messages to each other. The fact is, they are, but they are not using "snail mail," which is the term that electronic travellers use to describe sending something on paper through the regular mail.

People are instead writing personal communications using electronic mail, which has become so prevalent that even the nickname "e-mail" is fading online and "mail" is coming to mean messages sent from one person to another through electronic means. Any other means of communication needs definition, such as the moniker above, or "voice mail."

It's as simple as a regular letter but faster. It's as fast as a phone call but with a written (or at least computer disk) record. It's generally private (though future court cases will have to prove whether it is protected under the Fourth Amendment to the Constitution; and as far as international messages, who knows?) Communities of folks gather around certain networks, discussing topics dear to their hearts, and getting to know each other in a way that would not be possible otherwise. And did I mention that it's fast?

Suppose you're in a foreign country and you hear some very distressing news about home: the government is falling, or oppressing, or transforming. Do you write home for news of those dear to you? Might take too long. Do you call? Perhaps someone is listening, and perhaps you can't get through because of all the other people doing the same. But, you can get to the nearest university, and borrow their e-mail system long enough to send a message, and get one back, about what is really happening.

This is exactly what happened in 1989, when Chinese officials were trying to keep the Tiananmen Square uprising a secret, and even in 1991 when Gorbachev was being held by those who wanted to stage a coup. When ordinary means of getting the truth out were unavailable, someone posted the news on the Internet.

Suppose you want to sell a CDROM and the discs with it so that you can buy a used laser printer. With the money and time, you could advertise locally and nationally—this for sale, that wanted. A few phone calls later, and within a few weeks, you'll have made the deals. Or, with a Usenet connection, within a few hours you can accomplish the same thing.

Electronic mail has uses in the less-than-personal message, as well.

Suppose you want to let 10,000 people know about an important upcoming scientific seminar, in time for them to plan and budget to attend. Well, the traditional way is to do as in FIG I-1.

I-1 *The old way to send a message to a lot of folks.*

To explain this process briefly, the details are written up, sent to a typesetter, proofread, sent back, corrected, laid out by hand or by desktop publishing, sent to a printer, and printed as flyers. That part takes two weeks, if you are exceedingly lucky. Then the printed pieces are turned into letters and sent to the post office. Now, this part is very tricky. You could use one of three classes of mail, each with such complex, confusing and self-contradictory rules that a postal worker once told me even USPS lawyers can't explain some of them. But suppose you breeze through all that, and get them mailed. Then, trucks and planes deliver it to the 10,000 mailboxes. Best case for delivery: six weeks total.

Now this method has several substantial advantages:

- Almost everyone you would want to reach with this information has a snail mail-box.
- Color, graphics, and photographs of the speakers can be included in your information.
- The hard copy that arrives can be used to register for the seminar.
- The recipient is used to this form; it's friendly and familiar.
- Lots of companies exist just to take the difficult part over for you, and they do good work.
- And if you are a commercial, for-profit organization, it's still the best way.

But consider this: If you are a nonprofit organization, in research or education, or a government agency, you could take that written text file with just the information, and—using an electronic mailing program—get the information to those 10,000 people almost instantly by addressing it to a specific news group, using a mail exploder or simply posting it on the right bulletin boards. See FIG. I-2. Any computer or network of computers, through modems and other transmission devices, can put that text message on any other computer or network of computers which are also on the electronic mail system. The Internet is a term often used for this system.

Best case for delivery: as fast as you can type.

The advantages of snail mail mentioned above are not in e-mail. Pictures, color and graphics clog up e-mail. Not everyone is connected, though in this case your target audience probably will be. It's different, perhaps alienating, to certain groups. It is

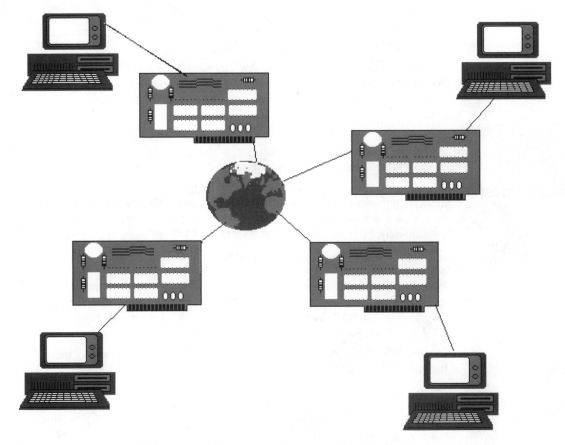

I-2 *This is the Electronic Underground way to send a message to a lot of folks.*

definitely do-it-yourself. And commercial traffic is prohibited on many e-mail connections.

So, the appeal of e-mail is not that there are no rules, complex or otherwise. It is not that there aren't competing pieces of mail for the transportation mode. It's not that it's free: someone somewhere is picking up the tab, through taxes or commercial connections, or both. It's not that it's foolproof; if it doesn't work (bad addresses, etc.) your message bounces back to you, sometimes with a note so terse a postal clerk would be shocked.

It's that such problems are most often solved by the software, "in the dark" to the average user. Computers, supercomputers, phone lines, satellites, and other hardware can handle large volumes of e-mail. Terse notes only come when the software cannot handle the problem; even then some of those terse notes are stored in text files and appended like a form letter to the returned packet, so it is still "in the dark" to the users.

What computer owner alive hasn't wished at one time or another to have more power? (Apologies to *Home Improvement*.) One of the ways to travel the Electronic

Remote computing

Underground is called remote computing, and the command you use is often (but not always!) rlogin or telnet. You might use this to log into a catalog's ordering system, or to look up an address, or to play a game.

It can be complex as a virtual reality site, where several people type messages, or even send pictures, to one another, playing roles in a drama they make up as they go along. The only rule is to stay in your character, which may or may not be your physical reality.

Some disadvantages here: Remote computing is not available at every nook and cranny of the Electronic Underground. It must also be used with caution, as carelessness can cause great grief on the other end, and vandalism can land you in jail.

File transfer

One of the great joys in traveling the Electronic Underground is the varied and interesting treasure hidden there. But taking a treasure home with you is not being greedy, as it will still be there for the next traveller, too. Best of all, if you're good at creating things, you can leave treasures for others to find!

How do you put the treasure in your knapsack, so to speak, and carry it home? That depends on where you have found it. On a bulletin board, you will download it right away, with your favorite transfer protocol. On many of the systems, you will send a message to a faraway computer. The message will contain the magic words, and the genies will deposit the treasure in your electronic mailbox. Well, that's almost what happens! ;-)

[What was that, you say? Why are those punctuation marks at the end of the paragraph? That, dear traveller, is something I'll explain in our voyages!]

And oh, the treasures you'll find! Icons for your Windows, GIF (Graphic Interchange Format, a standard for graphics) files of everything from Saturn to satyrs (and nymphs!). New programs, old program fixes, files describing program bugs that you never would have known about until your system crashed. Threads of messages on compelling topics. (Ok, so maybe cats repel rather than compel you, but the thread can be fascinating!)

But, no journey is without risk. And it is here, in the realm of file transfer, that the dreaded "micro"-organism, the Computer Virus, lurks. Inoculations are strongly recommended before using this mode of electronic travel. The unwary are doomed (or at least their computers are!).

Almost all the places I'll visit will have some version of these functions. Some places specialize in one, ignoring the others. Others try to be all things to all people. I'll go from the unimaginably vast to some that are downright insular. But whether quaint, or exotic or just interesting because you've not been there before, the places you'll find in these pages are worth a look.

Overview: Where we'll go

It is amazing how many people have decided to run a network or bulletin board, thereby using computers and modems to make their work more fun, and their fun (incidentally) more work. Choosing among them is not easy, but choose I had to: I could neither start nor finish the book unless I did.

This book is not going to cover the Big Three of online systems—GEnie, CompuServe, and Prodigy. For one thing, each already has more than one volume dedicated to mapping out their landscapes. For another, they are probably among the few places you have visited if you already have a modem because many modems come with an introductory package to one or all of them. Finally, they advertise nationally, and you can readily find out more than you need to know about them.

For similar reasons I won't take you to the heavy-duty online database research services. They're very expensive and hard to learn; and besides, I'm writing another book about them.

Yet there are other systems, full of wonders and interesting people, that you should know about. They don't advertise very widely; most of them are content to list themselves in the *Computer Shopper*. You almost have to know someone who is already a user to find out about some of them, where they are and how they operate. That's where this book comes in: It's your passport to the lesser-known virtual communities, the Electronic Underground.

I envision our journey as starting in the biggest cities and traveling to the farthest reaches of the empire, to towns and villages. The selection of systems here is very personal, reflecting what I know and enjoy. Although I have not covered, by any means, all the systems worth your notice, I think I have picked a representative sample.

Some of these systems are quite large, and have been around a while, with a cadre of loyal users. Others have just gotten off the ground. But the common theme among them is that they are not immediately visible to the novice electronic traveller. This might be because they don't advertise so widely, or because the sysops there are running the system more for fun than for profit, or because the profits have just started rolling in, or for other reasons. But they all have had some influence on what the Electronic Underground is today.

I'd like to clarify some more terminology before we take off.

Another semantics lesson

A *network* is what happens when several computers connect their CPUs together in some way to accomplish something. In the first section of the book, I'll look at the largest of these, which I'll call the cities of the Electronic Underground. These networks are unbelievably large, and the people and machines hooked onto them are literally on every corner of the planet. Some log on and log off, using them as virtual hotel rooms. Other large computers are the backbone of the networks. These machines are using these networks like apartments: through dedicated phone connections called *leased lines*, they are online all the time. Like an apartment, these network connections are available at any time for as long as the rent is paid.

I do want to point out hastily, dear traveller, that should you want an explicit guide to the Internet, *this is not it*. Ed Krol's *The Whole Internet User's Guide and Catalog*, from O'Reilly & Associates, is the ticket to extended, substantial exploration of this amorphous online entity. I shall merely whisk you through on a nonstop, galloping tour. Lunch is not provided.

Some smaller connections of computers are also called networks. They run over more conventional phone lines or over packet switching networks. These medium-sized towns of the Electronic Underground usually hope to be like the Big Three someday soon in terms of profit and influence. They are based on a set of computers in one place (unlike the "cities," based on computers spread miles or even *oceans* apart from each other) onto which you connect your computer for a while, for a fee.

These towns might have started out small, and may be so yet, but all started with a definite profit goal and a business plan. They were equivalent to planned communities from the start. They also usually started out with more than one phone line connection and more than one computer.

Then, we'll visit the villages of the Electronic Underground. Most of these are bulletin board systems, which will be defined in Chapter 13. Two things distinguish these systems: They usually started out with one machine, one phone line, and one dedicated sysop with a dream. Some of them later wound up with paid staff, computers and phone lines galore, and subscription fees; in other words, all the trappings of the towns and cities.

But others were content to stay smaller, hooking onto a loose confederation of like-minded BBS sysops, exchanging e-mail on a "network." These villages might charge for your visits, but usually only enough to help cover the costs.

So the villages I will visit include three that are just about to graduate to town status and three that are small villages on examples of larger email networks of BBS.

In the back of the book, I have tried to put some practical pointers. With the kind permission of the author, I have reprinted an article that describes a trip around the world using systems just like the ones in this book; an appendix about the Electronic Frontier Foundation; some tips on traveling on the Internet; and lastly, your phrase book, so you won't sound so much like a tourist.

Personal communications are evolving and transforming through systems like these. The Big Three of online services are much like the interstate: fast, reliable and predictable. But the back roads I'll show you here, like the back roads of William Least Heat Moon's *Blue Highways*, while less traveled, may be illuminating.

Part one
Cities of the electronic underground

We visit the largest collections of online communities.

Chapter 1 *The Bouncy, Brilliant Bitnet.* A small network open only to educational and research institutions. Someday your child's school might be connected!

Chapter 2 *The Immeasurable Internet.* All the time, everywhere, people have their computers logged onto the largest network you can imagine. A look at how and why.

Chapter 3 *The Ubiquitous Usenet.* The metaphysical part of the Internet; gossip, articles, messages and essays, around the clock from around the world.

1 The bouncy, brilliant BITNET

E-mail	*listserv@bitnic*
U.S. Mail	CREN Information Center
	Suite 600
	1112 Sixteenth St. NW
	Washington, DC 20036
Phone	(202) 872-4200 [voice]
Hours	24 hours a day
Basic rate	$2,000–$15,000 a year
Notes	Open only to educational and research institutions.

History

Its name, according to legend, came from "Because It's Time Network," or—in other versions—"Because It's There Network." Originally developed by New York City University in 1981, the network's original funding was from IBM, and the protocols and software on it are largely IBM-based. It is said that 3371 kinds of organizations are using this network.

It doesn't aim low: The network makes timesharing and electronic mail services available to universities, colleges, and academic institutions, with an ultimate goal to connect all academic networks in the US and abroad: Kindergarten through graduate school, and the government agencies that serve them. That's all.

BITNET is very popular; mostly university computers and several libraries also hook onto it. A study done in 1989 showed that its growth history proves you can predict how many people jump on the networking bandwagon by the number of existing subscribers and potential future subscribers. The success of BITNET shows, the study said, that the demand for national and international digital communications connectivity is real and growing, though in an S-curve, as technology struggles to keep up with the wishes and dreams of the users.

That nationwide high-speed backbone network we talked about in the Internet chapter—the Federal High Performance Computing Program, intended to link together the nation's biggest networks for more effective applications and information broadcast—is the driving force behind BITNET. Yet, because of its strongly academic flavor and firm emphasis on non-commercial use, it's been a bit of a backwater in the networking geography. And to be truthful, they sort of want it that way for now. Keeps the riffraff out.

The other reason for its odd-duck status is the protocols we mentioned earlier. It started off to the side of the Internet, and somewhat independently. It functions with both IBM and non-IBM computers; gateways and translators have connected BITNET to the Internet, but the transition is not always smooth . . . sort of like rounding the Cape of Good Hope.

Current backbone

When BITNET came under the direction of the Corporation for Research in Educational Networking (CREN) in 1990, the users wanted more than the pledged advisory role in managing the network. In linking up to the proposed backbone network, CREN users must develop the networks on their campuses, the last mile of the federal backbone. They wanted to enhance education on all levels, using the network, and so incorporated a 12-member Board of Trustees representing various elements of academia and industry.

It is now operated by EDUCOM, a non-profit organization that includes roughly 500 universities and colleges. According to BITNET Overview, that includes more than 3300 mini- and mainframe computers, spanning 46 countries. Its European counterpart is called EARN, and a great deal of traffic goes across the Atlantic on BITNET. Nearly 1000 discussion groups are on the BITNET, having from five to several thousand partakers each.

The CREN is open to higher education organizations at the campus level, with dues ranging from $750 per year to $10,000. For-profit members pay from $2,000 to $15,000. Each member is required to allow at least one other to connect to it and operate at least 20 hours a day, 7 days a week. Individuals and organizations not approved by CREN's board are not allowed to be sites.

The heart of the organization is the BITNIC (Network Information Center). Support, routing tables, information, the latest software, and policies come from the BITNIC. BITNIC lists these as advantages to BITNET/CREN:

- The interchange of ideas among the various educational institutions.
- Simpler addresses (as long as you stay within the BITNET!).
- Affordable connectivity, based on an institution's annual budget.
- The many servers on the network.
- Research and input to the developing standards.
- The dedicated volunteers who keep it running, solve the problems, and help newcomers connect and connect well.

Rules

BITNET is a little more conservative than the Internet. They are a publicly-funded organization and very aware of it. The rules are simple, but firm:

I. Thou shalt know thine own system before trying to use BITNET.

II. Thou shalt use BITNET for the purposes and goals of the Network, not your own. In fact, an anonymous send file access site was recently removed from BITNET because the group providing it was peeved with the amount of non-BITNET traffic it was carrying.

III. Thou shalt not interfere with the work of other users. This includes messages that damage other people's work or reputations.

IV. Thou shalt not disrupt the host systems.

V. Thou shalt not disrupt the network services.

VI. Thou shalt not clog the system with chain letters, picayune poppycock, or excessively large files (300K is the current limit).

VII. Thou shalt not advertise, market, resell bandwidth or conduct business on the BITNET. CREN allows you to provide services supporting the needs and purposes of the networks and charge for it, so long as it remains within the limits of the other commandments.

VIII. Thou shalt be aware of, and follow, the laws and regulations of information transfer. The CREN will be most especially p.o.'d over international messages that violate Department of Commerce regulations. They will act on such violations. Like a duck on a June bug.

IX. Thou shalt mind thy manners.

X. Thou shalt stick to the subject of the forum, digest, magazine, etc. Off-subject messages are rarely tolerated. Further, some people have been in deep yogurt over messages like "Thanks for the quickie!" See Rule III.

Who's there

Japan's major computer network for scientific researchers and the developers connected with BITNET in 1992. The Japanese network, called Tsukuba Net, has its host computer in Tsukuba Science City, northwest of Tokyo. It put 700 more researchers of science and high technology on BITNET, and created the potential for more joint research and development projects, including computer hardware and software ventures, between Japan and the U.S.

Hong Kong connected in 1989, when their Hongkong Academic Research Network (HARNET) connected to a leased line at Yale. This allowed about 200 academics, who had been dialing long distance for limited connections, to be a part of what's become *the* way to conduct academic business.

The European Academic Research Network (EARN) is BITNET's counterpart across the big pond. The SUEARN Journal was mentioned in the Internet chapter; many people receive that over BITNET.

As we mentioned, many libraries and librarians are on the BITNET. From card catalogs to newsletters and magazines devoted to library and research, BITNET has become the way to keep on top of information science. A list of catalogs, compiled at the University of New Mexico, is available at *LISTERV@UNMV* (.BITNET).

BITNET is also part dream, part nightmare for academics with ideas to try out. Many a dissertation or published study started out as a discussion on a mail list on BITNET. If the idea is moronic, obtuse, or otherwise dim-witted, the feedback on BITNET will be quick, honest and sure. If it has a grain of importance but the approach is wrong, you'll find the input pouring in. Collaboration by colloquy is becoming commonplace.

"It's become very important to academic life," says Chris Albright, the technical CREN representative at the University of Alabama in Huntsville. "It's a tool few can do without these days. If it goes down, I hear from our users at least twice an hour until I fix it. We're a small university and we get 500 messages a day over BITNET."

Dr. Walt Sullins, professor of psychology at the same school, is a constant user of BITNET. "A BITNET celebrity depends on the list you subscribe to. BITNET is a very focused group, with little overlap between the areas of interest. Communications tend to be person-to-person. But I'd say most faculty use it now. The interchange of ideas with people of similar academic and social interest is the most valuable thing about the network to me.

"It has had a great impact on the academic life . . . the ivory tower is not so isolated," he continued. "It has made academics more aware of the relationship between academia and the real world. It has speeded up some processes, but it has also made people in research more aware of how social issues affect their work, because you're open to more views than just your own campus'.

"But the worst part is that it's so slow, relative to the NSF backbone, I mean. It's still quite fast, mind you. But the limitation on access to the Internet, and its physical structure over slower phone lines, makes it a little harder to use."

At times, working through the night on BITNET, he has seen the postings come in from around the world, time zone after time zone checking in . . . it's neat, he says, to see Europe and Africa, the Mideast and Asia, Australia and Japan take their turns. And as Eastern Europe emerges from the old USSR, bits of information filter in from the Ukraine and Belorusse.

How to log on, how to send messages, how to receive

The system assumes that you are on some major computer, with a resident sysop or manager to ask questions. If you are part of any school with a modem and a computer, you probably can connect, at least by asking the nearest university to let you have a node on their host. Several software packages, some free, some cheap, some dear, give people connection to BITNET. Some of them are as follows:

- **Jnet**. This one shows a DEC VMS machine how to run NJE/RSCS protocol. It is available from Joiner Software, Internet address *JNET@Joiner.com*; BITNET: *JNET@JOINER*; phone (608) 238-8637.
- **PDMF**. This program works with VMS MAIL and Jnet to allow one to communicate with the Internet. It comes from Innosoft International, Inc., Internet:*sales@ymir.claremeont.edu*; BITNET:*SALES@YMIR*; phone (714) 624-7907.
- **MAILER Release 2**. For IBM VM systems, to add some smarts to your local mail program. This is called a Mail Transfer Agent, and it's just to make life easier. It's free from Columbia, Princeton, or Rutgers University.
- **UREP(R)**. This lets UNIX systems connect with BITNET's protocols. Remember, the IP/TCP protocols sprang from the UNIX environment. This is a bridge between the two. To get this one (it's $1200, US) contact *BEEKMAN@PSUVLSI* on BITNET or *beekman@cs.psu.edu* on the Internet.
- **BITNET II**. For the system who has everything, BITNET II was designed for sites on both the Internet and BITNET. Developed at Princeton, it is a new protocol to translate BITNET to Internet back to a BITNET site. Michael Gettes is in charge (*GETTES@PUCC* on BITNET). Now assuming you have the machine, the software, and the permission to use both, where do you go from here?

BITNET has three basic functions: electronic mail, list servers, and discussion lists (forums). BITNET has also interactive messages, called "chat," which we'll discuss in a minute.

Electronic mail on BITNET is pretty straightforward, as long as you don't wander too far from "home" (the actual BITNET itself). First find out how the local mailer software works: Does it ask for address, subject, etc. , or do you have to place each on the message properly yourself? Find out the steps to address, write, and send; put them in writing where you can see them from the keyboard and proceed. Figure out your keyboard pal's address. The easiest way to do this is call: no white pages project has started on BITNET yet.

A BITNET address is typically *PERSON@INSTITUTION*, or if you are sending from Internet, then *PERSON@INSTITUTION*.BITNET. Put that in the "header." Then supply the subject of the message and the text:

SUBJECT: BLACK HOLE IN MILKY WAY—WILL WE FALL IN?
This is the latest data. . . . . .

Note well that if you are composing in a text editor, be certain you have inserted carriage returns after each line (filling your screen across) because the program at the other end might or might not format for your keyboard pal.

Then send the message with the command from your end. Another useful thing about BITNET is the LISTERV e-mail discussion lists. A list is available from *LISTSERV@BITNIC*, from which you can choose interesting-sounding lists to query. If you want to know more about a certain list, send mail to *LISTERV@node* (the interesting one from the list) with no subject and this line of text:

REVIEW *list_name*

Now the answer will come back as "non-mail" that is not in ASCII. Your local computer master must help you RECEIVE the non-mail, according to the quirks of your system. But then you read the review, and decide to subscribe:

TO:*LISTERV@node*
FROM: YOUR BITNET ADDRESS
SUBJECT: Anything or nothing
SUB *list_name "your_name"*

Now, you can read the postings to that list for a while, decide to write someone there, and do as above. Or post something yourself to the whole list:

TO: *list_name@site*
FROM: YOUR BITNET ADDRESS
SUBJECT: Your heart's desire

In general, the mail you send will not echo back to you; you will only see what others have posted.

Documents and other files are on listerv, too. The most popular list server is on BITNIC, and you can find out about them by sending mail to request LISTERV FILELIST. On BITNET, because it is an IBM system, each filename has two parts: file-name file-type. So NETINFO FILELIST is the full name of the list of files on network information.

The format for your request is:

SENDME NETINFO FILELIST

Try this: send some messages to your favorite listserver with these messages in them:

HELP

or
```
INFO PR
```
or
```
INFO ?
```
or
```
SENDME LISTPRES.MEMO
```
You'll get back all the secrets of making LISTSERV serve you. One file you definitely want to get is BITNET USERHELP. It's a take-you-by-the-hand guide to basic BITNET services.

Can you get files FTP from BITNET? Well, there might be a Santa Claus, Virginia, but there is no standard for requesting FTP via E-mail. Therefore, the commands used at one site will not necessarily work with others.

BITFTP is one mail interface; it is the FTP portion of the IBM TCP/IP product ("FAL") on the Princeton VM system. It lets BITNET/NetNorth/EARN users FTP FILES from sites on the Internet. BITFTP speaks only to RFC822-format mail, IBM NOTE-format mail, PROFS-format messages, or files with no headers at all.

BITFTP returns the requested files as NETDATA-format files or as mail files in UUENCODE. If you specify "UUENCODE" or "NETDATA" on your "FTP" command, BITFTP will try to use that format. If you do not specify the format, BITFTP will try to choose the format for your node. VMS users should specify BINARY F 512 and should use RECEIVE/BINARY to receive the NETDATA-format binary files BITFTP sends them.

The files you request will be sent to you in NETDATA format or UUENCODED inside mail files.

Sometimes, BITFTP will send you a file that you cannot read. Before you panic, THE FIRST THING TO DO is to make sure that you specified ASCII if the file should be words or that you specified BINARY if the file should be binary data, executable programs, tar files, or the like. You can do this easily, because you'll get a return message. In that mail file, you'll find a secret code:

>   Your original commands
>>   Your commands as interpreted by BITFTP and passed to TCPIP
>>>   Your commands as interpreted by TCPIP and passed to the remote host
<<<   Messages from the remote host
>>>>   Completion messages from BITFTP

Suppose you want to use BITFTP from CIS. Send CompuServe Mail containing your FTP commands to the address:
```
BITFTP@PUCC.BITNET
```
The first command to BITFTP must be "FTP" or "HELP".

The recommended syntax for FTP requests is
```
FTP hostname
USER username password [or ANONYMOUS]
<other ftp subcommands>
QUIT
```

After the hostname on the FTP command, you tell BITFTPT the format you need the files to be in, say "UUENCODE" or "NETDATA." (If the username is "anonymous", no password is required; BITFTP will use your userid and nodeid as the password.)

Note that on many systems passwords are case-sensitive; that is, the password might be required to be in lowercase or mixed case or uppercase. (The same is true of directory and filenames.) The following is an example of an FTP request:

```
FTP f. ms. uky. edu
USER anonymous
CD /pub/msdos/Games
DIR
BINARY
GET robotron.arc msdos.robotron
QUIT
```

BITFTP uses a subset of the FTP subcommands provided in the IBM TCP/IP and uses the same syntax. The currently supported subcommands are:

ACCT   To send host-dependent account information.
         Format: `ACCT account-information`
ASCII   To change the file transfer type to ASCII.
         Format: `ASCII`
BINARY   To change the file transfer type to image.
         Format: `BINARY <FIXED record-len> <VARIABLE>`
CD   To change the working directory.
         Format: `CD directory`
CLOSE   To disconnect from the foreign host.
         Format: `CLOSE`
DIR   To get a list of directory entries.
         Format: `DIR`
EBCDIC   To change the file transfer type to EBCDIC.
         Format: `EBCDIC`
GET   To get a file from the foreign host.
         Format: `GET foreignfile <localfile>`
         If you specify `localfile`, it must be in the forms
         `filename. filetype` or `filename`, and the `filename` and
         `filetype` may each be no more than 8 characters long and may not
         contain periods.
LOCSTAT To display local status information.
         Format: `LOCSTAT`
LS   To list the files in a directory.
         Format: `LS <name>`
PWD   To print the working directory.
         Format: `PWD`
QUIT   To disconnect from the foreign host.
         Format: `QUIT`
STATUS   To retrieve status information from a foreign host.
         Format: `STATUS <name>`
SYSTEM   To get the name of the foreign host's operating system.
         Format: `SYSTEM`
TYPE   To specify Image, ASCII, or EBCDIC file transfer.
         Format: `TYPE <I|A|E>`

If BITFTP is unable to connect to the host you specify, it will send you mail after the first attempt, but will keep trying at intervals over three days. The only additional mail files you will receive will be when the connection is made successfully or when BITFTP gives up after three days.

The load on BITFTP is often very heavy, and network backlogs are often so great that it might take several days for a file to get to you once BITFTP sends it. Be patient and don't send multiple requests for the same file; you'll just congest the system.

Questions about BITFTP and suggestions for improvements should be directed to Melinda Varian, *MAINT@PUCC* on BITNET or *MAINT@pucc.princeton.edu* on the Internet.

Interactive Message ("CHAT") on BITNET is like CB on CompuServe. It requires that you and your keyboard pal both are connected simultaneously. Like a telephone conversation, it interacts between two people. (RELAY is how more than two people send real-time messages; more on that later.) If your intended target is not online, your message disappears. The syntax depends on which software is running on your computer, but usually it's SEND or TELL or something like that:

```
SEND person@institution "Where is the Black Hole?"
```

And that's about all, because you can only SEND (TELL) one line at a time, about 78 characters.

To get a file from another computer with Message, it's something like:

```
SENDFILE MyFILE Info person@institution
```

Now, RELAY lets the same thing happen with more than two people. Relay is a server, and each user signs on to one nearby. You can pick a channel, much like a citizen's band radio. You must first tell the relay server who you are:

```
TELL RELAY AT MYUNI /Register MY-NAME
```

and you "sign on" with your handle:

```
TELL RELAY AT MYUNI /SIGNON NETHEAD
```

Then using SEND or TELL as appropriate to your local machine, you can "broadcast" (so to speak) your one-liners to others on that channel.

All messages will be prefixed by the handle of the one sending it. As I am a faster talker than typist, I've never found this sort of online chat as useful as a telephone conversation. For one thing, you rarely finish a sentence of more than one line without someone else "walking" over your type. It gets most confusing. I once read an abstract of an article about how RELAY was *the* major security threat to the network, but I find it more annoying than threatening.

Message and Mail can both be used to get things from servers. Servers are programs, up and running always, waiting for requests. They have a mail address just like people do; but they do the easy stuff like send repeatedly requested files so that people can get some work done.

They respond to commands like tell and send, and you send mail to the server with commands. A request for a file that lists all the files will usually be your first message or mail to a server. Second, you might ask for HELP on that particular server, because they do vary slightly. Third, you can ask for a specific file listed on the response to the first message, using the commands you got by sending the message HELP.

We told you earlier BITNET has not yet launched a White Pages system. The closest thing they have are user directory servers, but they are disparate, dispersed, and disorganized. An institution *can*, but doesn't have to, have a list of people on it, with an occasional reference to disciplines, interests, or topics. If you know a person's real name, if you know that person's institution or school, and you know there is a user directory there, you have a chance of finding that person's BITNET address through the directory server—if that person registered. The syntax will be something like:

```
TELL [or SEND] NAMESERV AT PLACE SEARCH/NAME Keyboard-Pal
```

Name servers also can help you connect with people who have similar interests. You could send the message

```
TELL [or SEND] NAMESERVE AT PLACE SEARCH/FIELD BLACK HOLES
```

(you could use up to five keywords after field). You'll get back a list of people at that place who registered interest in black holes. To register yourself, pick the name server of choice and send the message:

```
TELL NAMESERVE AT PLACE REGISTER Your-Name keywords
```

As Prof. Sullins mentioned, one of the best things about BITNET is keeping people with similar interests in contact with one another with a minimum of travel and hassle. This is most often done by the forums, digests and magazines.

Forums, digests, & magazines

A forum is an automated mailing list with a specific subject. From aliens to COBOL to economic theory, you can find a forum on BITNET, with professionals, amateurs, dabblers, and innocents chiming in their views on various topics, posing questions, and posting answers. Anyone on that mailing list can send mail to a server (remember, that's an automated program to take care of things so that people can do important stuff) on a specific machine. The server explodes that mail all over the list, so to speak. Headers from forums will list the server as the return address, and it is to the server that responses should go.

All that openness is a two-edged sword. You can get all the information on laser research you wanted, but also hear the latest laser jokes, which you might not have wanted. In some forums, you could spend all day just reading the postings. And you probably have better things to do. In response to that, some subjects have "digests." In this setup, the server stores all postings to the forum subject on a moderator's machine. When that person has time, or wants to, she wades through the postings, editing and condensing, then sends it on to the mailing list. This greatly reduces the amount of mail over the lines. But due to vacations, job changes, flu season, and the like, digests can vary in their timeliness and effectiveness. The digest lives and dies by the moderator's graces.

Electronic magazines have all the features of print ones except pictures (and the advertising!) They are organized into departments, written by people who feel they have some expertise, and sent out only to those who request them. Frequency depends on the subject and the urgency the editors feel about getting it out.

Before we leave the realm of BITNET, we should point out that the BITNIC has a plethora of helpful files. If your BITNET connection is a university, the technical information or member CREN representative should be able to give you a copy of the basic documents. They are also available (for reasonable photocopying fees) from

CREN Information Center
Suite 600
1112 Sixteenth St. NW
Washington DC 20036
(202) 872-4200

Though BITNET is considered a small, isolated part of the Internet, it is important for this: a whole generation of college students, from liberal arts to quantum physics majors, are this minute using BITNET for their academic, social, and even sometimes spiritual pursuits. When they leave academia for the "real world," they might not expect employers to supply MTV, but they will cry "I want my NET!"

2 The immeasurable Internet

E-mail	*nsfnet-Info@nic.merit.edu* [Internet]
U.S. Mail	NSF Network Information Service Merit, Inc.
	2901 Hubbard, Pod G
	University of Michigan
	Ann Arbor, MI 48109-2016
Phone	(313) 936-3000 [voice]
Hours	All the time, everywhere
Basic rate	Depends on how you connect

I call it immeasurable because its "size" is fluid, changing each minute. When trying to understand the Internet, remember The Blind Men and the Elephant: No matter what part you hook onto, you don't have the whole story.

The Internet is UNIX-based but not UNIX-bound. And despite its use of UNIX, an AT&T product, it is an open system. That is, the specifications for using it are public domain, and anyone can build some software to communicate across it. It is private in places, public in places, and commercial in some places (but only in a very limited, restricted sense). Telling you all the things it is would take only a little longer than telling you the things it isn't.

Where it is

The Internet is everywhere, but not everyone is aware of it. That's because it is really a collection of networks, and few of the individual networks are famous. Also, in the past it was a somewhat exclusive club because you could only connect if you were heavily involved in research or education *and* heavily involved in computer telecommunications. Few people are both. The granddaddy of the Internet was the Advanced Research Projects Agency network (the legendary ARPANET), which from 1969 to 1990 was the central backbone of the Internet. In 1969, it (ARPANET) was the Internet. By 1980, all the major universities and research centers had signed on. By 1990, it had metamorphosed into the NSFNET (National Science Foundation Network) and all its children, cousins and acquaintances. A recent document, RFC1296, reported on Internet's growth from 1981 to 1991. It included this graph, FIG. 2-1.

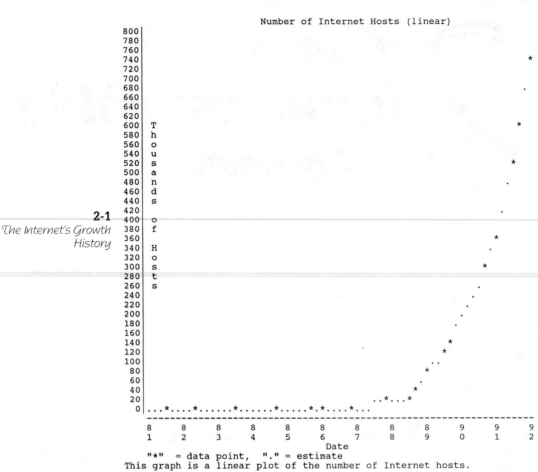

2-1

The Internet's Growth History

Number of Internet Hosts (linear)

"*" = data point,   "." = estimate
This graph is a linear plot of the number of Internet hosts.

Who's in charge here?

An article quite famous in Internet circles appeared in *InfoWorld*, February 4, 1991. "Just Who Owns the Internet?" by Sharon Fisher, postulated that lots of people own a piece of it, but no one owns the whole. Ownership, of course, can be defined as who foots the bill, in which case NSF and the state of Michigan and several major corporations have a claim, as we'll explain in a minute. Or one could define ownership as who controls the purposes for which it may be used. Under the precept "Them that does the doing gets to do the saying," then, the users themselves, whether or not they are paying for the infrastructure, can be seen as the owners. If this sounds like power to the people, that's just the way many Internetters like it. As we'll see, the freedom to say what one likes is cherished on all parts of the net.

Lest you think this enjoyment of anarchy means the Internet is out of control, let us hasten to note the existence of The Internet Society, chartered December 1991. A board of trustees was appointed at that time: Juergen Harms, Robert E. Kahn, and Kenneth M. King. These men were to oversee election of a new board in late 1992.

The society is a nonprofit organization for the following educational, charitable and scientific purposes:

- To facilitate and support the technical evolution of the Internet as a research and education infrastructure, and to stimulate the involvement of the scientific community, industry, government and others in the evolution of the Internet.
- To educate the scientific community, industry, and the public at large concerning the technology, use and application of the Internet.
- To promote educational applications of Internet technology for the benefit of government, colleges and universities, industry, and the public at large.
- To provide a forum for exploration of new Internet applications, and to stimulate collaboration among organizations in their operational use of the global Internet.

So the formerly open, freewheeling Internet seems to be growing up to an extent, although Little Orphan Internet is hardly wearing a three-piece suit.

Freewheeling though it is, Internet definitely isn't free. The connectivity takes a lot of hardware, software, labor, and telephone charges. This is paid for, as we noted, by some corporations and some public institutions.

Not a free ride

Congress funded it $93,000,000 for Fiscal Year 1992; even more, private companies have kicked in research, hardware, and labor to get it to the point where 45 megabits per second can pass through on some connections. Your average user won't get to use those, though.

University students who get hooked onto the Internet while completing their studies are loathe to give up the connection when going into the "real world." They often make a net connection a condition of accepting a job, and so their company pays for the connection. If your company or university has a connection, you probably feel it is comparable to the telephone or copier: something you use to make life easier, and something you don't expect the individual to be charged for per use. This might change soon.

"It's not always going to be free [to the user]," says Donald S. Retallack, Ph.D. As the Boeing specialist who runs the Alabama Supercomputer Network, he is verily a power user of the Internet, as well as an example of a private company helping to keep the Internet useful and well-used. "There are hidden costs. UAH picks up the tab for my connection to the network. It's like the library, a part of the university's overhead. Parts of the Internet are supported by our taxes. It is not per use now and that might change."

Retallack sees a day when digital switching might come to homes, allowing home access to the Internet. For say, $40 a month, you could have phone lines comparable to the local universities, getting you the network newsfeed whenever you want.

"It would allow me to do this from my home and vastly change how I work," Retallack said. "The problem with current voice grade lines is the speed. ISDN will change that, and change the Internet and how we work drastically. It's coming within 10 years."

An important Internet document, Request for Comments (RFC): 1206, explains it this way:

> The Internet is a large collection of networks (all of which run the TCP/IP protocols) tied together so that users of any of the networks can use the network services provided by TCP/IP to reach users on any of the other networks. The

Internet started with the ARPANET, but now includes such networks as NSFNET, ARPANET, NYSERnet (New York State Educational Research Network), and thousands of others. There are other major wide area networks, such as BITNET and DECnet networks, that are not based on the TCP/IP protocols and are thus not part of the Internet. However, it is Internet via electronic mail because of mail gateways that act as "translators" between the different network protocols involved.

Note: You will often see "internet" with a small "i". This could refer to any network built based on TCP/IP, or it might refer to networks using other protocol families that are composites built of smaller networks.

--- Gary Scott Malkin
--- April N. Marine

Which is only a beginning of an explanation.

The landscape of the Internet

The more than three million users have compared it to a (insert "giant" before each of these) brain, bulletin board, telephone system, mailbox, highway. All these terms imply transporting information from one place to another. The users also acknowledge it as a community of uneven terrain: environs of intellectuals, suburbs of sanity, regions of researchers, and outposts of the outrageous.

The Alabama Supercomputer Network, which connects major research centers concerned with supercomputers, is an environ of intellectuals. In a physically real community, this would be one neighborhood with very expensive houses surrounded by very high fences with guard dogs. The exclusivity is very evident here.

Suburbs of sanity would be represented by the commercial connections to Internet. While no commercial traffic is to traverse the Internet proper, selling connections to Internet is not only permitted but seen as the wave of the future.

Advanced Network and Services Inc. (ANS) was formed in June 1991 to supply one of the many business connections to Internet. Charging institutional network subscribers $300,000 per year for high capacity service and $55,000 per year for the slow (1.5 megabits a second) stuff, it is a consortium made up of MCI Communications Corporation, IBM, and Merit Network Inc. The presence of such powerful communications players should tell you the game is definitely afoot! Their competitors, places like PSI, Connect, Inc., and Portal, were started by Internet users who saw a need unmet in the marketplace. Giants like ANS move in when such small guys prove they were right. It's all part of the "privatization" of the Internet, which is the wave of the future.

Some information industry analysts have predicted that ANS's presence in the commercial Transmission Control Protocol/Internet Protocol and network services area will be one catalyst to change the previously exclusive Internet network into a national computer-backbone network. The Internet network, which now has connections spanning overseas, is becoming the National Research and Education Network (NREN). NREN will be a fast network for academic users and researchers, funded by the High Performance Computing Act of 1991. Now we have two sides to that question: can or should government pay for and develop this instead of private enterprise? The answer seems in the middle, with government handling the research end and private enterprise handling other traffic.

An example of the researcher's regions would be NASA's Spacelink. This is an unusual Internet address: one that is available ONLY through telnet. It does not accept or send FTP or e-mail. Though it can be dialed directly [at (205) 895-0028], teachers on the state of Texas' educational network, to name just one, can use an Internet address to get there:

> *spacelink.msfc.nasa.gov*
> *xsl.msfc.nasa.gov*
> *192.149.89.61*

Once on, they can download lesson plans on living in space, the latest press releases from NASA, .GIF images[1] from Hubble, Voyager, and Magellan, and programs for simulating space experiences. NASA Spacelink's connection is very limited; once in, you cannot connect to other NASA computers! But it is full of online, free information on space activities. The Saturn .GIF files are especially striking. Resources such as this were VP Albert Gore's vision when he wrote the HPCA of 1991 as a senator.

Though designed with education in mind, NASA/Spacelink is available to any users with access to the Internet or a modem. They have 32 TELNET ports.

In early spring 1993, the sysops were developing a File Transfer Protocol (FTP). You can use KERMIT protocol to try it out. Right now, only XMODEM or YMODEM will download the GIF files and programs over regular phone lines; you cannot do it through the Internet, or as their help file on the subject puts it, "Please don't attempt to download with XMODEM or YMODEM via the Internet. You'll lock up the Spacelink port you're using and nobody will be able to use it until we see what you've done and unlock the port manually. When we implement FTP, we will fix this problem."

So, if you want to use XMODEM or YMODEM (which are types of file transfer protocols), you'll need to call NASA Spacelink directly. But through the Internet, you can download great text files. When universities and other educational groups approached NASA about designing networks to offer teachers and students access to the services available on the Internet, it became clear that connecting to the Internet would reduce access costs for NASA/Spacelink's target audiences, teachers, and students. NASA/Spacelink reaches the Internet via the Southeastern Universities Research Association Network (SURAnet), a regional network that is under the National Science Foundation Network (NSFNET).

Graphics, high and low resolution, are available through Internet. Figures 2-2 and 2-3 are from NASA Spacelink.

An example of an outrageous outpost is furry. What is furry?

"Heh heh . . ." writes Morgan Schweers, a participant. "Furry fandom is a subset of science fiction fandom that is mainly oriented towards anthropomorphic animals (animals similar in shape to humans). FurryMUCK is a virtual reality dedicated to furry fandom. (Almost all the people there are in the form of one type of furry or another.) Furry can be used to refer to the fandom, a fan, or even a creature who *IS* anthropomorphic. The main attribute of a furry (referring to the actual being) is that it have fur. That's about it . . . *grin*

· · · · · · · · ·
[1]GIFs are high-resolution graphic files.

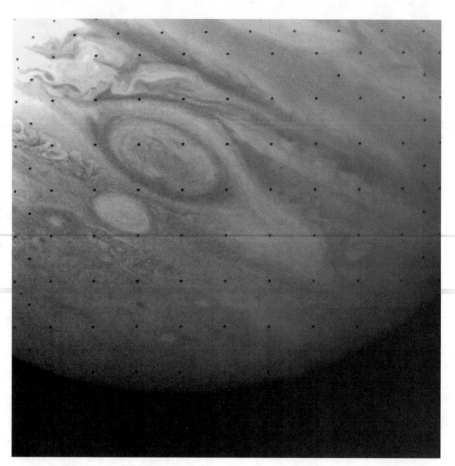

2-2
This can be downloaded from NASA Spacelink, but only by direct dialing the (205) 895-0028 number.

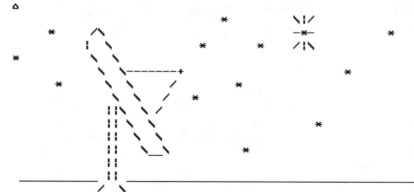

2-3
Some low-resolution graphics are on NASA Spacelink too.

A radio telescope allows scientists to view the universe
in wavelengths other than visible light.

"To get onto FurryMuck, you can use the 'telnet'[2] program, and type `telnet 128.2.254.5 2323` and it will connect you. Registration is necessary on Furry, but you can use the 'guest' account to go in and look around.

"Yeah, the Internet does have a lot of fun people!"

We've mentioned that the Internet crosses many boundaries, some of them political. The Space Physics Analysis Network is an example, as scientists from all over the world connect to it, post to it, and use it for trying out ideas they might one day publish. JANET and JUNET are connections that span the oceans, the former to the U.K., the latter to Japan. Business, science and education are conducted over these connections.

SUEARN has become the hot spot on the Internet since the political upheaval in what used to be the Soviet Union. The dearth of infrastructure in the Eastern European nations has held it back, but it will soon be a big player in the matrix of networks spanning the globe. (See FIG. 2-4.)

```
◆  File  Edit  Setup  Connect  Fax      Alt-H for help   VT100  2400-8-N-1

Newsgroups:   bit.listserv.su-earn
*****  *    * ******  ****  ****** *    **      ****  SUEARN-L is the weekly
*      *    * **      **  ** ** ** ** **  **     ** ** digest for discussing the
*****  *    * *****  ****** ****** ****** *** ** **  ** ongoing work on connecting
  *    *    * **      **  ** ** ** ** **  **     ** ** the USSR to Internet.
*****  ****** ****** **  ** ** ** ** **    *    ** ** Moderator: M.A.Meystel

This digest contains:

* Tutorials *

  X.25/X.400 (Steve Goldstein)

* Announcements *

  Electronic Networking (Joe Ryan)
  Rel-EAST (Esther Dyson)
  Communications Privacy (John Gilmore)

* Articles *

  On-line in the Soviet Union (Werner Klotzbuecher)
```

2-4
A sample header from SUEARN, an Internet newsletter.

It might not be stretching to say any country with telephone connections has at least one Internet connection. Connection to these international nets might be restricted in some cases because some of them are through very expensive connections (satellites and such) and they don't really want hobbyists on their connections.

But judging from the Internet's history, that might not be avoidable!

Experienced users will point out that the Internet is a great tool but is still easily frustrating sometimes. Looking up an address is not easy. The latest address list can be out of date in minutes. Users get frustrated by the syntax of the addresses; especially with the confusion of symbols in the addresses, things get hairy pretty fast. One wrong character in the address sends it to the wrong place as surely as one

The basics

• • • • • • • • •
[2]Telnet is a program to log onto another computer, using it as you would your own.

number dialed wrong in a phone number misdirects your call. Considering the vast amount of machines on the network, though, the system works surprisingly well.

Let's talk about Internet addresses. For e-mail, it's the one point you must understand. All addresses on e-mail are made up of the local part, the person's own mailbox, and the host part, generally the machine that will receive the message for the person. Even to people very used to the internetworks, address formats look chaotic, even haphazard. Well, they are.

The @ form of addressing is the most common. These addresses are signed from Internet's headquarters and look like this:

```
local-part@domain-name.type
```

or

```
###.###.##
```

The standard @ (commonly pronounced "someone at something dot something") is the first. A typical address is *elizabeth_crowe@cup.portal.com*, which roughly translates as Elizabeth Crowe at the Cupertino connection of Portal, a commercial system. By the way (or BTW in Internetese), technically that domain name describes a mail exchanger, not a machine name. Another common address might be *jstudent@cs.purdue.edu*, or Joe Student at the computer science department of Purdue, an educational institution system. So to interpret the most common address, assume everything before the @ is about the person (or server) receiving the message, and everything after is about the place. The final part will be the top level domains:

com	commercial organizations
edu	educational institutions
gov	governmental institutions
int	international organizations
mil	military groups
net	major support centers of the networks
org	miscellaneous organizations, usually research centers

Now those words, abbreviated as they are, are for human convenience. The machines use them only briefly, translating them quickly to a set of corresponding numbers. The numbers are what the TCP/IP program uses, and if you know the numbers and want to use them directly as in the Furry address above, that works great. But if another net is needed to relay the message to your recipient, then it might require other separators than the @. This is where the chaos begins, because many systems with different address schemes hook onto the Internet. For example,

::	Digital's EASYnet, and in this case, the format is `host::user`, the opposite of the Internet standard.
!	This is called "bang" and is used in the UUCP network. It often strings together the route the message must take to get to the user, instead of letting the system decide the path. A chain of hosts (not to be confused with heavenly hosts) in this format could look like this: `host1!host2!host!user`
%	This is sometimes put in as part of the user's definition, as everything on the right of the @ is considered locally important but not domain important. So, a university might assign a syntax of

```
guysname%lit@biguni.edu
```
You might have to combine syntaxes to cross networks such as `guysname%host.uucp@uunet.uu.net` to go from Internet to uucp, or `uunet!domain!user` to go the other way.

Which syntax to use? Well, the best bet is to ask the person to whom you are addressing the mail what the correct address is. Still, the most common, and most likely scheme, is the @. An excellent work to read is a document called

```
Subject: FAQ: How to find people's E-mail addresses
Followup-To: poster
Date: Thu, 7 Nov 1991 08:00:42 GMT
Archive-name: finding-addresses
Version: $Id: finding_addresses,v 1.17 91/10/28 19:32:30 jik Exp
$
```

This is available in the TELECOM forum at CompuServe, and on Portal.

For all that it seems omnipotent, mysterious and exclusive, the Internet exists for three functions . . .

The sending and receiving of private(?) messages, be they letters, files, or data. It is meant for short files. This is the most common use of the Internet, or any small lowercase internet. You would be amazed at the number of offices that simply close down when the e-mail doesn't go through. Usenet is the total of the mail and news that travels over the Internet. Sometimes e-mail is stored and forwarded, sent as traffic allows. In other cases, it is even more direct than a phone call, with the sending machine connecting to the receiving machine. An example of this: Logging onto Netcom (a commercial service we'll visit later) one Saturday morning, I decided to try an experiment. Using the "forward" command, I sent one letter in my file folder onto my address on Portal (another service). Now, keep in mind these are both in Southern California. (See FIG. 2-5.)

E-mail

```
Send the message to: elizabeth_Crowe@cup.portal.com
To: elizabeth_Crowe@cup.portal.com
Subject of message: Re: Help (fwd)
Copies to:
Please choose one of the following options by parenthesized letter:
e)dit message, edit h)eaders, s)end it, or f)orget it.
Send
Sending mail...
You can use any of the following commands by pressing the first character;
d)elete or u)ndelete mail, m)ail a message, r)eply or f)orward mail, q)uit
To read a message, press <return>. j = move down, k = move up, ? = help
Mail sent!
```

2-5
Sending the letter . . .

A few keystrokes later, I was logged onto Portal and found what's shown in FIG. 2-6.

Pretty good, but we're talking across town; well, almost. So let's try another experiment. From CompuServe, in Ohio, using their Internet connection, I addressed a letter to myself on Delphi in Cambridge, MA. (See FIG. 2-7.)

And then I signed on to Delphi to find what's in FIG. 2-8.

Now these are examples of best case. On many bulletin board nets, the store and forward feature will be used: late at night, the bulletin board dials a net host and

```
21313.13.-1.37 Re: Help (fwd)
2/1/92 07:50 libbi@netcom.netcom.com (Elizabeth Crowe)
Lines 1 to 14 of 66 (21%)
-----
Received: from portal.unix.portal.com by hobo.corp.portal.com (4.1/4.0.3
   1.7) id AA02274; Sat, 1 Feb 92 07:49:54 PST
Received: by portal.unix.portal.com (1.171) id AA12581; Sat, 1 Feb 92
   07:49:53 -0800
Received: by nova.unix.portal.com (5.65b/4.1 1.78) id AA16131; Sat, 1 Feb
   92 07:49:50 -0800
Received: from netcom.netcom.com by netcomsv.netcom.com (4.1/SMI-4.1)id
   AA00342; Sat, 1 Feb 92 07:50:16 PST
Received: by netcom.netcom.com (4.1/SMI-4.1)id AA07239; Sat, 1 Feb 92
   07:50:15 PST
From: libbi@netcom.netcom.com (Elizabeth Crowe)
Message-Id: <9202011550.AA07239@netcom.netcom.com>
Subject: Re: Help (fwd)

To: elizabeth_Crowe@cup.portal.com
-----
```

2-6

…And receiving it.

```
≡                     CompuServ  Information Manager
   File   Edit   Services   Mail   Settings   Special
                                                              18:20
┌──────── Name ────────────────── Address ────────
    To:   Electronic Traveller____   >INTERNET:etravel@delphi.com__ CC: 0
 Subject: Will it work?_____

 Can this message go from Compuserve to Delphi?




   Out Basket      Send Now    [ ] Receipt        File It       Cancel

 F1=Help  F3=Done Editing  Ctrl+U=Undo  Esc=Cancel
```

2-7

Going from Ohio…

```
MAIL>

   #1         27-FEB-1993 19:27:40.51                        NEWMAIL
From:   IN%"70007.5075@CompuServe.COM"  "Elizabeth P. Crowe"
To:     IN%"etravel@delphi.com"
CC:
Subj:   This is a test

Return-path: <70007.5075@compuserve.com>
Received: from ihc.compuserve.com by delphi.com (PMDF #3207 ) id
   <01GV87E214U0935TG5@delphi.com>; Sat, 27 Feb 1993 19:27:16 EST
Received: by ihc.compuserve.com (5.65/5.930129sam) id AA12493; Sat,
   27 Feb 93 19:27:06 -0500
Date: 27 Feb 1993 19:19:01 -0500 (EST)
From: "Elizabeth P. Crowe" <70007.5075@CompuServe.COM>
Subject: This is a test
To: <etravel@delphi.com>
Message-id: <930228001900_70007.5075_CHM74-1@CompuServe.COM>
Content-transfer-encoding: 7BIT

Can this message go from Compuserve to Delphi over the Internet?

MAIL>
```

2-8

…to Virginia

deposits mail. Quickly, it also picks up mail with the bulletin board's address. Then it hangs up. Similarly, the host will later dial a hub, and do the same thing. On it goes until working hours the next day. Then the mail waits on some disk until the working world's telnet, FTP, and e-mail is done for the night and it starts up again. If you'll notice, every e-mail message has a "header" that is a record of when, where, and how the message was sent and received. And reading those, you will see this is still usually faster than what habitual e-mail call "snail mail" (USPS).

Still, USPS has certain advantages. You cannot directly e-mail a check, for example, or your signature (unless you count faxes as e-mail, which some people do). But you can send a picture, scanned into the computer as a graphics file, and programs, *and* almost any text. Yet, and this is important, almost any file over 40K will tie up someone's phone lines, and some of these will be bounced back to you. This is because some nodes on the Internet have placed a limit on how many bytes can go through their connection, and they bounce back anything over the limit. Generally, these are non-profit nodes who have to watch their phone bills, even the Internet connection, carefully. Really large files of text or graphics or code must be sent snail mail.

Another USPS advantage is privacy, protected by the Constitution.

Now are e-mail messages private? That depends entirely on how you hook onto the Internet. Generally, a university's Internet administrator acts as postmaster, sending the proper mail from the machine that receives the mail to the desk of the recipient. As a practical matter, it would be hard for the administrator to read each e-mail message and still get any other work done. But as a security matter, he has the ability. Further, going through a government net, it is entirely probable that someone can read an e-mail message. On commercial nets, you must ask the management how they handle privacy. Policies change. If you posted to the Usenet on some newsgroup, you probably have given your message more widespread exposure than shouting it from your rooftop. We'll cover what that means to your reputation later.

Online zines

Many electronic mail publications have sprung up on different subjects. One example, and there are hundreds, is the MeckJournal, which describes itself this way:

MeckJournal, which is available at no charge to interested parties, is the latest service to be offered to Internet/Bitnet users. Issues will include an editorial, late-breaking news, and either a forthcoming feature article from a Meckler journal, a chapter from a forthcoming technology book, or a contribution from a Guest Editor.

Individuals with access to the Internet/Bitnet can receive issues of MeckJournal two different ways. A subscription to MeckJournal may be placed by sending a message to *Meckler@tigger.jvnc.net* with the following information in the body of the text:

```
Subscribe MeckJournal [Internet or Bitnet address]
```

Subscribers will automatically receive each monthly issue and other information as it is published.

Internet/Bitnet users may also access the journal through the following method: telnet to *nisc.jvnc.net*, and then type `nicol` [lowercase] at the logon prompt. No password is needed.

Another is the Merit/NSF newsletter called The Link Letter. To subscribe you send a message `subscribe yourname@yourhost.domain` to *nsfnet-linkletter-request@merit.edu*. You can also get back issues through anonymous FTP.

FTP, or file it right here

This is a direct file transfer protocol from one computer to another. The principle is the same as sending a CompuServe text file or downloading a shareware program from a local bulletin board. It is really not for use by humans but by programs, but it is interactive to a point (you can type `help`, for instance). This transfer of non-ASCII files from one site, through several others, to another can be by request of the receiver or a command from the sender. This is how NASA scientists get the latest data from telescopes, how a university professor in the U.S. can write a paper with one in the U.K., and how you can get the historical documents (RFCs) on the Internet and other networks. Also how public domain software travels, as well as viruses and worms. BEWARE!

In FTP, you are manipulating not only your computer but also the one to which you are logged on. And vice versa. Therefore, on a commercial connection, you USUALLY do not get real FTP; instead you send a mail message with the FTP request in it, to which the computer responds with a mail message.

"Real FTP goes over the lines in real time," says Carol Johnson of Portal. "You truly are connected. And we can't resolve the security problem of that to our satisfaction. So ours is a different system: you put in your request and it's sent later on the store-and-forward system."

Anonymous FTP is the term for signing onto a computer on the Internet and copying specific public files there. Generally these systems accept "anonymous" for the user name and "guest" or your last name for the password. An anonymous FTP can be real-time or a mail message, with the response sent to you back by mail. The following example is from Jerry Martin of Ohio State University, in his RFC1290, shown here:

```
FTP Internet-computer-name
When prompted for a userid, type anonymous
When prompted for a password, type your e-mail address
To get a listing of files, type dir
To change directory type, cd directory-name
To get a file, type get filename
To get a binary file, type binary, then get filename
To end session, type quit
```

Example

```
FTP pilot.njin.net
Username: anonymous
Password: yourname@computer.edu
cd pub/FTP-list
get FTP.list
quit
```

Telnet or RLOGIN

Telnet lets you run someone else's computer from your own. In effect, your terminal, wherever it is, is directly using the machine at the other end of the connection[3]. According to Steve Rubin (*support@netcom.com*), Technical Support Staff, Netcom-Online Communication Services, the syntax for telnet on Netcom is

```
telnet site.domain
```

• • • • • • • • •

[3]This is so you can play a game, order something, run a program that they have and you don't, or even look up a file or someone's address on a different machine.

For example,

```
telnet netcom.netcom.com
```

You could capture it locally using

```
telnet site.domain | tee capture.file
```

The commands will be similar but subtly different on different systems.

Specific sites allow certain parts of their system to be used this way. They are usually the archie systems; more about them later. Almost any Internet connection can theoretically be used this way.

"You can get to the door and knock," says Jim McCullars, a FIDOnet administrator. "But unless they have given you the key, you can't get in." However, it has been done.

In 1990, a computer vandal broke into a DEC site through the Internet, wreaking havoc. The experts said the problem was not the Internet but the individual systems on it: lax security systems and people using passwords found in the dictionary (or worse, their names!) The problem is endemic: the passwords are only as secure as the people who use them.

Despite the common security problems, Internet users despise nothing more than someone who abuses them, using another system without permission. If the site you use is not an archie or an anonymous FTP site, and you crack in, well, your name is mud. It's considered the most obnoxious, irresponsible thing to do, even if you did no harm beyond a sneering message that you got through the security system.

If you have ruined something, prosecutions are not unheard of. You probably remember the worm incident where a young man found himself in deep yogurt over a program that worked better than he expected at invading other systems. As John Dryden said, "Beware the fury of a patient man," especially if you have misused the system they have worked so hard on and for.

Yet, there are places where the stranger is welcome. Just a few of the places where anonymous connections are allowed:

Come on in

* Special Internet Connections: *

* Compiled By: Scott Yanoff *

- Archie telnet *quiche.cs.mcgill.ca* or *132.206.2.3*.
  Offers Internet anonymous FTP database. (Login: archie)
- Cleveland Freenet telnet *freenet-in-a.cwru.edu* or *129.22.8.82*.
  Offers USA Today Headline News, Sports, etc . . .
- Dante Project telnet *eleazar.dartmouth.edu* or *129.170.16.2*.
  Offers Divine Comedy and reviews. Login: 'ddpfrnet', password: 'freenet'.
- Geographic Name Server telnet *martini.eecs.umich.edu 3000* or *141.212.100.9*
  Offers Info by city or area code (Population, Lat./Long., Elevation, etc).
- Ham Radio Callbook telnet *marvin.cs.buffalo.edu 2000* or *128.205.32.4*.
  Offers National ham radio call-sign callbook.
- IRC Telnet Client telnet *bradenville.andrew.cmu.edu* or *128.2.54.2*.
  Offers Internet Relay Chat access.
- Library of Congress telnet *dra.com* or *192.65.218.43*.

Offers COPY of Library of Congress (Assumes terminal is emulating a vt100).
- Lyric Server. FTP *vacs.uwp.edu.*
  Offers lyrics in text file format for anonymous FTP downloading.
- Oracle. mail *oracle@iuvax.cs.indiana.edu.*
  Offers The Usenet Oracle! Mail with subject as "help" for more info.
- PENpages. telnet *128.118.36.5.*
  Offers Agricultural info (livestock reports, etc.) Login as 'PNOTPA'. Prefers your terminal to be emulating a vt100.
- UNC BBS. telnet *samba.acs.unc.edu* or *128.109.157.30.*
  Offers: Access to Library of Congress and nationwide libraries (login: bbs). Assumes your terminal is emulating a vt100.
- WAIStation. telnet *hub.nnsc.nsf.net.*
  Offers on-line documents. (login: wais) FTP *think.com* for more info.
- Weather Service. telnet *madlab.sprl.umich.edu 3000* or *141.212.196.79.*
  Offers forecast for any city, current weather for any state, etc.
  * NOTE: NO LOGIN NAMES OR PASSWORDS ARE REQUIRED UNLESS STATED OTHERWISE! *
  * Don't forget port numbers (example: the 3000 in Weather). *

--

--

```
 __      MILWAUKEE, WISCONSIN
! !/\_!\   A Great Place By A
!! _ !!_  Great Lake
!_! !! !!_ __ @_ __
! !! !! !! !__ _ @ __ ___ yanoff@csd4.csd.uwm.edu yanoff@miller.cs.uwm.edu
!!! _!! ___ __=ll_ ___ yanoff@convex.csd.uwm.edu yanoff@elvis.csd.uwm.edu
!! !! !____ _ \___/
!! !! __ __ __ ____ __ Computing Services Division
~~~~~~~
```

Not the guy in the comic books!

Now, what is an Archie? UNIX and Usenet people are more than happy to explain: Archie is a database manager. The data are names of files and the Internet addresses of machines that contain them. One accesses an "archie" site directly using the "FTP" program, or the telnet program. An FTP example is:

```
ftp archie.domain.address
```

The system responds by asking your name. You type anonymous. The system will use its standard ok and ask for a password. You type guest. The system will ok that. From there, you can type help, or else type get followed by the name of the file you want (for example, get RFC1118).

The system will tell you it's doing that; and when it's finished, you get the FTP> prompt. You type close. It says goodbye, or some such, and you type quit.

One can also use telnet: Telnet <closest archie server>. For example,

```
telnet archie.sura.net
```

would connect you to a server in College Park, Maryland. Login as user ARCHIE; no password will be asked for. Now type prog <topic>. If you wanted to find a file with Novell in the name, then type

```
prog novell
```

This will search the database and produce a list of every location that contains the word "novell." The list will include filenames and directories. Now, if you do not have Internet access with telnet, you are not totally out of luck. You can send a mail message to *archie@quiche.cs.mcgill.ca* with "help" in the body of the message to find out how to access archie via mail. Mail access to archie might not be as useful as the interactive access, but you will still be able to get some things.

By now, two big questions are in front of you: If you are not a UNIX user, how do you get the programs to do this? Further, how do you know which files to ask for if you have the programs?

Translation, please

Happily, many places now have MAC and DOS versions of these programs. On CompuServe, look in the UNIXFORUM, or TELECOM, or IBMFF, using the keywords FTP, TAR and INTERNET. On Portal, as will be explained later, you can use their system to do all the mysterious UNIX part. Or, you can sign onto Netcom or PSI to use their UNIX programs without having it yourself. On some bulletin boards you also will find small system versions of the programs you need.

It is important to note the form of these files. You can have a program mailed to you, but it will first be translated from ASCII. The program to do this is called "uuencode," and the name is often used as a verb. The program to undo the translation is called "uudecode," also a name often used as a verb. (You don't have to mangle the English language to be a telenetter, but it does seem to help!)

And this might be the place to mention tar, shar, and compress. They are programs to make files smaller, helping the transmission process. Like uudecode and uuencode, these programs started out UNIX and were rewritten for MSDOS, TurboC, MacIntosh, Atari, and many other systems.You can check your local user's group or CompuServe for the latest versions.

The program tar (all lowercase) is the most common archiving program. It can be used for text or for program files, most commonly the largest ones. Another program, shar (all lowercase), is only for text; it will damage executables. It uses a shell to extract the archive created with shar. Non-UNIX users need a program called unshar, as well. Finally, compress is a UNIX program that usually comes with the UNIX packages these days. All these programs help make the transmission of files faster and more efficient.

A good place to begin learning about these programs is the CompuServe UNIXFORUM. Download and study README.TXT in Library 2.

An important detail for those using DOS systems: if you get a file in the e-mail created on UNIX, you will notice something strange. Where DOS puts a CR-LF, UNIX puts only LF. You will generally need to fix this, manually or with a public domain program. One such is the program LineFix Package (FL20.ZIP, which unzips to CHR10.EXE v1.0 and CHR13.EXE v1.0) by George Spafford, and there are others. This is especially important in a file you are trying to compile, but it makes a text file considerably less annoying, too.

Now as in any culture, the Internet has a legacy of literature. Some of this is must reading, while some will merely enhance your enjoyment.

Must reading includes RFC1206, quoted earlier. As it says, almost everyone who ever signed onto the Internet had the same questions at first. RFC1206 is a collection of these (along with the answers) for beginners and intermediate users. Some of it won't make any sense until you have done some trial and error. Simply apologize profusely to those offended by your mistakes and move on. 1206 is available on CIS, in several forums. Telecomputing is a good place to start.

Required reading

Another important document is E. Krol's "The Hitchhiker's Guide to the Internet," RFC1118. (Also recommended is Krol's "The Whole Internet Guide and Catalog," O'Reilly and Associates). RFC1118 is more technical than it seems because it is written in a conversational style, as if you were in the room with Krol and he were looking over your shoulder as you stumble through. A sample:

> The Hitchhiker's Guide to the Internet is a very unevenly edited memo and contains many passages that simply seemed to its editors like a good idea at the time. It is an indispensable companion to all those who are keen to make sense of life in an infinitely complex and confusing Internet, for although it cannot hope to be useful or informative on all matters, it does make the reassuring claim that where it is inaccurate, it is at least definitively inaccurate. In cases of major discrepancy, it is always reality that's got it wrong. And remember, DON'T PANIC. (Apologies to Douglas Adams.)"

It goes on like that at some length. This document is available on almost any system with an Internet Connection. Look in America Online, under Computing and Software Department, Computing Forums, Telecommunication and Networks, Browse Individual Libraries, Miscellaneous and Text. On CIS, look in the TELECOM Forum Libraries with `Brow=all key=Internet`. Or send a request to any archive site for RF1118.TXT. (See an example below.)

Another must read is "Dear Emily Postnews", which will be on many systems under different names such as MANNERS.TXT. The file identifies itself as:

> Original-author: brad@looking.on.ca (Brad Templeton)
> Archive-name: emily-postnews/part1

Brad Templeton also serves as sysop for the Comedy RoundTable on GEnie. A satirical look at what not to do, this file is worth the time to get. It is on Compuserve, Portal, and Netcom, and can be retrieved with a request to an archive. It starts out:

> **NOTE: this is intended to be satirical. If you do not recognize it as such, consult a doctor or professional comedian. The recommendations in this article should be recognized for what they are—admonitions about what NOT to do.

A similar article is called MISSMANN, which is a Judith Martin-style satire on the same subject.

Information, please

Typically, much of the important stuff about how to connect is on the Internet. As it is all written by those who are connected, and stored in archives that are connected, one would think it difficult to find if you are not connected. However, there are ways of making them talk . . .

One is to call NSFNET Information Services at (800) 66-MERIT for names and administrative contacts for mid-level networks. Another is to call NSF headquarters at (202) 357-9717. But if you have any electronic mail capability outside your own building, you can use e-mail to contact them.

To obtain information on how to connect to the Internet through the NSFNET or an NSF-affiliated network, send the following mail message to the mail-server *info-server@nnsc.nsf.net*:

Request: NSFNET
Topic: CONNECTING

To obtain information on the documents currently available on the NSFNET from the info-server, send the following mail message to the mail server *info-server@nnsc.nsf.net*:

Request: NSFNET
Topic: NSFNET-HELP

Other RFCs you want to read are:

RFC-1175   A Bibliography of Internetworking Information
RFC-1173   Responsibilities of Host and Network Managers
RFC-1207   Answers to Commonly asked "Experienced Internet User"
Questions
RFC-1208   Networking Glossary of Terms
RFC-1290   There's Gold in them thar Networks!

These RFCs can be obtained by anonymous FTP from *nic.ddn.mil* or via e-mail server from *nisc.sri.com*. To use the RFC e-mail server, send an e-mail message with the subject line showing the RFC you want to *mail- server@nisc.sri.com*. The NIC service will e-mail the requested RFC back to you.

Source:

Anonymous FTP to nis.nsf.net
cd rfc
get $index.rfc
get RFC1118.TXT-1
get RFC1175.TXT-1
get RFC1173.TXT-1
get RFC1206.TXT-1
get RFC1207.TXT-1
get RFC1208.TXT-1

You can look up a person's address on several computers. The following is from "There's Gold in them thar Networks!" from Ohio State University:

```
WHOIS - E-mail white pages
```

WHOIS is a program available on many workstation/mini/mainframe computers that can connect to another computer. By supplying a person's name, it will respond with information it has on the person. A similar program called finger does the same type of thing, except it only supplies information on individuals with an account on that specific computer. Whois generally is operating on a database containing most of the individuals at the university, not just on the machine you connect.

The following is a list of universities that have a whois service working. It is not, by any means exhaustive, and I would be interested in knowing about others that might exist so I can add to this list.

The Ohio State University

Telnet to osu.edu or
Use Whois command whois -h osu.edu

Enter firstname.lastname
Example: `whois -h osu.edu jerry.smith`

University of Oregon

Use Whois command whois -h oregon.uoregon.edu
Enter firstname.lastname
Example: `whois -h oregon.uoregon.edu Rose.Smith`

University of Virginia

Use Whois command whois -h whois.virginia.edu
Enter lastname, firstname middlename
Example: `whois -h whois.virginia.edu Smith, John James`

University of Pennsylvania

Use Whois command whois -h whois.upenn.edu
Enter lastname, firstname
Example: `whois -h whois.upenn.edu Smith, Judy`

University of Wisconsin

Use Whois command whois -h wisc.edu
Enter firstname lastname
Example: `whois -h wisc.edu Jane Smith`

MIT

Use Whois command whois -h mit.edu
Enter firstname_lastname
Example: `whois -h mit.edu Robert_Smith`

Indiana University

Use Whois command whois -h iugate.ucs.indiana.edu
Enter firstname_lastname
Example: `whois -h iugate.ucs.indiana.edu Gerald_Smith`

end of quote from "GOLD"

PSIlink also has a "white pages" function that we will examine in another chapter.

Some Internet lore

Now all of this works quite well, and it might seem that it was always that way. Not so, dear reader. It took a great deal of teeth gnashing and garment rending for this system to get where it is today. For example, the privacy issue is with us and won't go away. Internet standards committees are working on privacy issues all around the world. The European Community is ahead of their North American counterparts, but sooner or later there will be international rules about how and when electronic mail can be read. But for now, your privacy is up to you.

Because replying to mail is so very easy (push a button and you're on!) you must consider well the message's origin and exactly to whom your reply will go. If you reply to a message on a forum, often the default reply is set to send your thoughts to all members of the forum. Be careful what you ask for in sending e-mail messages; you WILL get what you requested, whether or not that's what you wanted.

Just to cite one example, once upon a time, a forum message from the Government Documents forum was forwarded to a faculty member interested in the message's topic. He replied to the message, and added a postscript asking for a copy of a "Twin Peaks" episode. By replying to the forum at large, instead of only to the person who forwarded the message, he accidentally sent his whole text, including the postscript, broadcast to the entire Government Documents Librarians' forum. Now, not all librarians lack a sense of humor; still some on the forum thought "Twin Peaks" was a little frivolous for that network's discussion. Others, however, overlooked this obvious (but innocent) breach of their culture, and offered to supply the tape! So the moral of this little tale is to avoid what's been called "enter key regret." Understand your system, and be careful where you post. In replying to a message forwarded from a bulletin board, forum or newsgroups, start a new message to the person who forwarded it, or you'll send the same message to the whole forum.

This brings us to a serious note. E-mail is not strictly private. Your message can be edited and forwarded by anyone who receives it, with your name still attached. Further, if your message crosses privately owned lines, the owners of those lines might decide to inspect it. This is a gray area of the law with shadows longer than the light. Once you send a message out there, it's public property.

Watch your language

The Electronic Communications Privacy Act of 1986 offers some protection. But although it has some privacy protection against the government's interception of electronic communications while in transmission and government's unauthorized intrusion into e-mail stored on a system, the court cases have held that companies may look at anything on their equipment and systems. Outsiders to the company are not allowed access, you understand, but if the messages are on a company's system, they're as open to examination as stuff coming out of the copier or taped from a phone conversation. Two court cases—one involving Epson, one involving Nissan— have held that employees fired for what they said in e-mail messages did not have their privacy rights violated. So, company snooping and Big Brotherism are entirely legal, especially if the company has published a policy that it intends to do so.

An eye-opener to another bit of e-mail history is *The Simple Book* by Marshall T. Rose (1990). If you want to be a user but not a mover and shaker on the Internet, skip the middle part of this book, written for graduate-level programmers. But read the Foreword, Preface, and Introduction, then read the chapter "The Future."

Rose details (in the areas marked with a soap box) what might be called the Standard Wars. To quickly sum up Rose, who writes from substantial experience, the Internet was growing even as those using, running, and designing it were arguing on how and where it should go. Different groups flung their standards into the fray, each proclaiming to have found the Holy Grail of a truly useful protocol standard. This led to some mind-numbing exercises in futility, according to Rose, and some of it has yet to be resolved. The many committees running the Internet (and we won't go into them here) have a checkered efficacy record, some doing wonders and blunders, some merely reading documents and tossing sops to different factions, some doing both at different times. But in all, Rose concludes that "The 90s should be a productive and exciting time for . . . internets of all kinds!"

Make it so.

3 The ubiquitous USENET

E-mail	*info@uunet.uu.net*
U.S. Mail	UUNET Technologies, Inc.
	3110 Fairview Park Dr., Suite 570
	Falls Church, VA 22042
Phone	(800) 488-6384 [voice]
Hours	24 hours a day
Basic rate	About $40.00 per month, depending on volume.
Notes	It's everywhere; this is just a place to get started.

Remember the game "Gossip?" One person whispers to another and the comment goes around the room. . .

USENET is the result of a game of gossip gone wild on certain business computers using the UNIX operating system. It is a system, a program, and an institution all at the same time.

The USENET is the message and news part of the overall Internet. The Internet is much more than text, but USENET is all text. While the Internet is physically a set-up of computers, wires, satellites, and phones, the USENET is simply a bunch of text that travels specific pathways on the Internet. The Internet is physical; the USENET could be considered metaphysical. It is the software and keystrokes to communicate person-to-person, while the Internet is machine-to-machine.

"It [USENET] is not a hardware thing at all," says Carol Johnson of Portal, one of the USENET connections. "It's all these ideas flowing all around the world, all these great conversations."

USENET is comprised of e-mail, and articles, all sorted into hundreds and hundreds of "newsgroups," which are sort of like magazines (you subscribe) and sort of like late-night dorm discussions and sort of like a symposium. Its flavor depends on newsgroups you subscribe to. There are seven major newsgroups:

- COMP, for computer-science related topics.
- SCI, for science not related to computers.
- NEWS, for network software topics of interest to system administrators.
- REC, for recreation.
- SOC, for social interaction and discussion of social issues.
- TALK, for talking to others.
- MISC, for miscellaneous items.

More about these later.

Tom Czarnik, who is administrator of FTP on the Internet, says ". . .let's make a distinction between Internet and USENET. Internet has come to mean the sum of the regional nets, while USENET is a system for the exchange of newsgroups, mostly via UUCP. . ." It's also sort of like those clubs you started in your neighborhood as a kid: secret passwords, code names, magic words, and a special way of talking that only the "in" crowd understands. However, it's more democratic and less snobbish than a kid's club. A bit.

You might have heard of USENET and not realized it. Chinese students on USENET in North America communicated with the folks at home in May 1989. They were able to get the news of what was really happening and to tell the media in the US.

We were invaded by the dreaded "worm" in 1988. How many people use USENET? In 1989, there were 16,000 sites and over half a million users. It's still growing.

USENET got started, according to legend, in 1979, when a group at Duke University in North Carolina wanted to exchange data on research with some other universities. This group was in on the ground floor of the development of UNIX, an operating system. (This story holds that UNIX is a pun on a preceding program called MULTICS. . .Get it? MULT. . . UNI. . .) Anyway, soon they had written programs in UNIX to allow them to exchange data and analysis back and forth to other universities running the same programs.

In some cases, they even began to do remote logins—that is using someone else's computer as you would your own, from a remote site. (Remote sometimes being across campus, and sometimes thousands of miles away.)

And then they began to send each other messages to discuss hardware and problems, and industry gossip, and how to fix certain bugs, and current events. And jokes. And dreams. And dirty pictures.

Then they began routing the more interesting stuff through an automated program. This program's duty is calling other UNIX sites while people sleep, leaving off packets of data and programs and messages, picking up others destined for other places, and calling another site. More than 3000 articles a day are routed this way today.

Now, this was all by the way of work, and the people involved hard-core UNIX techie types. But, no one said it couldn't be fun. Meanwhile, nonuniversity types who also ran UNIX got in on the loop from colleges, research centers, and high-tech corporations connected with those to government agencies. In the South, the phrase for what happened next is "It grew like kudzu." Now there are public access sites and commercial connections. In fact, by simple numbers, there are more business connections than educational. A list of free USENET sites is available from Phil Eschallier, in the pubnet.nixpub newsgroup. Because he updates it every month, any list I could put here would be outdated before the book went to press.

The "management" of this was, and still is, all "volunteer." As hard as the work must be to coordinate all this traffic, moderate the newsgroups, make improvements and document them, and keep it all up to date, "slave" might be a better word, though the administrators certainly don't feel that way. (See FIG. 3-1.)

```
/Gateways/Usenet/misc/misc/Net.Module.Manual Being Compiled
1121.3.4470
Read article (Usenet)
/Gateways/Usenet/misc/misc/Net.Module.Manual Being Compiled
1121.3.4470.1 Net.Module.Manual Being Compiled
12/16/91 07:59 21/828 smash@oucsace.cs.OHIOU.EDU (Scott Mash)
-----
I am in the process of compiling the Net.Module.Manual.  All submitted
manuals should be complete, not just a plot.  All plots should be sent
to the keeper of the Net.Plot.Manual which is now in its 3rd edition.
Please put your name and email address at the top of your manual.  I am
accepting modules for all rpg games (adnd, dnd, cyperpunk, gurps etc).
Your module should be in either ascii or postscript, maps in postscript
have much greater detail so I have decided to also accept postscript.
Please take the time to write even a small module.
Thanks in advance,
Scott Mash
!   Scott (Smasher) Mash        !  My expressed opinions do not
!   smash@oucsace.cs.ohiou.edu  !  necessarily represent those of
!   smash@bigbird.cs.ohiou.edu  !  Ohio University or the
!   cs819@ouaccvmb.bitnet       !  Computer Science Dept.
```

3-1
An example of the hard work done by USENET volunteers.

Each USENET site has an administrator, and along the backbone a committee tries to keep everything standard and current. This is done with no financial compensation. But, people do use this for their work, and when it doesn't work, things could get serious. So the people who got it all started volunteer their extra time to make sure that it runs well. And surprisingly, it still does. These volunteers are an intrepid lot. As the system grows, they insist on certain rules in their newfound land of free exchange.

Some of these are covered in "A Primer on How to Work with the USENET Community" by Chuq von Rospach. This is a file you can get from almost any USENET node, and it's worth reading. The file is not an official RFP but a text file. You can find it under

Newsgroups: *news.announce.newusers, news.answers*
Followup-to: *news.newusers.questions*
Archive-name: *usenet-primer/part1*
Original-author: *chuq@apple.COM (Chuq von Rospach)*

His main points are condensed in this next section. . .

Primer excerpts

Rule #1 Never forget that the person on the other side is human. You're using machines to upload and download, so your interaction with the USENET might seem pretty dry and impersonal. But the whole point of the net is to connect people, and what they're thinking and doing. Don't treat the people out there as machines. Remember they have feelings, and failings, too. (See FIG. 3-2.)

```
Read article (Usenet)
/Gateways/Usenet/misc/misc/Hello world !
1121.3.4460.2 Re: Hello world !
12/16/91 23:45 9/208
Lines 1 to 9 of 9 (100%)
-----
                        /  7:34 am  Dec 12, 1991 / writes:

>I am born again

So, why don't you get on with your new life - instead of wasting your
time bragging about the fact to the world?
```

Rule #1.a A corollary to this is to be aware how your postings reflect on you. Never write anything you wouldn't say at a party or in a crowded room. Those postings are all many, many people will know about you, and you never know who is out there reading. The world is in constant motion today; no matter where they are right now, people on the USENET might someday be clients or work with you or meet you in other circumstances. And they might remember your postings. In the end, you can't really hide behind the modem.

Is e-mail private? Well, that depends on your system administrator and the other guys. Generally, yes. Be aware, however that rumors regularly circulate about government snooping on ALL the nets.

This very public nature of postings can stand you in good stead, however.

For example, "A net celebrity is a person who is well known enough that a substantial number of people on the network are aware of them, and can recall reading an article by them," says Morgan Schwers (*mrs@net.com*).

"Keith Petersen is one of these people. When Keith's job was threatened by funding cuts at Simtel-20, the network exploded with people 1) offering him jobs, and 2) offering to donate funds so he could continue working as the software archivist. Partly due to the public outcry, he retains his job still."

Rule #2 Humor and sarcasm are best used cautiously. This is part of remembering that there are people out there, not just a connection of machines. Subtle humor, especially satire, is hard to get across with no facial expressions, body language, or hand signals. Really well-done sarcasm so closely resembles the attitude it belittles it is sometimes taken for a genuine attitude, when delivered only in written form. So it is polite to clearly label all humor. How? Well, some conventions are (tilt your head to the left):

:-) or :-]	A smiley face
:-D or HAHAHA	A laugh
;-)	A wink

What goes around comes around!

Other expressions besides humor are:

:-o	Surprise
:-/ or :-\	Frustrated or puzzled
:-P	Sticking out your tongue
:-(or :-[	A frown

The book *Smileys* by David Sanderson (O'Reilly and Associates) lists loads of these emotions. It might seem silly, but these symbols can help prevent misunderstandings. And should you be tempted to become incensed over something you've read, remember some people on the net consider themselves above using these silly symbols. Don't "flame" the author unless you are sure he was serious. All this leads to another rule. . .

Rule #2.a Rotate messages with questionable content. This means writing them in code. You write your joke or whatever, and a UNIX command will encrypt it. The standard encryption method is to rotate each letter by thirteen characters so that an "a" becomes an "n". (Yes, just like those secret code wheels you used to get in cereal boxes!) This is known on the network as "rot13." When you rotate a message, the word "rot13" should be in the "Subject:" line. Most of the software used to read USENET articles have some way of encrypting and decrypting messages. Your system administrator can tell you how the software on your system works, or you can use the Unix command

```
tr [a- z][A-Z] [n-z][a-m][N-Z][A-M]
```

Similarly, certain graphics files, whose names will NOT be mentioned here, are encrypted, and must be laboriously unencrypted to be viewed. If you're interested in such things, you will find the necessary code in the newsgroups carrying the files.

Rule #2.b Mark or rotate answers or spoilers. That is, if you are telling people what you thought of a movie or book, and your discussion discloses a surprise ending, use rotate. If a review has "rot13" in the title, assume it reveals something similar. And if a puzzle, joke, or riddle has been posted, and you post an answer, rotate it too.

Rule #3 Be brief. Everyone is busy. Postings on the network are huge in number. With so many going so far, only the most important bytes of information should be included. Also remember that somewhere, someone down the line is paying a long distance charge to send your postings on. And you know yourself that the briefer the article, the more likely you are to take time to read it.

Rule #4 Use descriptive titles. Respect people's time (and lack thereof) by being quite clear about the subject matter in your title. See also rule 2.a.

Rule #5 Target your articles. When posting an article, you have a choice of how wide the distribution will be. Choose wisely, for the same reasons you want to be proud of your postings, and use descriptive titles. Usenetters consider it bad form to post both to misc.misc or misc.wanted and any other newsgroup, for example; if it fits in the latter, it has no business in the former. It's also annoying to find an ad for a meeting in Seattle posted worldwide. Finally, certain newsgroups have rules about what can be posted and how it must be worded. You might inadvertently break some rules by posting it to the whole world. This is the reason for alt. groups, discussed later. But the tackiest trick of all is to test out your first posting ("This is a test.") in a worldwide newsgroup. This is the sign of a rank amateur, and a rude one at that.

Rule #5.a A close corollary only post a message once. This is an obvious courtesy to those trying to control the traffic.

Rule #5.b Think before you post. Don't post announcements regarding major news events (e.g., "The World Trade Center just got bombed!") to newsgroups. By the time most people receive such items, they will long since have been informed by conventional media. If you want to discuss such an event on the net, use the misc.headlines newsgroup.

Rule #6 When you see something you want to answer, comment upon, or discuss, your reply is called a "follow-up" on USENET. A tradition is to summarize the message in the following format:

Joe Usenetter said in *{here put the title of the article}:*

>*{Here you quote what he said with one arrow each quoted line..}*

>>*{Two arrows mean Joe was quoting someone else from another article.*

My answer to this is. . .{etc etc}

and so on. If someone didn't get on in the beginning, he can take the time to look up the original or take your word for the direct quote. However, do not directly quote the whole article! Only truly pertinent parts, at most four or five lines, should be repeated.

Rule #6 Use mail to answer a question posted at large. Instead of posting an article everyone reads, post a mail response only to the person who asked the question. Also, check to be sure no follow-ups have already been posted; someone might have already given "your" answer. The questioner is then expected to follow. . .

Rule #6.a If you asked a question of the newsgroup at large, post all the answers you received in an edited, summarized form. Editing means strip the headers and signatures, combine duplicate responses, and quote only the original question in brief. Summarizing means a short condensation of the results.

Rule #7 Be careful about copyrights and licenses, and cite appropriate references. Copyright law is complicated and no clear-cut case has defined the use of copyright in electronic versions of text. Further, no one "owns" the USENET. You might be personally guilty of plagiarism unless copyright laws and rules are carefully followed. Posting licensed software to USENET is a another good way to get flamed, if not sued. Remember, a very large percentage of the users make their living writing code, and they do not care for pirates! Very close to this subject is citing references. If you give statistics or quotes or a legal citation to support your position, you are much more believable if you have given the source of same, and give full credit to the source.

Rule #8 Don't start, or get involved in, a spelling flame. Von Rospach puts it very well:

"Every few months a plague descends on USENET called the spelling flame," he writes. "It starts out when someone posts an article correcting the spelling or grammar in some article. The immediate result seems to be for everyone on the net to turn into a 6th grade English teacher and pick apart each other's postings for a few weeks. This is not productive and tends to cause people who used to be friends to get angry with each other."

It is particularly unfair when you remember that many USENET members are using English as a second language and solely as a courtesy to those of us in North

America and the UK. Yes, things are not always under control on USENET. Occasionally, net-wide versions of shouting matches flare through the net. Sometimes these are over really important issues, such as criminal activity over the net. These you might not be able to resist. But, when you jump into one, please remember rules #1, #1.a, and #2.

Rule #9 Don't overdo your signature. Some programs allow a user to compose his signature and store it to be appended to every e-mail, article or file he sends out. The purpose, of course, is the same as a rubber stamp or a gummed label with your name and address. However, just as some of those are decorated, some signatures are too. A simple statement of philosophy is sometimes added. ("Freeze dried instant coffee is the work of the forces of darkness.") However, some people go overboard, making their signatures longer than some of their articles. This is bad form. Proper form is to make your signature your real name and your USENET address. (See FIG. 3-3.)

3-3

A nicely done signature— informative and attractive.

```
+=+=+=+=+=+=+=+=+=+=+=+=+=+=+=+=+=+=+=+=+=+=+=+=+=+=+=+=+=+=+=+=+=+
Joe Backo
Sun Microsystems Internet:  joe.backo@East.Sun.COM
6716 Alexander Bell Drive Usenet:  ...!uunet!sun!sundc!jback
Suite #200 AT&T:  (410) 290-1234
Columbia, MD 21046 FAX:  (410) 312-1799
+=+=+=+=+=+=+=+=+=+=+=+=+=+=+=+=+=+=+=+=+=+=+=+=+=+=+=+=+=+=+=+=+=+
```

Rule #10 Von Rospach does not spell this one out, but Gene Spafford of Purdue University does. Thou shalt not ask over the Net what is more easily, efficiently and quickly done over the phone. Such as someone's address. Or whether a certain company has a site. Or whether Joe Blow from your college dorm is out there somewhere. Call and ask these questions. The net cannot be the only means of communication; only the most fun.

Your next step

So. You're ready to become a Usenetter. What next?

As we emphasized, USENET is a UNIX-based, noncommercial conferencing system that uses UNIX's UUCPs communications facility. USENET sort of sits on top of UUCP. There are three ways to hook into USENET. Set up a feed through UUNet, the nonprofit organization that helps people use USENET; monthly maintenance is $35 and per-hour use costs $2. Or call a local university or large local company and ask if they provide news feeds; becoming a branch on that site's backbone costs only phone charges. Finally, several commercial enterprises are on the USENET news feed.

Let's look at them one-by-one.

UUNET is one: A nonprofit corporation dedicated to helping people use the USENET, helping newcomers get started and helping the USENET stay useful. Its computer is devoted to sending mail and news. As of February 1992, UUNET had 2400 sites, many of them old-timers on the USENET. Besides that, UUNET has an amazing archive of public domain software. More than 6 gigabytes. Be warned, however, that much of this is uncompiled, not user friendly, and takes expertise to use. Be that as it may, there are real solutions to real problems here.

UUNET is popular as a mail site. Store and forward as well as immediate delivery to local sites are offered. In special cases (and for special prices) UUNET can offer instantaneous service between two remote users as well.

Yes prices. UUNET is not free, although it is affordable. One way to hook up is to subscribe by writing to

UUNET Communications Services
3110 Fairview Park Dr.
Suite 570
Falls Church VA 22042
(703) 876-5050 [voice]
(703) 876-5059 [fax]

The Net Domain address is *info@uunet.uu.net*.

If you have a UNIX computer, and $.40 a minute, you can get the free UUNET software by using your modem to dial 1-900-GOT-SRCS and use the command `uucp uunet!~/help`. Set up your UUCP Systems or L.sys file first.

Piggybacking on another's system is a good bet if you have good connections in the USENET world. The cost will probably be reasonable, but you might have to obey strict rules about time limits, when you're allowed on, and so forth.

Other services offer connections to the USENET, too. Besides a large USENET library on CompuServe's Telecomputing Forum (GO TELECOM), there are

The Well (see Chapter 12)
Portal Communications (see Chapter 10)
PSI (see Chapter 11)
BIX (see Chapter 5)

As far as mail and news reads on USENET, many bulletin board systems are on the USENET. Ask around at computer clubs for one near you. Some sources of software for USENET are:

Tim Pozar
Late Night Software
671 28th St.
San Francisco, CA 94131
UFGATE for MS-DOS.
(415) 788-2022 [voice]
(415) 695-7727 [voice]

Vortex Technology
P.O. Box 1323
Topanga, CA 90290
UULINK for MS-DOS
(213) 290-3920 [voice]

Ross M. Greenberg
Software Concepts Design
594 Third Ave.
New York, NY 10016
RAMNET for MS-DOS
(212) 889-6431 [voice]

DECUS
219 Boston Post Rd. (BP 02)
Marlboro, MA 01752
VMS software
(508) 480-3259 [voice]

Also, check out the Unix forum on CompuServe for some public domain utilities. There are also useful files on how to use DOS with USENET. (GO UNIX). Portal's USENET Archives has the CBIP Starter's Kit, which has code and explanations. (GO 9449.3).

For the minimum, you will need a form of uudecode to work with your operating system, be it UNIX, MS-DOS or Mac. You will also need an archive extractor. ARC-E, or other extract only programs will take up less space on your disk. Portal's USENET Archives is a good place to look for text files on where these are located, and for instructions on how to use them. Some local bulletin boards might also have such software.

Say you want to know if a file you want is on wuarchive, one of the largest anonymous FTP sites. A typical way to find out is write a message that says

```
reply elizabeth_crowe@cup.portal.com
connect wuarchive.wustl.edu
dir
quit
```

Address it to

```
ftpmail@decwrl.dec.com
```

This request will give you a listing (directory) of the root directory on *wuarchive.wustl*.edu. This is like getting a directory of C:\ on your IBM. If you would like a different directory, use something like:

```
dir /ibm/new_uploads
```

Having received the directory, you can send similar messages to retrieve interesting files. This will work to retrieve the program by substituting the program's file name as you find it in the directory. But remember well that UUCP will send programs (binary) files translated into gibberish-looking ASCII. You will need the program that translates the gibberish back into binary: uudecode.

Other current software is obtainable from almost any major USENET site. Source to the 'rn' newsreader program is also widely available. The following sites have sources to the current news software available for anyone needing a copy:

```
Site Contact
```

munnari kre@munnari.oz.au
osu-cis postmaster@tut.cis.ohio-state.edu
philabs usenet@philabs.philips.com
pyramid usenet@pyramid.com
rutgers usenet@rutgers.edu
tektronix news@tektronix.tek.com
watmath usenet@watmath.waterloo.edu

Sources for both news 2.11 and "rn" are also available in the *comp.sources.unix archives*. European sites should request the sources from their nearest Eunet backbone site.

For beginners, at home with no system administrator to help, the best bet is probably to sign onto a bulletin board system with a USENET feed in order to get an idea of the newsgroups. Also, many FIDOnet BBSs are on the USENET e-mail system.

BBS systems on the USENET will run different programs to connect; this depends on what the BBS system is. The SYSOP will have or can tell you how to get the program to use USENET with his board. If it is Fido system, check out UFGATE. If the BBS is compliant with UUCP you might find Waffle. If you want a mechanism to move the news onto your system in USENET format, check out FSUUCP. Both Waffle and FSUUCP can also operate in a standalone mode for personal use. UUCP is also usable in standalone mode, but at this time does not support news.

A system like Portal or UUNET costs more, but you can use their shell to get started. Follow the help menus and read all the background material you can online. Look for files that begin with FAQ. That stands for Frequently Asked Questions, and these files are usually compiled by those who have answered them too many times. Their fond hope is that in compiling the files, they can avoid answering them in the future, except to update lists and the like. (See FIG.3-4.)

```
/Gateways/Usenet Archives/comp/binaries/ibm_pc/Volume 6
15823.3
-----
0   -   Test posting [collection]
1   -   Status: RO [collection]
2   -   Display the "Face on Mars" photos on VGA [collection]
3   -   pax - tar and cpio for MS-DOS [collection]
4   -   Linear programming solver [collection]
5   -   Sharetax 89 [collection]
6   -   vuimg210, a GIF and TIFF viewer [collection]
7   -   FRAC, a tetris-like game [collection]
8   -   fstat, list file status for MS-DOS [collection]
9   -   vidutils, video utilities for CGA [collection]
10  -   scanrs58, TSR to scan for virus while you run [collection]
11  -   scanv58, scan a disk for a virus [collection]
12  -   tskerm24, Kermit utilities [collection]
13  -   PC-TAX89 v1.3 [collection]
14  -   Telix, [collection]
15  -   Telix, docs and support [collection]
-----
```

3-4
Archive sites are a good place to look for files of frequently asked questions.

We mentioned the international aspect to USENET. One example, taken from press reports, is that in March 1991, the Direct Connection (TDC) online service unveiled its custom software to help users sift through the myriad of USENET newsgroups— a customized version of the standard USENET newswire feed. In addition, it allows subscribers to originate and reply to USENET messages.

This is more effective, not to mention faster, than having each subscriber log on to USENET and dredge through the thousands of messages manually.

TDC, which is available on dial-up on (081) 853-3965, costs a flat fee of UKP 10 a month, regardless of how much subscribers use the service. TDC supports modem speeds from 300 to 2400 bits per second (bps) with MNP error-correction and data compression. I was not, unfortunately, able to test it out for this book.

A good explanation of downloading software is in the December 1991 issue of *UNIX World,* volume 8, number 12, page 95. "Get yer free software here!" by Rick Farris, shows how users can download free software from archive sites. Farris discusses UNIX modem configuration, dialing, and permissions. He also presents sample communications scripts.

Most of the time, a binary (program) file can be sent to you with a simple mail message. Addressed to one of the sites you have determined has the file you want, send the appropriate message such as

```
send your-usenet-address filename
```

Then use the system you are on to send the mail.

As an example, if your USENET connection is a FidoNet bulletin board, you can send a message to anyone on USENET providing that

- You know the exact USENET address of the recipient. A bad net address is exactly like a wrong phone number. You must know the site name of his node, and his user name on that node.
- Whether the BBS has a "smart" mail program or whether you must route the message yourself. The latter is rare, but not unheard of.
- Which FidoNet node forwards mail to UUCP nodes for your network.

To send the message, using the BBS netmail section, compose and address the message, indicating when asked that you want the message sent to the node that forwards for you. If it is a request for some file from a server, and the BBS allows such an option, have the message erase itself once received. The first line is the address that the gateway will look at; this is where you will put the address of the recipient:

To: *Usenet address with !s*

Then follow with the message, such as:

```
send help.file
```

To send a message from the USENET to a friend on FidoNet, you must know which FidoNet node to send it to, the path from UUCP to that system and whether that site has map entry (that is, a program that knows how to get there from here). If not, the path will be

TO: *UFGATE_site!zone!net!Node!firstname.lastname.*

Otherwise, take her login name and her FidoNet address and turn them into a USENET address. Jill User at 1:501/66.9 would become *jill.user@f66 .n501.z1.fidonet.org.*

The domain of fidonet.org will include only those sites that are listed in the official FidoNet nodelist. Also remember the rules: no advertisements going across the net to get there! Be sure to subscribe to the newsgroups that interest you. There is more out there than you can possibly read, so be selective.

Gene Spafford, NSF/Purdue/U of Florida Software Engineering Research Center, Dept. of Computer Sciences, Purdue University, W. Lafayette, Indiana, Internet:*spaf@cs.purdue.edu*, compiles a list of USENET newsgroup three or four times a year. His forward to the list reads as follows:

"World" newsgroups are (usually) circulated around the entire USENET—this implies worldwide distribution. Not all groups actually enjoy such wide distribution, however. The European USENET and Eunet sites take only a selected subset of the more "technical" groups, and controversial "noise" groups are often not carried by many sites in the US and Canada (these groups are often under the "talk" and "soc" classifications). Many sites do not carry some or all of the comp.binaries groups.

There are groups in other subcategories, but they are local to institutions, to geographic regions, etc., and are not listed here. Note that these distribution categories can be used to restrict the propagation of news articles. Currently, distributions include

world	Worldwide distribution (default)
att	Limited to AT&T
can	Limited to Canada
eunet	Limited to European sites
na	Limited to North America
usa	Limited to the United States

There might be other regional and local distribution categories available at your site. Most US states have distribution categories named after the two-letter abbreviation for that state or category (e.g., "ga" for Georgia, "nj" for New Jersey). Please use an appropriate distribution category if your article is not likely to be of interest to USENET readers worldwide. A companion article to this lists all of the regional distributions and their newsgroups.

The "world" groups have been gatewayed with the listed Internet lists. Some of them might not still be gatewayed due to broken software and/or gateways; such groups are marked with an asterisk ("*") in the following list. Please contact me if you should know of their current status. Also note that the group comp.lang.forth is gated with the bitnet discussion list *umforth@weizmann.bitnet*, andrec.railroad is run from *railroad@queens.bitnet*. Some of these lists are gated one-way into USENET groups; those groups have been marked with a ">" symbol in the following list. If you are reading this article from a site not on the USENET, you may subscribe to Internet lists by writing to the request address. You form such an address by putting "-request" before the "@" symbol, as in *unix-emacs-request@bbn.com*. This gets your message directly to the list maintainer instead of broadcasting it to all the readers of the list.

Also note that moderators of USENET groups might not be in charge of the corresponding mailing list or gateway. For example, the moderator of comp.sources.unix does not have anything to do with the unix-sources mailing list; matters concerning the mailing list should be addressed to unix-sources-*request@brl.mil*.

Also on the USENET, you'll find less "traditional" newsgroups—some moderated, some not. Because of their size (volume of articles and messages), specialized or unusual audience, or a different set of administrative rules and concerns, these groups do not travel over the entire network. They are carried through use of the distribution mechanism. Sites must support them and find a feed to send them on in order to include them; that is they are "invitation only" feeds. They are "hierarchal" and are usually preceded by "alt." Your best bet to finding them is a service like PSI that lets you subscribe to any feed you want, or a BBS that delights in the shock value of some of these. The purpose of these alt groups is to give free rein to any and all exchanges people might want to make. That's exhilarating to some, exhausting to others. A file on CompuServe for new Usenetters (in the UNIX Forum, Library 4) says in part:

WORDS TO LIVE BY #1:

USENET AS SOCIETY

Those who have never tried electronic communication might not be aware of what a "social skill" really is. One social skill that must be learned is that other people have points of view that are not only different, but *threatening*, to your own. In turn, your opinions might be threatening to others. There is nothing wrong with this. Your beliefs need not be hidden behind a facade, as happens with face-to-face conversation. Not everybody in the world is a bosom buddy, but you can still have a meaningful conversation with them. The person who cannot do this lacks in social skills.
—Nick Szabo

WORDS TO LIVE BY #2:

USENET AS ANARCHY

Anarchy means having to put up with things that really piss you off.
—Unknown
—Gene Spafford

What might this include? Well, alt.censorship, for discussion about restricting speech/press. Or alt.cyberpunk, a group devoted to high-tech and low-life. How about alt.fan.dave_barry, an electronic fan club for humorist Dave Barry; or if you're feeling argumentative, alt.flame, a group who enjoys literate, pithy, succinct screaming. If you absolutely must break rule 8, look into alt.flame.spelling, "Fore piple whoe kant spel." How to subscribe depends on where you are. If your system at work or home has UUCP's news or notes software and is actively participating in transferring news, find the groups you want. A list of groups and their corresponding mailing lists is at the beginning of the file "active-newsgroups/part1" on *pit- manager.mit.edu*. Retrieve that file and use those addresses to contact the list administrators (be sure to use the "-request" address). Then get on their "mailing list."

It is important to remember that individual Usenetters don't really belong to USENET; their machines do. Each machine "joins" the network when the administrator agrees to store and forward news messages. Those messages are stored on local disk at each machine and remain there for some number of days. Usenetters read the articles from local disk or over a network connection from the machine with the articles on disk, in whatever order and according to whatever selection criteria they want to use. Thus, in general, a user "gets" a group if a machine at their location (site) ``gets'' the group.

Recently, Sterling Software, a US company, put the world's monthly USENET output on CD-ROMS called NetNews/CD for about $35 per disk. This was greeted with cheers and howls. The cheers came from those who felt this was a cheap price for a great deal of convenience. The howls came from those who felt that somehow it was violating the privacy and property rights of the people who posted these articles for all on the USENET and most of the Internet to see.

The solution, fortunately, is simple. The company, upon receiving a registered letter stating that you do not want your postings ever included in their CDs, will have the software delete your contributions to the net from their CD.

One possible advantage to such a route: should you break all the rules 1–10 mentioned before, you perhaps can prevent the occurrence from becoming engraved on a CD for infinite replay. But then, if you had the foresight to send the letter, you probably have the foresight not to post stupid, nasty, or hasty words.

To have a machine become a site on the USENET, you must obtain a copy of the news software, compile it, and install it on your machine. You also need enough disk space to hold the articles as they come in—a complete feed of USENET and related groups requires about 10Mb of overhead, and up to 15–20Mb per day of storage (as of late 1991, volume tends to double annually), plus up to another 20Mb of batch space per feed. Thus, in the worst case, if your site gets a full feed, will supply one other site, and will keep all news articles for 10 days, it will need about 300Mb of disk space. And then move it on, which will require some heavy modem machinery, and possibly large phone bills if the next site is not a local call. Obviously, this is better done by some institution.

How to

So, if you can't install news, or don't have that sort of hardware, you might be able to find a sympathetic news admin who will feed you selected newsgroups by mailing postings to you.

Gene Spafford has this advice: "You also might install one of the NNTP newsreaders and read the news remotely from their systems. Both of these mechanisms are costly in terms of resources, and you have to know exactly who to ask to get it done. This varies depending on your network connectivity, local operating system, and the willingness of other site admins to let you do this, so I can't offer you any specific advice on how to make arrangements. You can try posting to 'news.misc' and the groups you want to get to find a feed. Of course, if you don't have the ability to post to the news, that doesn't help much—sorry."

Spafford says these are some very common questions he receives, and his answers are as follows:

Q. Where can I get more information on news software and news readers?

A. This depends on your operating system and form of network connections (if any). There is an article posted to the net on a regular basis entitled "USENET Software: History and Sources" that tells where to find most of the popular news software. It is normally posted to the news.announce.newusers group on the USENET. If you can't access the news to read this article, you can get a copy from the archive on the machine *pit-manager.mit.edu* using either FTP or mail.

To get the information by FTP, connect to *pit-manager.mit.edu* (18.72.1.58) using anonymous FTP. Retrieve the file pub/usenet/news.answers/usenet-software/part1. You might want to get a copy of the pub/usenet/site-setup file there too.

To get the information by mail, send an e-mail message to *mail-server@pit-manager.mit.*edu containing `send usenet/news.answers/usenet-`

software/part1 (Send a message containing help to get general information about the mail server. The server on pit-manager contains copies of lots of other interesting articles about the USENET—you might want to read some of them.)

Q. What does it cost to receive news?

A. Nothing, except the cost of your disk space, CPU time, and communication costs to transfer the news. This can be expensive, but there is no formal fee.

Somewhat more facetiously, there are some intangible costs: People get cranky when their newsfeed is down or when management decides to restrict a feed—deprive people of their rec.humor.funny or censor alt.sex and you might have an angry mob on your hands!

Employees will spend a part of their day reading netnews instead of doing real work. Your disks will fill up and you'll have to buy more. Your system will spend more time on the phone every day, and if you only have a 2400-baud modem or a very congested leased line, you might have to upgrade. A full feed from a commercial site can cost you in the hundreds of dollars per month if you're not careful. Graduate students will graduate six or more months later than if they didn't read news. Employers should note that misc.jobs.offered is one of the more popular groups, and your employees might find a better job elsewhere.

Q. How do I find a feed?

A. Locate another site on the same network you are and that is already on the USENET. Ask the admins there if they will provide a feed.

Admins of sites on the Internet can send mail to *nntp-managers@ucbvax.berkeley.edu* to ask for a newsfeed *after* they have tried finding nearby sites to act as feeds.

Q. I'm on Bitnet—Can I connect to the net?

A. Yes, but . . . Some BITNET sites are running software that doesn't work particularly well with USENET so you need special configuration to support it. Contact your favorite BITNET LISTSERV and get the list NETNWS-L. That list carries info on the necessary procedures and software. (See Chapter 1).

In general, once you get on, however you do it, the best way to proceed is to READ. Lurk in the background, noticing what is said, how, and by whom. After a little of this, jump in with a posting (to the moderator if this is a moderated newsgroup) or a personal letter to someone who impresses you.

As we mentioned, more USENET sites are at businesses than anywhere else. Therefore, it is important to note here that announcements of professional products or services on USENET are allowed; however, because someone else is paying the phone bills for this, be absolutely certain it is of benefit to Usenetters at large, not just yourself. Post (or look for) such notices in the appropriate newsgroup—say, comp.newprod.

Never post product announcements to a general purpose newsgroup (e.g., misc.misc). "Product Announcement" or "Service Announcement" will be your subject line. Never repeat these—one article per product at the most; preferably group everything into one article. You will get the net version of rotten tomatoes thrown at you for advertising hype, so stick to technical facts. If it is particularly obnoxious, the moderators might remove the announcement altogether. If you post something thoughtful, or a question politely phrased, you will probably get a reply in an amazing space of time. Below is a typical routing message at the top of a letter. The top shows when it reached the destination, the bottom when it left. It was posted in Central Time Zone, received in Pacific Time Zone. Note where it went, and how fast. (See FIG.3-5.)

```
Received: from portal.unix.portal.com by hobo.corp.portal.com (4.1/4.0.3
    1.7) id AA09032; Wed, 22 Jan 92 13:05:47 PST
Received: by portal.unix.portal.com (1.165) id AA19966; Wed, 22 Jan 92
    13:05:43 -0800
Received: by nova.unix.portal.com (5.65b/4.1 1.76) id AA10867; Wed, 22 Jan
    92 13:05:31 -0800
Received: from uther.cs.purdue.edu by arthur.cs.purdue.edu
    (5.65c/PURDUE_CS-1.2)id <AA15314@arthur.cs.purdue.edu>; Wed, 22 Jan 1992
    16:05:25 -0500
Received: from localhost.cs.purdue.edu by uther.cs.purdue.edu
    (5.65c/PURDUE_CS-1.2)id <AA19634@uther.cs.purdue.edu>; Wed, 22 Jan 1992
    16:05:21 -0500
Message-Id: <199201222105.AA19634@uther.cs.purdue.edu>
```

3-5
This header shows where a message started, how it travelled, and when it arrived.

To sum up, USENET is the people. Again quoting Schwers:

"(The best part is) the anarchy. It's not a controlled system, where only people 'authorized' can post, etc. It's a free exchange of ideas, limited by nothing but people's own common sense. The network exists because people *THINK* usually before they post. The ones who don't are criticized, often heavily. BUT THEY ARE NOT TOLD THAT THEY ABSOLUTELY CANNOT HAVE ACCESS. There is freedom here, freedom unlike almost any other available at this time."

Part two
Towns of the electronic underground

We visit the medium-sized online communities, many of which hope to compete commercially with the Big Three (CompuServe, GEnie, and Prodigy).

4 The Dew Drop Inn
America Online

E-mail	*cs@aol.com*
U.S. Mail	8619 Westwood Center Dr.
	Vienna, VA 22182-2285
Phone	(800) 227-6364 [voice]
Hours	24 hours a day, but cheapest 6 p.m. to 6 a.m. your time
Basic rate	Free start-up, $5.95 first hour, $4.00 per hour after that at night.
	$8.00 an hour daytime. More for overseas.

America Online is an independent provider of online services; so far only the United States and Canada are connected. Any review you read places it squarely between CompuServe and Prodigy in price, depth, interface, and ease of use. Personally I found it light years ahead of Prodigy because the front end is so crisp, fast, and useful; and for entertainment, dead even with CompuServe. The business and research facilities are not in CIS's class; for instance, you can't search some of the news texts, or save a clippings file.

History

"We were Quantum Computer services to start; now we're America Online, Inc.," said Kathy Ryan. Originally a Mac service, America Online was unveiled by Quantam in 1989; DOS users were welcomed in February 1991. The company offered public stock in early 1992.

Scope

"Our central features are the departments and e-mail—that's where it shines. It's a good interface. The graphics aren't just pretty, they're useful!" says Ryan. "You really don't need to understand a bunch of arcane stuff to use it. But it's powerful enough for online junkies."

How to sign on

The only way to get on is the front-end program. The free software, available by just calling 1-800-227-6364, was designed by GeoWorks and shows the MacIntosh heritage. While a mouse is not required, it was designed with one in mind.

AOL signon software is included with any version of GeoWorks, which is a Windows-like program. However, the version supplied with GeoWorks is different in two respects. For one, in the GeoWorks version, you don't have a button to tell the program to log off as soon as this download is over; you must babysit the download and push F3 yourself when it's done. The other is that the graphic showing you how far you've come and how far you have to go on the download is different; the stand-alone front end draws a blue bar graph, while the GeoWorks version simply prints the numbers. The main advantage to the former is that it's easier to see from across the room if you've decided to go do something else!

I found the program delightful because I had been hacking my way through so many difficult systems in researching this book. But I realized that I had also gained some significant moxie in dealing with these programs. So I got myself a guinea pig: I asked my father to go through the new member hoops, and tell me what he thought. His response:

"It was not designed with a laptop computer in mind! The installation procedure on a laptop is a tad challenging because some of the boxes for filling in text (the name box in particular) will fall off the bottom of the screen. The graphics also assume a color monitor. On a typical laptop's screen, you'll have to squint a bit to tell what exactly is highlighted.

"Also, the program was designed for a mouse. Without a mouse, you must use a sometimes confusing combination of the space bar and the Tab key to move among the selections. Trial and error will be the only guide as to which will work where you are right now.

"But if you have a full-color screen and a mouse, assume you'll have little trouble!"

AOL is one of the better bargains in the online underground if you are in the continental U.S. Your first month is free; after that, it's $5.95 for the first hour on evenings or weekends. Regular rates are $4.00 per hour after that for nights and weekends and $8.00 an hour for daytime (6 a.m. to 6 p.m. your local time) usage any weekday. The free areas are What's New & Online Support during evening and weekend hours; at prime time, it's $4.00 per hour. Hawaii, Alaska, and Canada pay $16.00 per hour; $12.00 in What's New & Online Support. (See FIG. 4-1.)

In the spirit of the place, you can count on some "free" time, and maybe get some "credited" time, too. Besides the free area mentioned, and the fact that your first hour is free each month, you can earn "credited" time in various areas. One is the weekly Opinion Poll, where you can post a question you feel is of current interest. If it's chosen for the next week's poll, you get a credited half hour. Further, any uploads to a software library will get you credits, applied back toward the time it took you to upload. (See FIG. 4-2.)

Of course, some things get you extra charges, too. The Quantam Space play-by-mail game will rack up a charge every move; some vendors online have additional fees for using their services. Still, overall, it's less easy to go broke visiting America Online than most places the Electronic Traveller could go.

The program installs itself, asking you questions where appropriate. Answer the questions, and before you know it, you're on. You have several choices, and COM3 and COM4 are supported. One of the choices is to make the modem be quiet while it's connecting. You might want to opt for that, but we'll discuss an exception later. (See FIG. 4-3.)

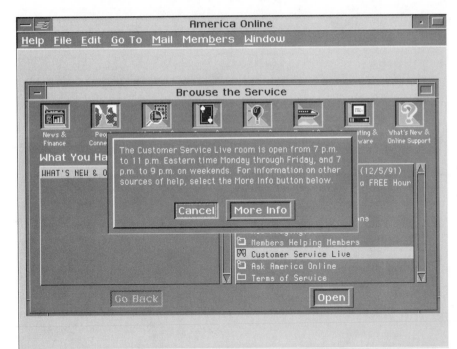

4-1
The Customer Service Screens explain the charges.

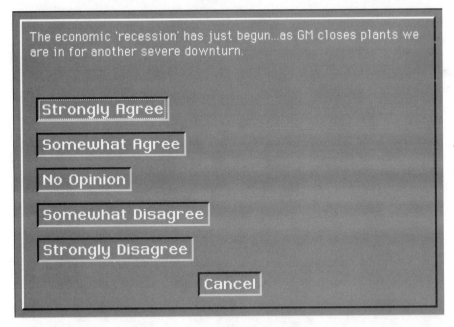

4-2
You can win free time in the Opinion Poll.

When you see the welcome window, you are online! Clicking (or with a keyboard, highlighting and hitting Return) on What's New might be your first best bet. Or Browse the Service, which shows you the categories you can choose. (See FIG. 4-4.)

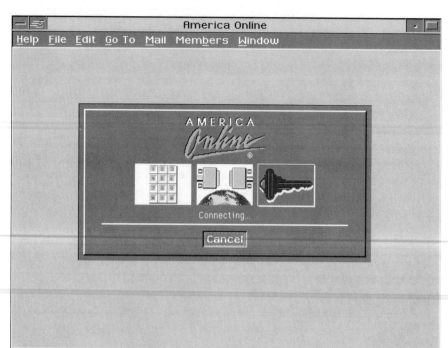

4-3

The connect screen lets you know you're on.

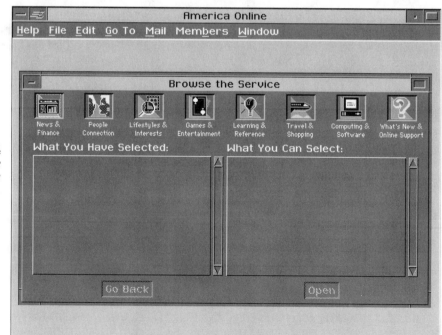

4-4

The Browse the Service screen shows what you can choose.

Because the front end is so graphical and easy to use, I couldn't successfully mess up. The structure is very intuitive and logical. One nice feature is the Keyword Menu. Choosing GOTO, you can EDIT THE GOTO MENU and install your favorite keywords. Then the control key plus one digit will take you where you want to go. Your welcome kit will have a list of keywords; a more current one is online, choosable from that same menu.

What to see

America Online sees itself as a personal productivity tool. It has some business areas and a plethora of personal ones. Not strictly entertainment or business, it aims to be both. Publications such as PC World, Home-Office Computing, and USA Today are online, with varying degrees of searchability. The PC World area is especially interesting, with their collections of programs and tips.

Vendors online include Broderbund, Microsoft, and GeoWorks; more are being added all the time. Microsoft has several helps for the business-minded; many of the others are consumer-oriented areas, for questions on tips for using the products, grousing about what was not included, and so on. Some sample programs are there; so are articles singing their praises.

Each area has moderators to answer questions and host online discussions. The online community seems to be middle-class in taste and education. It's a comfortable place, with a small corner for almost everyone.

People from all walks of life are here, and some have rather esoteric tastes. The child pornography case got much attention. In December 1991, AOL called in the FBI because a user tipped off management that pornography and sexually explicit conversations were cruising around the service.

AOL considers itself a family-oriented and law-abiding organization. But as is usual in cases of electronic crime, which law applies was the big question. The Fourth Amendment ensures privacy, but it is also illegal to own or transfer child pornography.

But as experts will tell you, AOL owns the lines and can control what goes over them. During a chat on AOL, I posed the question "Is e-mail private?" to ProfJB, an expert of the homework help section. His response? "Yes and no."

He cited the case of a woman fired because she questioned the right of her employer to read e-mail on the company's system, when the messages she sent were meant to be "private." The courts supported the company because the hardware and software to send the messages belonged to the company. Anything on the e-mail system was held to be as open as anything on one of the company's copying machines.

Because most e-mail goes over someone's private system at some point, these messages are more like cable television programs than like mail or phone messages. So if a message is going through a privately-owned system at any point, then it is no longer a personal paper or effect, covered by the Fourth Amendment to the Constitution. You have, in effect, broadcasted it, asserted ProfJB.

In a similar vein, Steve Case—president of America Online, Inc.—wrote an open letter to all users of the system. "Our goal is to foster the development of an 'electronic community' that honors the principles of freedom of expression, while also recognizing that some community standards are needed for the service to grow . . . The laws and decorum will be obeyed. Those who disagree can 'shape up or ship out'."

Still, don't think that means this is a stuffy, straight-laced place.

Almost any Chat you get into will have some double entendre going on, even (especially?!) at 9 a.m. when everyone is paying premium. It's all meant in good fun, and rarely gets too ribald. Still, it can get in the way of a more meaningful conversation. As one person put it, "There ought to be someplace for the married-with-children types like us to chat in peace!" Of course, there is: you choose the Private Room icon, name the room (that morning we called it Serious Writers . . . Serious Gays were in another room all their own!) Then you can chat without the distraction of people desperately trying to twist your dull typical language into something witty about fooling around. Another option is to highlight the responses of people whose words you do want to read, and "ignore" those you don't or your own if you like! (See FIGS. 4-5 and 4-6.)

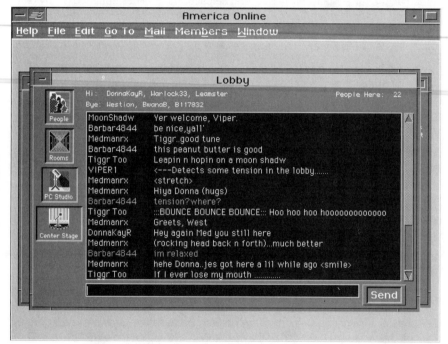

4-5
You can watch all the conversation in a chat . . .

"It's really a community. Probably because it's so easy to use and we have set it up to promote interaction, it is a real community," says Ryan. The staff promotes the interaction, too, by sending real-time messages to people they see online. This is called Send Instant Message and is usually used when the chat is getting so hectic, one person needs to "whisper" to another. The first time that happened to me, I didn't know about that menu item, and was shocked to have a "HI LIBBI" window pop up suddenly. Staff also uses Send Instant Message to announce the beginning of an online discussion. A window will pop up telling you who, when, and the keyword to go there. A Ctrl-F4 will get it out of your way.

"A lot of people hang around in the People Connection. This is the central communication region. Lavona runs the Online Pub," says Ryan. Other popular

4-6

... Or you can ignore certain people, if you like.

features are the lively developer sessions, and nightly homework help sessions. Inside Technology also has stimulating discussions.

If you've got the laid-off blues but still have the money to sign on, there's a Job Listing area (Keyword JOBS). You can search it for your geographical preferences, your skills, or the company you'd most like to work for. (See FIG. 4-7.)

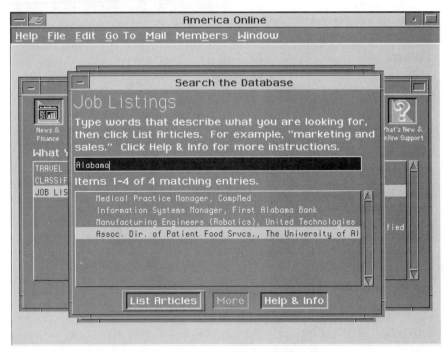

4-7

The Job Listing (Keyword JOBS) is searchable by town, state, or job description.

Tymnet and SprintNet are the communications networks. When you first get your software and install it, the program dials a 1-800 number to determine the best numbers to dial for your location and modem speed. It writes them into the setup screen for you, and unless the numbers change, you have no more worries.

Networks

Of course, the numbers do sometimes change. In early March, I could not connect for two days in a row. On the third day, I left my modem set to speaker on until connect and heard an announcement that the number my setup was dialing had been changed. This was without any prior warning.

So every now and then, go *Keyword* ACCESS NUMBERS and see what the latest numbers for your locale are.

The first half of 1992 was spent in fine-tuning the Internet mail option for America Online. Ryan says the Internet connection will open for mail only. As an AOL subscriber, your Internet address will be *accountname@aol.com*. Internet Mail access was scheduled to be available by June; the USENET newsfeed is still being looked at. Anonymous FTP will be for text files only.

Electronic mail is one of the nicest things about AOL. You can compose your mail offline and save on connect time charges. To send a letter, choose COMPOSE MAIL before you have signed on. Fill in the Address (you must have the ONSCREEN name; to find that, you can go ONLINE to keyword NAMES and follow the instructions). Type your letter. Then from the menu bar, select Sign On. Window will pile upon window in this process, but you can click on the "Empty" part of the screen to send your letter. This only works one letter at a time, of course.

Another way to do it is to compose the letter offline as a text file and save it. Then, while online, type in only the recipient address, and use the ATTACH FILE option. The file will then be sent with the letter.

You can do neat tricks with this such as blind copies. You can also send FAX and snail mail.

How to sign off

Hit F3. It asks you if you're sure, and then gives you a screen with your time online and some newsy tidbit. (See FIG. 4-8.)

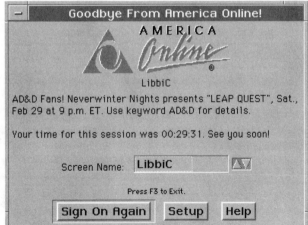

4-8

A newsy tidbit to entice your next signon.

5 BIX
The programmer's paradise

E-mail	*info@bix.com*
U.S. Mail	One Phoenix Mill Ln.
	Peterborough, NH 03458 USA
Phone	(800) 227-2983 [voice]
	(603) 924-7681 [voice]
Hours	24 hours a day
Basic rate	$13 per month
Notes	Chat, e-mail and files. Internet mail connection. FTP, telnet as of summer 1993.

Perhaps you think you know about BIX. Byte Information Exchange, after all, has been around quite awhile. It's for the diehards, the professionals, the people who are more serious about their computers than they are about their mothers. All the BIX administration will tell you about size is that it has more than 10,000 users, less than a million, with about 100 new daily messages on the average conference.

Put your thinking cap on before coming to BIX. This is a very hi-tech atmosphere, probably the epitome of such systems.

"We're a little stuffy. If you're used to a lot of other commercial systems, you'll find us quite a stuffy bunch. We're into intellectual hobnobbery. We do have fun, but we're serious folk about our computing. We like to say we have a high signal-to-noise ratio," says Tony Lockwood, editor-in-chief of BIX. That tell you something? But pause. Things are happening at BIX. BIX is more organized. BIX is friendlier. BIX is available with—now sit down—a graphical interface!

The beginnings of BIX were auspicious. It was launched in 1984 as an electronic extension of BYTE magazine. As Stephen LaLiberte, director of BIX puts it, "We started officially as a commercial system in 1985. We were testing in 1984. The day we started, we had this real small announcement, at the end of an article, that the program discussed here would be available for downloading at our Peterborough number. We had two phones on the line of that number.

"Two weeks later, the phone police came: we had the northeast section bottlenecked and there was just not enough trunk capacity to handle the calls to our Peterborough line. The whole system was backed up. We had to move the phones to Boston."

And that was just the beginning. BIX prides itself on being the place where the movers and shakers of computerdom reside. BIX users and operators see themselves as vastly different from the general online public: more astute, more serious, more avante garde. BIX is still in Peterborough, NH, and draws heavily from the technological centers of the northeast for their membership. For years (eons in the Electronic Underground) BIX was owned and operated by BYTE magazine, owned and operated by McGraw-Hill. Then, in February 1992, BIX was sold down the river, so to speak, to General Videotex Corporation, the parent company of Delphi, one of those general computer services.

This was hailed by the GVC folks as a chance to show that they could support the serious computer user. They were already involved in distributing information to cable TV, telex, and other data networks. It's possible, though certainly not announced as of this writing, that all these services of GVC could someday tie with BIX. Be that as it may, BIX definitely still has Steve LaLiberte, who has been and for the foreseeable future will be the director of BIX.

Help lines, voice lines, administration, voice mail and LaLiberte remain as they were before the GVC deal.

So this is still a place to log on and meet people from all over the world to chat about the latest concepts in computers, languages, artificial intelligence and other technology; the place to read BYTE online back to 1988; the place to download files of software in BYTE and other public domain and shareware programs; still a good place for electronic mail and chat, and for McGraw-Hill News if you've got the bucks for it.

How to dial . . . how to log on

Let's first cover the old-fashioned way.

You can connect to BIX directly at (617) 861-9767, or through your local Tymnet number. (Plans are in the works for a regional network to hook into BIX, the NEARNET, which serves the northeast. Only these people will be able to telnet in and out of BIX; more on that later.) Access from countries outside the US and overseas through a packet network account. Consult your local provider for details there.

Before logging in, check out the useful information in FIG. 5-1.

If you are dialing direct, set your system to 8 data bits, 1 stop bit, no parity, full duplex and 300 to 2400 baud. If you are dialing through Tymnet, set your system to 7 data bits, 1 stop bit even parity and full duplex. In both cases, set parity checking to off. If you are connecting through Tymnet, you will be asked for a terminal identifier. Type

    a

You will be asked to log in. Type

    bix [or BIX]

When prompted, type in your assigned BIX name and password. How do you get same? Well, you sign up. BIX is available for $13 per month for a year's subscription. (It used to be $39 a quarter, but they changed their billing cycle in

```
New York        (212) 797-5620    San Francisco  █ 10:09  Mon 04-06-1992 █
Toronto         (416) 960-3187    Washington, DC  (202) 463-4920
Hightstown, NJ  (609) 426-7110

.More..
Log-in to BIXnet by dialing the local access number and responding as follows:
                Prompt              You enter
                service>            bix
                name?               new

Log-in to Tymnet by dialing your local access number and responding as
follows:
                Prompt                      You enter
                Enter terminal identifier   a
                Please log in:              bix
                name?                       new

You may charge your BIX subscription to a major credit card -- American
Express, MasterCard, or VISA -- pre-pay with a check, or have it billed to
your company (send us your company's purchase order).

For more information, call BIX at (800) 227-2983 or (603) 924-7681.
```

March 1992.) Or you can choose an hourly plan: pay $59 for a whole year and add $4 for every hour you actually use the service.

Now, if you have a credit card, log on as above, but type in `bix.deal` when prompted for your online name. Complete the online registration, choosing your online name and password.

Tymnet connect fees are $3 an hour additional on week nights and weekends, and $6 an hour additional weekdays in the lower 48 states.

There's also BIXNET, which is available for the same rates. Call 1-800-336-0149 for local access numbers.

JLBLINK is the new interface: it's worth a try if you have Windows. It automates your online sessions, organizes your mail and conference messages for offline reference. You can download it from BIX, or for $9.95 have them send you a diskette with all the necessary software. You can send electronic mail to "bixbilling" to order. JLBLINK comes with a telecommunications program, macro-key capabilities, and a word processor.

"The great thing about this new front end is that there are no commands. It's all icon-driven," says LaLiberte, who was responsible for the project. "The first cut is IBM Windows 3 only. It's a totally windows-integrated program. It creates a BIX icon for you, dials, logs you in. Then there's a board of icons . . . that's your BIX options." (See FIGS. 5-2 and 5-3 to see the JBLINK Windows front end and the mailbox.)

"Amiga is our next target. Macintosh or DOS users shouldn't hold your breath. Unix users can look forward to their own version soon," LaLiberte says. "It's pretty zippy."

"There's a couple of unique things about this: You can attach a binary file to a mail message. To your editor for instance, you can write: 'Here's my editorial, attached, in a WordPerfect file,' and you just attach. On goes the binary. It's just like a memo or Post-It note on top of a disk."

"The front end knows how to do all this, you don't have to choose a protocol or anything. Just push the button. It's totally canned."

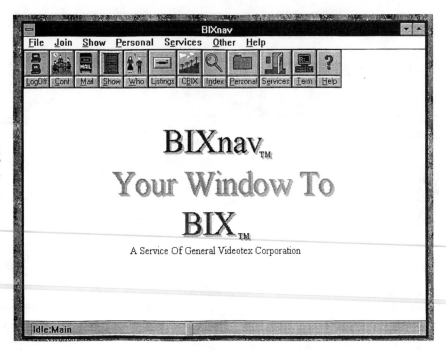

5-2
The new JBLINK front end for Windows presents your choices.

5-3
How your mailbox looks in JBLINK.

One of the reasons Windows was the first version of this new slick end is that Windows sort of lives and grows on BIX.

"Our Windows conference has gone through the ceiling and we are about to launch the Windows Information Exchange, in connection with "Windows Magazine", just as we did with BIX. The editor-in-chief is Ed Larya, formerly of Byte. He was instrumental in launching BIX and is now doing the same for Windows."

And the reason the next iteration will be an Amiga version, says Lockwood: "Our Amiga and IBM forums are really active. We simply have the best forum for Amiga that money can buy, including Commodore technical development teams. Our IBM forums offer the big names in the IBM business, and the developers of Windows." Another thing to check out is the "BIX User Manual." It outlines in black, white, and red what you can and cannot do. For $14.95, it can save you a bunch of time and frustration.

Sights: Libraries, special interest groups, messages

"From our formal and informal surveys, what the users find most important is the element of intellectual camaraderie. The global high technology reach is key," said Lockwood.

Who's there?

The populace online at BIX is significantly male, about 10% women. The staff is 50/50, though.

Online personalities include Jerry Pournelle, Hugh Kenner, Joanne Dow, Barry Nance, Rick Cook, Steve Sterling, Arthur Bozlee (expert on the former USSR's space program) and a few astronauts.

The regular Monday-Sunday schedule, as well as today's events, scroll as you log on. They generally include month CBITS (online chats with a moderator), sometimes special "kick the manager around" on-line meetings, a few appearances of UFO specialists, former Soviet scientists, and so on.

"We have the usual assortment of watch-your-language rules," he added. It's a very mature crowd: "Flame the content, not the writer" is the golden rule at BIX. Lockwood says it's fairly well followed, "but part of my job is to intervene when needed. We have sysops, and so on, but I'm the 600-pound gorilla. The collegiality is cherished here."

"And this is a PG system," said LaLiberte. "We try to be open, but we're not going to tolerate nonsense. No aliases. No obscenity. These are real people and professionals. That sets us apart. We don't get a lot of adolescent stuff around here; the customers drive them out faster than we can!"

Another thing has changed at BIX: they announced in April 1992 their Internet mail gateway. As a BIX subscriber, your address will be *jdoe@bix.com*. *jdoe* is your BIX signon name.

You will receive mail from the Internet and the USENET just as you do from BIX. To send mail, you use the commands of the BIX mail system, using the Internet or USENET address for your correspondent. You can upload the message or type it online, but it has to be short, a maximum of 2 megabytes. It costs 25 cents per message, still cheaper than snail mail.

"There will be no telnet or FTP," said LaLiberte. "We may join a regional net (NEARNET) and those people will be able to telnet. But absolutely we will never allow FTP . . . that's how you get viruses and so forth."

Two fun features that make BIX a friendly place are show who and show resume <bixname>.

The first will show you the names of the people online at the same time you are, and where they are on the planet. If someone's name and location interest you, the second command will tell you what that person is willing to tell other BIXen about himself. You, too, can have a resume, chock full of interesting tidbits about yourself. (See FIG. 5-4 for sample resumes.)

```
    mm Main menu

Enter a menu option or ? for help: 3
Username? liberty
This is a sample resume:

liberty, Steve Laliberte, Peterborough, NH
Last on: Sun Dec  9 14:16:42 1990
Steve Laliberte
BIX Director
BIX/McGraw-Hill
1 Phoenix Mill Lane
Peterborough, NH  03458
work phone (800) 227-2983 or (603) 924-7681

Resumes can be more than just your name and address. You can put
almost anything about yourself and family in here.

What sort of things can you write about?

Family
Hobbies
Employment
Education
.More..
```

5-4

Resumes on BIX are one way to introduce yourself.

You can use BIX as a business and personal network this way. Yet, privacy on BIX is good: "Your mail is private," said LaLiberte. "We don't mess with it. Messages are another thing. We are a publication, and as such we are responsible for what appears there. We reserve the right to edit public messages. If you read Folio, you expect to see articles on magazines. A story about walking your dog just wouldn't fit. That's the same thing with our BIX. Our charter is for the hi-tech professional, whether that's a programmer or a writer who lives and dies by the word processing program. That theme is necessary to everything we do. And, if in a hard-core programming area a question about turning on a printer should appear, we reserve the right to put that message where it belongs.

"That's how we keep the quality of our system so high."

The quality stretches across a wide spectrum of interests. Let's look at the conference subsystem.

If you are into computer industry news at all, check out the MicroBytes conference first. As with all conferences, you get there by choosing the join command at the main menu, or at a command prompt type

```
join microbytes
```

See FIG. 5-5.

For further information on BIX and our growing community of computer-using professionals, in the U.S. and Canada call 800-227-2983. In New Hampshire and elsewhere, call 603-924-7681, 8:30 a.m. to 11:00 p.m. EST (New York City time) weekdays.

Again, welcome to BIX. Thank you for your time and interest.

Tony Lockwood, Managing Editor

```
     BIX Main Menu

  1  Electronic Mail
  2  Conference Subsystem
.More..
  3  Listings
  4  CBix
  5  MicroBytes - Industry News Briefs
  6  Subscriber Information
  7  Individual Options
  8  Quick Download
  9  Command Mode (abandon menus)
 10  Logoff (bye)

Enter a menu option or ? for help:
```

5-5
At the main menu, type join microbytes.

MicroBytes is a read-only conference (the sysops can post, but you can't). You get there by pressing 5 at the main menu and will be shown the first three messages of the group. Messages are displayed from oldest to newest. You can get around that with several commands:

First   Look at the oldest
last   Look at the newest
again   Look at the one you just saw
Look at a specific message by number

The "Bix User Manual" has a long, technical explanation about its pointers system. It boils down to this: BIX knows what you've read. Unless you ask it specifically to do so, it won't show you a message, article or posting more than once. (See FIG. 5-6.)

This can get quite elaborate, skipping forward and back as much as you please. In MicroBytes, you'll be shown the topics available in that conference, which range from specific products to industry trends. If you want to make a comment about something you read in MicroBytes, join *tech.news* and add a comment. Other conferences, however, are exchanges of messages, just as on other systems we've visited. Some conferences are open: you have new users of various systems, lifestyle interests from cats to astronomy to comics, and professional conferences to choose from. Some of these, however, are "closed." You will see a "c" by such conference names when presented in a menu (and an "o" for open conferences). You enter conferences by typing join <conference>, and next time you sign on, that will be on your list of

```
      1   Electronic Mail
      2   Conference Subsystem
      3   Listings
      4   CBix
      5   MicroBytes - Industry News Briefs
      6   Subscriber Information
      7   Individual Options
      8   Quick Download
      9   Command Mode (abandon menus)
     10   Logoff (bye)
```

5-6

Microbytes is a must-see on BIX.

```
Enter a menu option or ? for help: 5

      MicroBytes News Service Menu

      1   o microbytes         Daily news briefs about technology and computing
      2   o microbytes.hw      New hardware products
      3   o microbytes.sw      New software products
      4   o short.takes        Hands on looks at new products by BYTE editors
      5   o reviews.hw         Formal reviews of new hardware by BYTE editors
      6   o reviews.sw         Formal reviews of new software by BYTE editors
     mm   Main menu

Enter a menu option or ? for help:
```

places to go. Should you decide you're tired of being part of a conference, type `resign <conference>`. Closed conferences aren't impossible to join. If you choose 1 from the writer's menu, for example, you can get the description of the *writers.pros* and the BIX name of the person to request membership from. Simply write that person outlining who you are and why you'd like to join. (See FIG. 5-7 for a conference listing and FIG. 5-8 for specific conference groups.)

```
 ◆  File  Edit  Setup  Connect  Fax      Alt-H for help   VT100   2400-8-N-1
Contact: AddStor, 3905 Bohannon Dr., Menlo Park, CA 94025,
(800) 732-3133, fax, (415) 688-0466.
Return for next, m for menu, or message number: m

      Conference Action Menu

      1   Read next message
      2   Read this message again
      3   Read comments to this message
      4   Read original message
      5   Contribute a new message
      6   Comment to this message
      7   Skip to a message
      8   Search messages
      9   Change to a different topic
     10   CBix
     11   Search BIX subscriber list
     12   Show a subscriber's online resume
     13   Show members of current conference
     14   Show last login time of current conference members
      p   Previous menu
     mm   Main menu

Enter a menu option or ? for help:
```

5-7

Conferences are listed this way.

If you are not sure about what is where, type `join index`. This menu system will scan all open BIX conferences for a keyword or phrase you choose. The results can be downloaded to read offline. Another good command is `show <topic>`. For example, if you need to know what's what with ozone, type `show ozone`. After a minute, BIX will show you all the conferences with messages with that string in it.

```
▪ ◆ File  Edit  Setup  Connect  Fax      Alt-H for help    VT100    2400-8-N-1
mm Main menu

Enter a menu option or ? for help: 11

     Join Conference Menu

1  Show information about a conference

2  o desktop.pub       Using microcomputers for publishing
3  o journalism        Reporting and writing news
4  o lexicon           About words
5  o new.writers       Getting started in the writing business
6  o poetry.prose          Writing both types of English
7  o sf                For Science Fiction, Star Trek, and fantasy fans
8  c sfwa              Meeting place for the Science Fiction Writers of America
9  o word.processor    Word-processing programs
10 o writers           The original writers conference
11 c writers.pros      Interaction for professional writers only
12 o writers.talk      Insights and conversation from professional writers
p  Previous menu
mm Main menu

 (o=open,c=closed)
.More..
```

5-8

*A specific group of
conferences look like this.*

Conferences are grouped under exchanges. The conferences are too numerous to
list, and besides they change a lot. But some of the highlights are as follows:

Exchange	Sample conferences
Software Libraries	amiga.games
Amiga Exchange	amiga.dev
The Associations, User Groups	medicine
and Professional Exchange	law
	sysops
BIX/BYTE Magazine Exchange	microbytes
Entertainment	chess
and Leisure Exchange	sca
	washington.dc
IBM Exchange	IBM.pc
	ibm.vendors
	ibm.repairshop
MacIntosh Exchange	mac.desktop
	mac.external
	ma.sandbox
Other Exchange	cd.rom
	international
	philosophy
	robotics
	unclassified
Programmers Exchange	ada
	gem
	rwars
	tech.support
Tojerry Exchange	chaos.manor
(That's Jerry Pournelle)	contact

	disasters
	space
Writers Exchange	new.writers
	writers
	writers.talk
Vendor Support Exchange	desqview
	borland
	logitech
	ataricorp

This is just a smidgen; the list goes on and on.

Mail has some neat features on BIX. One is that a message you have sent remains in your out basket, with a marker detailing whether it has been read by the addressee. (See FIG. 5-9.)

```
  7   Individual Options
  8   Quick Download
  9   Command Mode (abandon menus)
 10   Logoff (bye)

Enter a menu option or ? for help:
Enter a menu option or ? for help: 1
    From            Mail * Date
 1 lockwood         2377   Tue Dec 7 07:53   Welcome to BIX!
 2 helper           2382   Tue Dec 7 08:04   I can help
 3 sysmgr           2863   Tue Dec 7 12:58   Welcome aboard
 4 liberty          2881   Tue Dec 7 13:58   Yet Another Welcome

    Electronic Mail Menu

 1  Read mail
 2  Send mail
 3  View inbasket
 4  View outbasket
 5  Delete mail
mm  Main menu

Enter a menu option or ? for help: 1

Return for next, m for menu, or memo number:
```

5-9
This is what your mailbox looks like without the Windows front end.

And of course, as Lockwood mentioned, there's the ability to attach a binary file to a text memo.

CBIX is a popular feature. As pointed out, it is often used in a formal fashion as an online meeting, with a moderator. But free-form conversations go on, too. The realtime chat will have interesting people speaking their minds on whatever you can imagine. You'll find specific conversations on current events, fantasy role-playing games, trivia, and technology. Type join cbix and follow the menus.

If you just want to play around, there's rscards. This is a three-dimensional maze, which you zip around in your turbo pod. You've got your power generators, blasters and repair microbots. The object is to move through the complex and deadly maze in search of other BIXen (as the BIX users call themselves). Type `join rscards`.

Science fiction is another one of BIX's landmarks. From Star Trek to Twin Peaks, you'll find discussions and event announcements; stores, clubs and libraries; and of course the leading writers in this field. Join any or all of sf, animation, television, arts, elfquest, or leisure to check these out.

And you'll find conferences for people involved with adoption (parents and adoptees); the handicapped and those trying to develop software and hardware for them; and a large selection of software for downloading.

Speaking of the last point, don't forget to set your quick download protocols: after you tell BIX your preferred style of downloading, it's not necessary to tell it again.

How to logoff

You type `bye`, and you're gone, but not before you get a screenful of information. You'll be reminded of the numbers to call for voice support, as well as other useful bulletins.

In sum

You won't use BIX to shop, or manage your portfolio, or do your homework. But for the latest on what's what in computer technology, and camaraderie among an intelligent, intrepid group of techies, BIX is worth a visit.

6 DASnet delivers

E-mail	*[11]mktg, 460-4510* [MCI]
U.S. Mail	DA Systems, Inc.
	1503 E. Campbell Ave.
	Campbell, CA 95008
Phone	(408) 559-7434 [voice]
	(408) 559-0148 [fax]
Hours	All the time
Basic rate	Included with some online services; about $8.00 a month plus a per-message fee for individuals.
Notes	They deliver e-mail, the whole e-mail, and nothing but the e-mail.

Say you want to exchange e-mail with someone. As we've learned in our travels, typically, you must first jump through the hoops . . .

First hoop: What is the addressee's system? CompuServe? Internet? Some other?

Next hoop: The format of the message and the address. Can she receive graphics? Files? Simple text? Is the address @ or ! or some combination?

Next hoop: Is her system connected in any way with yours through some gateway, and if not, can you compute a route that will connect with her anyway?

Next hoop: Can you assure that the addresses coming and going are letter perfect?

The final hoop: Do you remember what you wanted to say before you started the loop through the hoops?

Enter DASnet As usual in the computer/telecommunications marketplace, the need created a product. DASnet is one such product.

You might often hear about DASnet in your travels. A privately owned company, it was formed to solve the problem of every commercial mailing system's having its own sheet of music to sing from: syntax, editor, connections, and nodes. While certain connections did exist, people on MCI couldn't talk to any other e-mail system except CompuServe, and some e-mail systems had no connections with other systems at all.

Then came DASnet. Launched in July 1987 by DA Systems, this subscription-based service was created to meet the needs of people who wanted to send e-mail messages across different e-mail vendors' systems. The parent company is a privately held for-profit concern. The corporation, DA Systems, Inc., has been around since 1974.

How it works

Of course, the first concern was security. E-mail security is improving, but the potential for disaster exists. DASnet is careful about this: DASnet modems only dial out. You post your message on your own e-mail system, with DASnet in the address field and the recipient's address and e-mail system in the subject field. DASnet dials out to several different systems several times a day. It downloads your message and sends it on.

Only one of you has to subscribe to DASnet for this to work, but you both must subscribe to some other e-mail system. Within a couple of hours, your message is delivered. This costs $30.00 for startup, $7.75 per month, plus 60 to 75 cents per message. Until the computer version of the interstate is in place, this toll road is about the best choice you have for traveling the e-mail pathways to unknown places. The reach is considerable: MercanFax in Hong Kong and Tokyo, MCI, AT&T mail, BIX, the Dialcom network, EasyLink, Envoy 100, MCI Mail, the SprintMail network, UUCP, and domain-addressable sites, e.g. ".EDU" and ".COM," and many more.

But on some systems, DASnet is part of your subscription package at no extra charge. These include (and more are added each day):

Alternex (Brazil)
Bookmail (Germany)
CESAC (Italy)
CIGnet
ComNet (Switzerland)
CONNECT
Deutsche Mailbox (Germany)
Euromail (Germany)
FredsNaetet (Sweden)
Galaxy
GeoNet (hosts in Germany, UK, USA)
GreenNet (UK)
INFOTAP (Luxembourg)
Mailbox Benelux (Holland)
MBK Mediabox (Germany)
MercanMail (Asia)
Nicarao (Nicaragua)
OTC Dialcom (Australia)
PeaceNet/EcoNet
Pegasus (Australia)
PINET
PsychNet
San Francisco/Moscow Teleport (USA/USSR)

Telehaus Nordhorn (Germany)
Telerede (Portugal)
Telexphone (France)
TEXTEL (Caribbean)
TWICS (Japan)
UNISON Web (Canada)

and organizations whose internal e-mail systems use the DASnet Service. So if you know anyone on any of these systems, you can use DASnet to send messages back and forth across e-mail systems.

Figure 6-1 shows how it works.

NOW! DASnet® Service for LANs

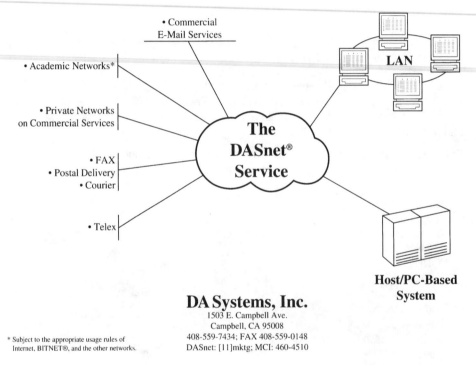

• Commercial E-Mail Services

• Academic Networks*

• Private Networks on Commercial Services

• FAX
• Postal Delivery
• Courier

• Telex

The DASnet® Service

LAN

Host/PC-Based System

DA Systems, Inc.
1503 E. Campbell Ave.
Campbell, CA 95008
408-559-7434; FAX 408-559-0148
DASnet: [11]mktg; MCI: 460-4510

* Subject to the appropriate usage rules of Internet, BITNET®, and the other networks.

6-1 *You could be a host/pc-based system on the loop that includes all the other elements.*

You can sign on by writing

DA Systems, Inc.
1503 E. Campbell Ave.
Campbell, CA 95008
(408) 559-7434 [voice]
(408) 559-0148 [fax]

DASnet e-mail address is *[11]mktg* from any DASnet-connected system. The MCI address is *460-4510*.

The gospel according to DASnet is that their service fits your current setup. No additional hardware or software expense is involved, they say, if you already have a modem and a computer, or any configuration thereof. Most of their services are aimed at businesses with lots of both hooked together, but if you have in place a phone line, leased line or packet switch, you are ready. You contact DA Systems and tell them your location, the hardware and e-mail software you use, and they fit you on. Other services include Telex service, FAX delivery and postal delivery, each with a set of charges.

You can use distribution lists: that is, sending the same message to many boxes, on many systems at once.

If you are on a system hooked up to DASnet as a standard feature, you simply follow the directions for that system, using the DASnet address according to the instructions online.

Anna Lange, marketing manager for DA Systems, says DASnet really opens up e-mail for companies and individuals.

"Different e-mail systems differ widely, even wildly. DASnet people on Unison and BIX can enter the DASnet address to ATT mail, *JSMITH@ATT*, in the 'to' field. Other systems are much more complicated, needing careful addressing. But this message format applies from ATT to other systems.

"You're looking at different kinds of service packages. We have constellations of services put together for people who use e-mail systems."

One constellation of services is for business e-mail systems, as listed earlier. They use it for internal business or projects. As an example, Lange says, certain religious service organizations use DASnet for communications among other churches. Another example is an economical way for export-import companies to communicate among offices. Other examples include, Lange says, "Attorneys. Both for-profit and nonprofit. Relief organizations. Most of them are customers of other customers. It has great general business use. A lot of publishers. A big customer is BookMail—a publisher's net in Germany."

But the real strength is what it does for the individual, she says. "It's electronic mail as it could have been from the beginning: wonderful!" Because it's easy to use, the point becomes sending a message, not figuring out the system.

"Even though you are a hobbyist, your e-mail concerns have other interests as well that this is the right address. Social, business, religious, and educational interests are served by this well. I'm aware of several families who communicate with their children via the DASnet services," she said. In the main, however, she said, most applications are business, nonprofits, and other more pedestrian pursuits.

DASnet has different service packages aimed at individuals and small groups. The easiest way to connect is to join the commercial service that offers DASnet as a feature. Or pay $33.50 for a setup and $4.75 per month plus a charge per message. Other packages hook on the on-site to a LAN or computer service, if you can talk your boss into it. Other constellations of services are for internal e-mail only. When set up for a company's wide area network or local area network, DASnet does not allow other users to connect.

How to use DASnet

Out of many, one

Why hobbyists might be interested

"People use something because they see something in it for them. They have family to correspond with, overseas or wherever. Naturally the ongoing communication is more possible by e-mail than by mail or phone," Lange said.

"I've known of people carrying out the postal chess idea through DASnet. The average user should possibly think about projects he is engaged in, things that make a difference to the world. For instance, Amnesty International distributes express alerts through DASnet. Timeliness really makes a difference in that situation. If you want to have immediacy and availability of your e-mail, coming and going, regardless of where you are at the moment, this is for you," she said.

"Everybody should sign up!"

7 DELPHI
Creativity & rationality in one

E-mail	*username@delphi.com*
U.S. Mail	1030 Massachusetts Ave.
	Cambridge, MA 02138
Phone	(800) 695-4005 [voice]
	(800) 365-4636 [modem, to join]
Hours	24 hours a day; evenings and weekends are cheaper.
Basic rate	DELPHI has two membership plans: the 10/4 Plan is $10 per month and includes the first 4 hours of use; additional use is $4 per hour. The 20/20 Advantage Plan is $20 per month, includes 20 hours of use, and is only $1.80 per hour for additional time. The Internet service option is an extra $3 per month including transfer of 10 megabytes (the equivalent of about 3000 typewritten pages). Access during business hours via Sprintnet or Tymnet carries a surcharge.
Notes	Interface much like BIX, its sister system, but a cozier, more casual feeling.

Creativity & rationality

DELPHI is a service of General Videotex Corporation, a developer of interactive and online services based in Cambridge, Massachusetts. For more information, either call the above number or send e-mail to Walt Howe, Internet SIG manager at *walthowe@DELPHI.com.*

DELPHI has been around longer than many online systems, but it's not very well known. It was the first online encyclopedia, started in 1983, but they have been growing and adding services steadily, ever since. Of course, it was named for the site of the famous Greek Oracle. For the Greeks, Delphi was the center in which opposing creative forces—the rational creativity of Apollo and the irrational creativity of Dionysus—merged and from which all creative forms emerged. There's a little more of Dionysus than Apollo here, but both are amply represented.

At its sister service, BIX, we discovered, the atmosphere was stuffy but active with dozens of conversations going on at once. DELPHI, though running basically the same software, feels more like the cafe around the corner: not nearly so straight-laced and technical; more chatting going on, games, and shopping. The software and the people are friendly and relaxed. And it's just more casual here. An example: though BIX might someday have an astrology area, DELPHI's is a very busy place indeed.

DELPHI uses an informal software setup. It has large file libraries containing both documents and software; fun is an important component. DELPHI is one of the few on-line services that does not require a special interface to make the service usable; however, should you feel the need, you can download a shareware program (PC or MAC) in most SIGs, called Messenger. Registration for this program is $45.

Logging on

DELPHI is on SprintNet, Tymnet, DataPack in Canada, not to mention its DELPHI/Regional services in Boston, Kansas City, Miami, and Argentina.

Set your parameters to 8-N-1 and your terminal emulation to VT100 or VT52. In my experience, my computer in an ANSI terminal setting just didn't like DELPHI's way of talking.

The best way to join is to call voice (800) 695-4005 and talk to the representative who can give you a password, user name, and the nearest phone number to dial. User names on DELPHI are all lowercase, no spaces. Your user name need not be representative of your real name; but once you have it, you're stuck with it unless you close that account and start another. When you order something online, though, and at certain SIGS, you will be asked your real-life name before you can participate.

Your username also becomes your Internet address: *username@DELPHI.com*.

An entire book has been devoted to navigating DELPHI. Originally written by Michael Banks, a new edition is out.

"Our guide has recently been revised and reprinted," says Russell Williams, Jr., vice president of sales and marketing at DELPHI. (You can reach him online as "rusty.")

"We bought the rights from Michael Banks, so it's now published by General Videotex Corporation. The title is 'DELPHI: The Official Guide' and the price is $19.95, but discounts are available to new members. (Right now, we're selling it during the signup for $12.95 plus $3 shipping and handling.)"

Vocabulary of DELPHI

Typing online, realtime messages to others on DELPHI is called "conference" here. You can "conference" from any menu, setting up several conversations at once. You can block out people, leave to check something out [a buffer will tell you what was said while you were "gone"], and even upload a file in conference mode.

The place to exchange messages and files is a "forum." That's usually in a menu for a "SIG" (Special Interest Group) or club.

"Mail" from the main menu is not just e-mail (that's MAIL MAIL from the main menu). In DELPHI, mail comes in many forms: telex (extra charge); translation to and from English to and from many languages; the workspace; and fax.

"Workspace" is available from almost any menu. It has a different prompt [WS>], and it lets you transfer, store, edit, copy, delete, view, and backup files. You can use it with e-mail, conferencing, forums, and databases.

"Database" is the name for files areas (analogous to "library" on CompuServe). Most files downloads are free. Transfer protocols include ASCII (tricky in VT100 mode), Kermit, Xmodem, Ymodem, and Zmodem. Uploading is free of connect charges.

A SIG is a special interest group, like a Forum on CompuServe or a RoundTable on GEnie.

DELPHI provides full access to the Internet, including real-time electronic mail, file transfers with "FTP," and remote logins to other Internet hosts using "Telnet." DELPHI is as of this writing the only leading consumer online service to offer such a wide variety of Internet features.

Before, anyone interested in accessing the Internet had a very limited number of options. In most cases, you had only e-mail connectivity unless you were connected directly through your company or school. DELPHI is now a low-cost access option available to home computer users. Anyone can connect to DELPHI with a local call from over 600 cities and towns throughout the US and, in many other countries, for $3.00 a month over the basic DELPHI charges.

DELPHI's connection to the Internet works both ways: In addition to offering access out to other networks, DELPHI offers services to people already on the Internet. Any user of the Internet can access DELPHI to use services such as Grolier's Academic American Encyclopedia, the Dictionary of Cultural Literacy, Reuters and UPI news wires, stock quotes, computer support, travel reservations, special interest groups, real-time conferencing, downloadable programs, and multi-player games. All these services can be reached through the Internet simply by joining DELPHI and then telnetting to the address *DELPHI.com* via the commercial Internet.

If you are a new user to the Internet, you can ask questions in DELPHI's Internet Special Interest Group (SIG). The Menu (reached by typing GR INT) includes an active message forum where members and staff can exchange useful information. (See FIG. 7-1.) Comprehensive guide books, downloadable software, and information files are also available, some of them for a price.

Internet is here

```
              THE

 _ /  /_/ \ /_ _/ \  _ /_/ \_ /_/ \ /_/ \
 /_/  /_/ /_/ /_/    \_/ /_/ /_/ /_/ /_/ /_
 _ / /_/ /_ /_/ _ /\ \ / /_/ /_/ /_/ /_/ /_/
 _/  /_/ /_ /_/ /_/ \ \/ /_ /_/ /_/ /_/ /_/


         SPECIAL INTEREST GROUP

     Helping you connect to everywhere!

     Walt Howe, INTERNET SIG Manager
       Jim Monty, Assistant Manager


NEW TO THE INTERNET? Select "Using Internet Services" on the SIG menu,
and read the file, "I'M NEW! WHAT DO I DO?

COMING TO A JANUARY CONFERENCE: Hope Tillman, Director of Libraries at
Babson College and Chair of the Special Libraries Association Networking
Committee. Talking about "Information on the Internet." WATCH FOR IT!!!

Press RETURN for Internet SIG Menu:
```

7-1
The Internet Special Interest Group helps ingenues with FTP, telnet, and other Internet intricacies.

Initiation to the mysteries

When your username and password are accepted, you come into the main menu (see FIG. 7-2), which might or might not have some announcements.

```
Find out what this year will bring for you in Astro Predictions.  Type GO ENT
ASTRO, and choose OUTLOOK.

Chapter 1 of THE MOTE IN GOD'S EYE sequel THE GRIPPING HAND, by Larry Niven and
Jerry Pournelle, is on DELPHI!  See GROUP SCIENCE, then DATA UP, and READ 245.

Parsons Technology has just updated it's store on DELPHI, including new Windows
programs.  For quality software at reasonable prices, type GO SHOP PARSONS.
```

7-2

The first menu you see on DELPHI.

```
MAIN Menu:

Business and Finance       News, Weather, and Sports
Computing Groups           Reference and Education
Conference                 Shopping
DELPHI/Regional            Travel and Leisure
Entertainment and Games    Using DELPHI
Groups and Clubs           Workspace
Internet Services          HELP
Mail                       EXIT
Member Directory           BOSTON Services

MAIN>What do you want to do?
```

Notice from these bulletins that you can chain commands. You could type ENT for entertainment, then ASTRO at the next menu for Astrology. But you could type GO ENT ASTRO, then choose OUTLOOK at the Astrology menu. At any menu, usually the first three or four letters of a menu choice will suffice. You can EXIT *GROUP-NAME* from one group to another directly, without intervening menus.

A quick rundown of your choices from the main menu:

- Business and Finance is where you'll find UPI Business News fees, a SIG for business minded people, stock and commodity quotes, an online brokerage and Dow Jones averages, plus other economic news and advice.

- Computing Groups are the SIGs, forums, and databases for several brands and flavors of computers.

- Conference, as we explained, is chatting online with people who are in the same menu you are at the moment.

  First, type WHO to see who else is around. Their usernames will be displayed, and whether they are conferencing. If they are, the conferencing group will have a name. To join a group that is conferencing type JOIN *groupname*. To page someone to come and enter a new group with you, type PAGE *username*.

  Most of the Conference commands are prefixed with a slash, "/", so that they can be distinguished from text when used from within a conversation. To see a list of all of the commands, enter /HELP.

  /Send allows you to send a direct message to any user currently on the system, unless they have used the /GAG command to prevent interruptions. The best way to learn about conference is to go in there and try it out. Don't be shy: ask questions. You will find that other users are very helpful and genuinely enjoy sharing their knowledge with new people.

- DELPHI/Regional will take you to gateways to the regional setups of DELPHI. Each has some unique features and often tie in with local universities.

- Entertainment and Games (the menu is shown in FIG. 7-3) include forums, real-time games, e-mail games, and more.

```
Entertainment & Games Menu:

Adventure Games            Poker Showdown
Astro Predictions          Quest
Board and Logic Games      SCRAMBLE Word Game
Collaborative Novel        Stellar Conquest
Critics' Choice Reviews    TQ Trivia Tournament
FlipIt!                    VT-52 & VT-100 Games
Hollywood Hotline          Yacht Club
Movie Reviews by Cineman   Help
Penn & Teller              Exit

ENTERTAINMENT>Which Selection?
```

7-3
The Entrainment and Games menu on DELPHI.

- Groups and Clubs: from Games to Writers, from Flight Simulators to the Environment, the general interest SIGs are here.
- Internet: from here you can visit the Internet SIG, as well as telnet and FTP. The telnetting menu is in FIG. 7-4.

```
◆  File  Edit  Setup  Connect  Fax               VT100   2400-8-N-1
INFO: Rutgers University Pilot Campus-Wide Information System
Main Menu Commands...

Command              Purpose
-------              -------
About_Rutgers        General Information about the University
Academics            Courses, Schedules, Registration, Special programs
Computing            Computing facilities, services and network information
Campus               Courses and events specific to each campus.
Directories          Phone directories, Faculty research info., Univ. Forms
Using_INFO           <<What is INFO, how to use it, how to send suggestions>>
Library              Libraries, information resources, reference material
News_n_Events        News, Weather
Services             Students,Faculty/Staff services, police info
University           University , Community
For other info, call the Student Info. and Assistance Center at (908)932-9090.

Find                 Search for keywords for Goto command.
Quit                 Exit from information system

INFO: Rutgers University Pilot Campus-Wide Information System
Main Menu>
```

7-4
DELPHI's Telnet is supported by Rutgers University. You must know the telnet address you want before you get here.

- Mail: as explained earlier, this is a wide range of communications services, hard copy and e-mail.
- Member Directory: look up someone on DELPHI by username or real name. Also, you can read short biographies of users here, and leave one of your own to introduce yourself to the other members.
- News, weather, sports: news wire feeds on these subjects, movies, and more.
- Reference and Education: Here is where you'll find New Parent's Network, encyclopedia, medical topics and SIGS, and for a surcharge, DIALOG research service.

- Shopping: Unlike BIX, DELPHI has quite a lineup of merchants online, many of them related to computer software and hardware, but you'll also find greeting cards, gifts, books and so on.
- Travel and Leisure: not only the Official Airlines Guide and Eaasy Sabre, but profiles of cities and countries you might want to visit, lodging and ground transportation, tours, cruises, and convention services. You can even apply for a travel visa online!
- Using DELPHI: This should be the new user's first stop. Set your capture on and download all 31 of the TIPS from this menu. If you have a specific problem, there's a new user SIG where sysops and administrators will help you. You're not billed for DELPHI time while in this menu, so make good use of it.

  Using DELPHI is also a good place to tell DELPHI your favorite settings. Type USING DELPHI SETTINGS, and you'll get the screen in FIG. 7-5.

```
USING-DELPHI>(Please Select an Item)> settings
Some of your temporary settings are being restored to their initialization
values.

SETTINGS Menu:

BUSY-Mode                      PROMPT-Mode
DEFAULT-Menu                   SET-High-bit
DOWNLOAD-Line-terminators      SLASH-Term-settings
ECHO-Mode                      TERMINAL-Type
EDITOR                         TIMEOUT
FILE-TRANSFERS                 UTILITIES
KERMIT-SETTINGS                WIDTH (Columns)
LENGTH (Lines/page)            XMODEM-SETTINGS
NETWORK-PARAMETERS             HELP
PASSWORD (Change)              EXIT

SETTINGS>What would you like to set? busy

The system default is that you are NOT BUSY.

You will now receive all messages.
Change this? y
```

7-5

The settings menu where you can set line length, whether you want to conference with people, and so on.

This menu is also available from forums. It is a powerful customization: you can determine which menu comes up first, whether you want menus or only command lines, your default file transfer protocols, your password, and more.

- Help will get you short descriptions of the commands from any menu you have at the moment.
- Exit: From the main menu, exit will log you off. From any other menu, it will take you back one menu.

Chain of command

You can get along just fine with DELPHI's menus, but don't forget that you can chain commands and selections to move past several menus at once. The "Go" command is the easiest way to do this, and it works with all the menus except e-mail. Exit, as mentioned before, can take you from one SIG to another.

You can change from one database topic to another using "set."

Conclusion

By far, the most popular feature is the conferencing. It makes DELPHI seem small and cozy, and newcomers are warmly welcomed. But this is a large and powerful service. Explore and confer, research and recommend. It's not the navel of the universe yet, but you can definitely increase your wisdom here.

8 Online crusaders
The IGC networks

E-mail	*support@igc.org* [Internet]
U.S. Mail	18 DeBoom St.
	San Francisco, CA 94107
Phone	(415) 442-0220 [voice]
	(415) 546-1794 [fax]
	(415) 322-0284 [modem, 8-N-1]
Hours	24 hours a day, cheapest after 6 p.m. and on weekends
Basic rate	One-time $15 sign-up fee. $10 per month after that for one hour off-peak. Internet connections at many locations for $3.00 per hour; otherwise $5/hour off-peak, $10/hour peak. Some gateways and storage space extra.
Notes	This is the calling-for-causes network. If you have a (liberal) axe to grind, get online here.

This is the activists' online realm, and the list of conferences takes up two dozen pages in small type. From legislative and informational resources to indigenous peoples' movements; from the Greens to the National Writers Union, you'll find people here who want to change the world in 1000 different ways.

Eco, peace, & conflict nets

The Institute for Global Communications runs the several networks, all with Internet/USENET connections. The three most popular are EcoNet, PeaceNet and ConflictNet.

EcoNet has conferences and files for those working for environmental preservation and sustainability. You'll find subjects such as global warming, energy policy, rain-forest preservation, legislative activities in many countries, water quality, and environmental education.

PeaceNet serves peace and social justice advocates around the world. The files and conferences center on human rights, disarmament, international relations, alternative news services and other topics, especially if they involve antiwar movements.

ConflictNet seems just a little different from PeaceNet, at first. The key here is that armed conflict and physical violence are rarely the focus, unless, say, a labor strike turns violent. Social conflicts, such as legal disputes, are more the crux of the matter. The message conferences and files concern guidelines for choosing a neutral third party, case studies in conflict resolution, exhaustive bibliographies on conflict resolution, legislative updates, educational materials and resources, and newsletters from around the world.

The three nets are all available once you're online, and only a keystroke away.

Other nets include

- LaborNet, a network for labor activists to collect information, collaborate efforts, and enhance organized labor's activities. Organized by Michael G. Stein, it so far is all volunteer. Check in here for in-depth discussion of the Free Trade Agreement.
- HomeoNet, for those interested in homeopathy, a self-help holistic philosophy of medical care.

Who's there Tucked in here and there under these generous umbrellas are Druids, gays, Kurds, UN workers, and novelists. Organizations online—and there are hundreds—include the Alaska Department of Education, Catholic Social Services Bureau, Global Action & Information Network (GAIN), National Geographic, and Zero Population Growth. Again, the list goes on for pages and pages. Name a cause, a minority group, or a third world nation, and they're represented here somewhere.

IGC networks provide sending and receiving of private messages, including fax and Telex, as well as the public conferences.

Within the conferences, you'll find events calendars, newsletters, legislative alerts, funding sources, press releases, action updates, breaking stories, calls for support, and peace and activism-pertinent USENET news feeds. You can search lists of speakers, get the address of US and world leaders, find grant making foundations, and more.

The whole purpose of IGC is to promote international cooperation and partnership, and discuss peace and environmental problems. IGC works to develop low-cost access to computer networking from outside the US, especially in the Southern Hemisphere. They played a major role in starting nonprofit computer networks in Brazil, Nicaragua, and Russia, and are working to develop similar ones in Bolivia, Costa Rica, Ecuador, Uruguay and Kenya. Australia, the UK, Canada, and Sweden have partner networks connected, too.

So who needs a passport?

Signing on If you have a SprintNet account, hit Enter at the Terminal= prompt. Then at the @ prompt, type c igc and Enter. When you see IGC CONNECTED, continue the login as presented.

You can log onto IGC directly, and with your credit card, register right away. On connecting, type new at LOGIN prompt, hit Enter at the password prompt, and fill in the blanks. It looks like FIG. 8-1.

```
 ◆ File  Edit  Setup  Connect  Fax              TTY   2400-8-N-1

AT&FE1V1X4&C1&DZS0=0S7=60
OK
AT
OK


login: new
Password:
Login incorrect
login: new
Password:
Last login: Mon Dec  7 14:54:40 from ing3.med.nyu.edu

Please wait a moment...
```

8-1
Logging in as "new."

The full registration process asks for name, address, phone number, and your major areas of interest. You can get a brochure with an application form by calling or writing the office as shown.

Within two business days, you'll get the screens shown in FIG. 8-2 and FIG. 8-3, welcoming you as a new member.

```
 ◆ File  Edit  Setup  Connect  Fax              TTY   2400-8-N-1
Welcome to EcoNet! You are now part of a rapidly growing community of
people who use the network to share information and to work together to
preserve and sustain the planet.

With EcoNet, you can prepare joint projects with partners all over the
world, read and discuss the latest environmental news and send private
messages nearly anywhere. You can even send a telex or fax directly from
your EcoNet account to people who do not have computer network access. See
your IGC user's manual for easy instructions.

Browse EcoNet's electronic conferences. EcoNet's support staff has set a
"visit list" of conferences in your account to start you off. To visit
these conferences, choose "Conferences" from the main menu, then type the
letter "v" and <Return> or <Enter> at the "Conf?" prompt. Once you're
visiting, refer to your user's manual for instructions to add or delete
conferences on your visit list to suit yourself.

Be sure to (g)o to the 'conferences' conference, which lists and describes
the conferences for EcoNet, PeaceNet, ConflictNet and our international
partner networks. You have access to any of these conferences by typing the
 conference name at the "Conf?" prompt.

-- Hit <RETURN> for more --
Mail?
```

8-2
This screen is sent to newly confirmed members.

Once you are on, you might notice that you are in Unix. This system works much like Portal, with batch downloading of messages and file uploading for replies. Not as handy as a QWK mail reader, but workable. The opening menu you see as a member is in FIG. 8-4.

the conferences for EcoNet, PeaceNet, ConflictNet and our international
partner networks. You have access to any of these conferences by typing the
conference name at the "Conf?" prompt.

-- Hit <RETURN> for more --
Mail?
The Institute for Global Communications staff is ready to serve you.
Contact us or our support staff (e-mail: support) with your suggestions or
for help using the system. Reach us by phone on weekdays in San Francisco
at (415) 442-0220 from 6 a.m. to 5 p.m. Pacific Standard Time.

Don't be shy about posting public messages in the "test" conference, and
then in others. Your participation will help the environmental movement,
in the U.S. and elsewhere, make this a healthier, happier planet.

Sincerely,

Anthony Whitworth and Michael Stein, EcoNet Program Officers

8-3

This screen is sent to newly confirmed members.

Mail: (i)ndex (u)nread (w)rite (c)apture (d)elete (s)ave (h)elp (q)uit:

Last login: Tue Dec 1 09:29:53 from mace.igc.org
You have new mail.
Terminal = generic (hit <RETURN> or enter new terminal type): tty
No such terminal type. Assuming terminal is generic.
Press the key used to delete a character, followed by <RETURN>: ^H
Your delete key is: BACKSPACE

    Welcome to EcoNet II. For help, type "?"

You have new conf entries in en.alerts en.announcements en.calendar ...

You have new mail messages.

        EcoNet Command Menu:

        c   -- Conferences
        m   -- Electronic Mail
        s   -- Setup: Change your Password, Language, Terminal Type
        u   -- User Directory
        d   -- Online databases
        h   -- Help
        bye   -- Logout

Your selection:

8-4

Your EcoNet opening menu shows whether you have mail waiting, as well as the commands to get started.

Usually, you'll go to mail first, then to conferences.

Handy commands to keep in mind

At a conference and mail command line, you can type c for capture, with a
subcommand of d for download. To download the titles of the messages (or
"articles") choose i for index, then % to show you only new items. You can
download the index, read it offline, then log back on. Then use r and the numbers
of the messages that interest you, and again download them. You can then read the
messages and compose answers with your favorite editor.

To upload replies or a new message you have written offline, at "Hit enter to enter/edit text, type 'u' to upload a file," the u command has these options:

a   for an ASCII on TEXT only documents. You watch the letters stream across the screen

aq   for ASCII without the letters echoed to the screen

k   for Kermit, text, or binary

x   for xmodem, text, or binary.

Choose your option, then manually start the upload from your end. See FIG. 8-5. Notice that with cc, you can send copies of any message to anyone or any list of people. In fact, many organizations on these nets use this as a way to send many people the same message for the price of one.

```
 ◆  File  Edit  Setup  Connect  Fax                    TTY   2400-8-N-1
Do you want: (r)eply message  (n)ew message  (s)end copy? r
Reply to (s)ender or (e)veryone in list? s
To: jillaine
Subject: re: NOW I remember


Hit <RETURN> or <ENTER> to type in a message, or 'u' to (u)pload a file:
---------------------------------------------------------------------
Begin typing; End with a line containing only a Period.
---------------------------------------------------------------------
Jillaine:

Had figured that out by the time I read your message. Will write jsneed
about the article.  Thanks, hope you are well very soon!

Libbi
 .

Hit <RETURN> or <ENTER> to send text, 'e' to edit:

Cc:
Message sent.

Mail: (i)ndex (u)nread (w)rite (c)apture (d)elete (s)ave (h)elp (q)uit:
```

8-5
A letter I sent to Jillaine. Notice the "cc," which will send carbon copies to anyone on the net.

Anywhere in the system, q will quit the current menu and return to the previous menu; ^S will pause scrolling text, ^Q will resume scrolling text, and ^C interrupts whatever is going on at the moment.

Usually, after reading and answering your mail, you'll want to <v>isit your favorite conferences. But let's take a little detour, and look at EcoNet's databases. To do this, you hit "d" at the main menu.

Wandering around

Figure 8-6 shows the databases menu. Each of these is searchable by keyword, and using the capture and download functions, you can have gargantuan amounts of information at your fingertips.

These databases are immense. The first one, sending political action messages to world leaders, is especially popular, but it entails a slightly higher cost.

The databases behave like "doors" on a BBS system: the EcoNet software steps aside, and in some cases you are actually patched through phone lines to an

Your selection: d

EcoNet Databases:

```
1 ..... InterACT        A Utility for faxing to World Leaders & Others
2 ..... UN NPPA         UN List of National Parks and Protected Areas
                           (from WCMC / IUCN)
3 ..... Harbinger File  A directory of citizen groups, government agencies
                           and environmental education programs concerned with
                           California environmental issues
4 ..... DEER            The Directory of Environmental Education Resources,
                           a project of the Colorado Alliance for Environmental
                           Education and the Colorado Department of Education.
5 ..... RG-ENERGY       Energy Cost Analysis System (from REAL GOODS)
7 ..... EVENTS          General calendar of events for the IGC online
                           community; post your own organizational events here!
8 ..... EPA             Bibliographic citations compiled by the US
                           Environmental Protection Agency library Network.
```

```
q ..... Quit from Databases & Return to Main Menu
```

Choice?

8-6
The EcoNet Database menu.

entirely different system (DEER works that way), with new command lines. Most have good online help, though.

So, let us now saunter through the maze of conferences.

As with any system this large, it would be impossible to read each and every message here. So you select the ones that interest you most and put them on a list. The EcoNet computer remembers your list, and the order you want them in. Then you will be taken through your chosen conferences as you type v.

Say environmental alerts is on your list. In FIG. 8-7, a v would take you there.

```
Conf?  v


Visiting en.alerts...20 unread topics, 4 unread responses
'u' to see next unread item, '?' for command summary, 'h' for more help
Conf: (i)ndex (u)nread (w)rite (c)apture (v)isit (g)o e(x)it (q)uit (?)
Conf?  i
```

8-7
The "v" command from the main menu takes you through your list of favorite conferences.

```
en.alerts

11/08/92    15*Norway: Natural Forests Threatened      econet
11/20/92    17*Alaska: Oppose Aerial Wolf Control      econet
            18*Earth First Activist Denied Parole      econet
11/24/92    20*URGENT: Gatt Debate in French Parl      chasque:pmccully
            21*New Zealand: Maori Fishing Rights       econet
11/28/92    25*Alaska: "Emergency" Timber Sales        econet
11/29/92    29*Maxam/Pacific Lumber Log Owl Creek    1 econet
12/07/92    31*Open Letter on the Demolition of t      gn:mahk


        **** End of Topics ****
Conf: (i)ndex (u)nread (w)rite (c)apture (v)isit (g)o e(x)it (q)uit (?)
Conf?
```

But how do you know what conferences will interest you? Well, when you sign up, you'll get a brochure with all the conferences listed. But, online, you can use (l) to search a directory by a keyword. Figure 8-8 shows the result of such a search. Then, in the conferences command list, choose "m" for maintain your list. There you can add, delete, change the order, and list your current preferences.

```
◆  File  Edit  Setup  Connect  Fax                    TTY   2400-8-N-1
Enter name, keyword, or <RETURN> for all (? for help): children
Do you want: a (b)rief, (m)edium or (c)omplete listing (? for help): b

Conferences marked with a `*' are privately listed to your group `enmisc'.

     This may take a while...
child.abuse     hr.child         youth.activism   child.rights    cc.childnews
fgc.child2000   child.discussi   child.research   education.2000  green.train
kids.only       bitl.kidsnet     kids.92          kids.93         kids.act
kids.cafe       kids.plan        kids.project     kids.response   youth.online

-----

(l)ist to look again, else <RETURN> to quit:

=======

Enter conference name (? for list of conferences): g kids.cafe


Visiting g...
No such conference: g  --  Use (l)ist to search the Directory.
Conf: (g)o to a conference (v)isit regular list of conferences
Conf?  g ki
```

8-8
If you want conferences dealing with children, do a keyword search. Then, from the conference command "m", you can change the list of default conferences you will visit each time.

So let's pretend that kids.cafe is on our list and visit. The conference rules are that kids.cafe is for children from all over the world to post messages to. Figure 8-9 shows a typical index to kids.cafe.

```
◆  File  Edit  Setup  Connect  Fax                    TTY   2400-8-N-1

kids.cafe -- kidcafe

12/07/92  955*to Cullen                        KIDCAFE@VM1.NoDak.EDU
          956*To anyone in Norway              KIDCAFE@VM1.NoDak.EDU
          957*MILES GARY/TERESA STANLEY        KIDCAFE@VM1.NoDak.EDU
          958*To Heimir Rafin in Iceland       KIDCAFE@VM1.NoDak.EDU
          959*** ANYONE **                   1 KIDCAFE@VM1.NoDak.EDU
          960**** ANYONE ***                   KIDCAFE@VM1.NoDak.EDU
          961*Robert Cory in Cathedral School N.Y  KIDCAFE@VM1.NoDak.EDU
          962*to Sheilds in Roanoke from Mary in   KIDCAFE@VM1.NoDak.EDU
          963*to Preston from Mary in Texas    KIDCAFE@VM1.NoDak.EDU
          964*to Adam Reed from Alexander in Texa  KIDCAFE@VM1.NoDak.EDU
          965*to Mike Richards in New York from J  KIDCAFE@VM1.NoDak.EDU
          966*Re: To anyone in Gainesville, Tx.   KIDCAFE@VM1.NoDak.EDU
          967*Holiday Parties & Fashions       KIDCAFE@VM1.NoDak.EDU
          968*To Andrea Lewis                  KIDCAFE@VM1.NoDak.EDU
          969*TV TV TV TV TV TV                KIDCAFE@VM1.NoDak.EDU
          970*To Tod Cox                       KIDCAFE@VM1.NoDak.EDU
          971*To Sergio Chavex                 KIDCAFE@VM1.NoDak.EDU

        **** End of Topics ****
Conf: (i)ndex (u)nread (w)rite (c)apture (v)isit (g)o e(x)it (q)uit (?)
Conf?
```

8-9
Kids leave messages at kids.cafe and kids.only.

And in kids.only, you'll find the charming message in FIG. 8-10.

Among these conferences for children are the projects, where a yearly activist project (letter writing campaign, or a national clean-up day) is organized online.

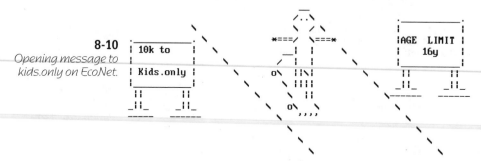

8-10
Opening message to kids.only on EcoNet.

A must-read from the conference is the message from Alex Brozan, *ABROZAN@PEARL.TUFTS.EDU*, the conference host, entitled: "Subject: WELCOME TO YOUTH ONLINE!"

In this message, Brozan reminds you that "this conference echoes an Internet mailing list with many subscribers who receive it as e-mail, so please exercise discretion when posting loooong posts, etc. . ."

He goes on to explain that this conference is based at Tufts University in Boston. It is also echoed as the conference youth.online on the IGC networks (EcoNet, PeaceNet).

Youth Online is an interchange for conversation and action relating to young people and "Electronic Activism." Electronic Activism, as defined by Brozan, is the use of computers and computer networks for organizing social change. "Youth" in general use is a broad term, but for the purposes of this conference, it refers to students and young people under the age of about 30. "We make this distinction," Brozan writes, "because activists in this age group (which in itself is quite broad) have agendas, needs, goals, obstacles, and potentials that are unique to them and different from the so-called 'adult' community."

Brozan notes that in the past decade, youth activism has increased dramatically, despite widely perpetuated myths of an apathetic generation. He cites students and young people actively involved in movements on a wide variety of issues, including racism, poverty, sexism, gender discrimination, homophobia, the environment, hunger, development, peace and militarism, free speech and censorship, education, reproductive freedom, human rights, and many others.

"Today's youth activists are more knowledgeable, more educated, better skilled, and, most important, have access to tools never available to activists in the past," Brozan writes. They are comfortable with new technologies that have revolutionized the way they are educated and take action, and computers are having an important effect on these movements. At the same time, people of all ages who are working for positive change around the world have discovered the enormous power of computer networks to aid them. They get limitless and speedy information on important topics, communicate with other people worldwide, debate and strategize, coordinate campaigns and projects thousands of miles apart, and respond quickly to urgent situations.

"Students and youth have also put these tools to great use. The Youth Online list/conference is intended for discussions of how students are using computer networks for organizing and how they can best put them to use," he writes. This includes general discussions; issues of access and equity; news and notices; updates on projects; strategizing; action and collaboration; and any other issues of interest to the members of the list.

"If you or your organization is using computer networks in your work, or if you have projects related to this topic, please send a description to me, the moderator, at the address below. I will post a summary of all the projects I receive," Brozan concludes.

The important electronic mail addresses for this conference are as follows:

To send to the moderator (for subscription requests, questions about the list, comments, administration, etc.), use the address *YOUTH-ONLINE-REQUEST@PEARL.TUFTS.EDU.*

To post to the list On EcoNet, PeaceNet, and other APC networks, send to *youth.online*; on Internet, use *YOUTH-ONLINE@PEARL.TUFTS.EDU.*

In all my travels in the electronic underground, I was sometimes discouraged to see adult people acting childish. These wonderful conferences, by, for, and of children, inspired me. It was nice, I must say, to see an online community that welcomes childishness in its most honest form, from those who have a right to be so!

Besides the ability to upload one message at a time, you might want to "burst" upon the ICG scene with several documents at a time. You can here, with the command burst.

Special features

First, say you have three articles you want to upload to a single conference, each with a separate "topic" or subject line. While off-line, use your editor or word processor in ASCII mode to write all three articles in one file. Follow this format:

```
.TOPIC
THIS IS MY TOPIC
.TEXT
This is my text. It goes on for about 200 words . . . . . .
.TOPIC
THIS IS MY NEXT TOPIC
This is my next text. It goes on for about 150 words . . .
.TOPIC
This is my last topic
.TEXT
This is my third text. It goes on for about 250 words . . . .
```

.TOPIC and .TEXT must be all capitalized, and the topics lines are limited to 34 characters. Everything after .TOPIC should be the text of your posting. Save this file as ASCII. Then log onto ICG, and when you get to the main menu of the network, type burst. You'll get step-by-step instructions, and your three files will be posted.

Another money-saving tip from the sysops at ICG is to use scripts, if your communications software allows. The conference apc.scripts has messages and files about how to do this, covering many different communications programs, commercial, shareware and so on. All this is important for the nonprofit organization as well as the lone activist.

Conclusion

In all, for the activist of a certain stripe, ICG is the place to be. If you're conservative, you'd be happier listening to Rush Limbaugh.

9 Netcom
For notorious UNIX nabobs & notables

E-mail	*bobr@netcom.com*
U.S. Mail	20 Harold St., Suite 42
	San Jose, CA 95117
Phone	(408) 554-8649 [voice]
	(408) 984-7524 [voice]
Hours	24 hours a day
Basic rate	$17.50 per month
Notes	Very Unix oriented; USENET newsfeeds. E-mail, FTP, and chat.

Netcom is a UNIX user's "died and gone to heaven."

It is VERY UNIX-bound. Three UNIX "shells" are offered; and to the uninitiated, one is as confusing as the other. To the UNIX head, it's a candy shop. It is also, let us say, staid. Sedate. Earnest.

A legend in the underground has it that once upon a time the WELL had a series of unexplained downtimes, capricious and annoying in the extreme to the WELL users. And during this time of frustration for the WELLians, the cry was heard, "Why can't this place be more like Netcom?! Netcom is run like a BUSINESS!" and variations thereof.

But you'll notice that means those crying in the wilderness were using BOTH Netcom and the WELL. I think that says something about needing a little steadiness as well as adventure in one's life. Netcom is for the steadiness.

This is not to say they don't have occasional hardware problems themselves. Once or twice the logon message in January explained that the system was down because of an equipment glitch. "Amazing how [an inexpensive] piece of hardware can bring a system to a halt," it said.

John DeBert, a friendly Netcom user, when asked about the very serious atmosphere there said, "I agree: Netcom is highly technical! I doubt that the 'business meeting' analogy would apply, though, because of the presence of what I call 'whiners' who complain about almost everything instead of accommodating things—rolling with the flow," so to speak.

"People use Netcom for several reasons," he continued. "There are programmers, 'hackers' (not meaning the media's 'definition'), explorers, businesses and people who just like to read news on the net. It's not set up for much of any social interaction. Two people can chat one on one, but there is no facility for group chats as there is on Portal, Compu Serve, etc. I rarely get involved with social stuff, anyway, 'cause most of the stuff quickly gets dull and the interesting stuff in netnews groups, such as soc.women (or whatever it's called now) is too one-sided: Most of the space is devoted to people fighting it out with each other and justifying this or that."

The only thing he doesn't like about it, he said, is something indigenous to the USENET, not necessarily only Netcom . . .

"Re, 'brats" I refer to users who haven't grown up. Sometimes, they do upload things that shouldn't be. They tend to be belligerent, openly hostile to other points of view, intolerant and inconsiderate of others, and tend to be the biggest complainers. When things do not suit them in the slightest, they react by writing long, drawn-out harangues about it. They also never apologize—voluntarily, at least," he said.

The details Netcom's Internet node is *@netcom.com*. They are also available through PC Pursuit.

The standard monthly rate is $17.50, but you can opt for your account to be billed to your credit card automatically and save 12% (monthly rate of $15.50).

Robert J. Reiger, known on the system as bobr (Internet address *bobr@netcom.com*), is the network operations manager. He's friendly and helpful, and a consummate UNIX user.

If you live in Southern California, it's a UNIX user's paradise because Netcom is not a long distance call. As yet, this is only a local network; anyone outside the 408 area code has to pay long-distance charges to connect. "We are working on CALnet allowing local access for Netcom users all over California," he said.

Reiger noted the system has a lot of games online, but they are text-based, as "graphics over nodes is still a trick." But many Netcom users play the multi-user dungeon games over the Internet.

"In the last few months we've seen some more nontechnical uses," he said. "Several areas used by our clients all the time: USENET and Netnews. We have all 1500 or 1700 newsgroups. Subjects range from adult topics to laser technology. The major headings are the main draw, the electronic forums. Rec.Humor is also popular."

"We have many games online," Reiger said. "Not the typical ones because the graphics don't go over the net well. IRC (the Internet Relay Chat) is online— interactive 'conversation.' I've gotten on at 3 a.m. and seen 20–40 people on it."

He noted that the flames on his system have to do with people breaking the "no business or profit" rule on newsgroups. "Someone posted a pyramid letter on the Internet, trying to get everyone to send him a dollar. They really don't like you to use the Internet newsgroups for commercial or profit purposes. His mailbox was so clogged with hate mail that it filled up!" Reiger said.

Security is a very high priority with Reiger. In the last of 1991 and beginning of 1992, Reiger posted several notices directing all users to change their passwords immediately.

"But Internet is a vast undiscovered territory. Just for an example, we have a security problem right now. I got on the Internet and with one command had a list of the newest code to fix the problem, all of it free. I can FTP to the sites listed and get what I need to solve the problem.

"Security is a problem, but 99% of it must be handled by the system people. What the regular user can do is not use any word or name in the dictionary. Use lower- and uppercase letters with symbols and special characters. Then no one can use your account," Reiger said.

"Our passwords are case-sensitive. I don't recommend that you automate your logon at all," he said, "but especially don't automate your password."

The best thing to do is write to Netcom and sign up your account. Then dial the proper number for your modem. See FIG. 9-1 for an example of the resulting login.

How to dial . . . how to log on

```
netcom login: libbi
Password:
Login incorrect
login: libbi
Password:
Last login: Mon Jan 13 04:06:39 from CALNet-sj1.netco
SunOS Release 4.1.1 (SERVER) #3: Sun Jan 5 13:55:30 PST 1992

 Netcom - Online Communication Services

  >>>>
  >>>>   New lines added to the SF POP
  >>>>
  >>>>
You have new mail.

Account Verification
  Account Status :  Active
  Account type   :  Complimentary temporary account
```

9-1
The login screen at Netcom.

If you followed Bob's advice on your password, you might have to try more than once. After three mistakes, you're logged off.

"The Netcom User's Guide", which comes with your registration package, details some of the UNIX commands. It doesn't really explain what "csh", "ksh", or and "sh" are: they are the UNIX shells you can use. For online telnetting and such, you really must learn one of these. For normal everyday use, though, such as mail and newsgroups, make your first command MENU. (See FIG. 9-2.)

```
   N e t c o m   - Online Communication Services
              Public Access UNIX System
SunOS 4.1.1 ------------------------------------------------------
```

```
          1   -   Check E-Mail
          2   -   Send E-Mail
          3   -   Who's on the System
          4   -   Talk to another user
          5   -   Read News
          6   -   Post News
          7   -   UNIX Command Level
          8   -   Account payment status
          9   -   File Transfer Utilities
          E   -   Exit Menu Program
```

9-2

The basic Netcom menu.

From here, things are pretty simple. Choose 1, and the mail reader shows you a menu of letters, which you can read, store in a file, forward to others, and so on. (See FIG. 9-3.)

```
Reading in /usr/spool/mail/libbi, message: 9
Mailbox is '/usr/spool/mail/libbi' with 9 messages [ELM 2.3 PL11]
   N  1   Jan 12 Elizabeth Crowe    (19)    editor saved ``/usr/tmp/snd.18840''
   N  2   Jan 12 David Feustel      (23)    Re: Help
   O  3   Jan 12 Elizabeth Crowe    (20)    editor saved ``/usr/tmp/snd.18247''
   O  4   Jan 10 Parag Patel        (67)    Re: Help
   O  5   Jan 9  Marvin Raab        (39)    Re: Help
   O  6   Jan 9  Tom Czarnik        (57)    Re: Help
   O  7   Jan 9  Yifun Liang        (43)    Re: Help
   O  8   Jan 9  Dave Smythe        (70)    Re: Help
   O  9   Jan 9  John Nagle         (23)    Re: Help
```

9-3

A Netcom mailbox menu.

```
You can use any of the following commands by pressing the first character;
d)elete or u)ndelete mail,  m)ail a message,  r)eply or f)orward mail,
q)uit
To read a message, press <return>.  j = move down, k = move up, ? = help
Command:
```

Choose 2, the mail sender, and things are a bit trickier. I did learn that a . on a line by itself will send the message, and that the easiest thing to do is reply to a letter sent to you. But it all depends on whether you are using elm (don't! unless you know UNIX really well) or mush (a bit more online help) or mail.

Choose 3 to find out if anyone is online you'd like to talk to. You'll get a listing like that in FIG. 9-4.

The names listed are the names you use to "call" them. Choose 4, and if the other person answers the "ring," you can have an online chat.

The first time I tried this, I got another person who was new to the system. Neither of us could figure out how to get off and do something else. In frustration, we agreed to just turn off our machines. In the ohnosecond (one minuscule fraction of a nanosecond, the time it takes to realize you just made a BIG mistake) that followed, I realized my log of the conversation was lost.

```
bobr      console Feb  8 05:20
alm       ttyp0   Feb  8 07:03   (CALNet-pa1.netco)
libbi     ttyp1   Feb  8 07:09   (CALNet-sj1.netco)
craigh    ttyp2   Feb  8 06:33   (CALNet-sj1.netco)
ubik      ttyp3   Feb  8 03:34   (CALNet-sj1.netco)
damon     ttyp4   Feb  8 02:06   (tsx-wsec103.unl.)
astroman  ttyp5   Feb  8 06:26   (CALNet-sj2.netco)
ngee      ttyp6   Feb  8 07:03   (CALNet-sj4.netco)
rbowman   ttyp7   Feb  8 04:58   (CALNet-sj4.netco)
masimo    ttyp8   Feb  8 07:07   (CALNet-sf1.netco)
cowpatti  ttyp9   Feb  8 05:12   (silver.ucs.india)
ernulf    ttypa   Feb  8 07:08   (CALNet-sj4.netco)
stevew    ttypb   Feb  8 07:09   (CALNet-sj2.netco)
payner    ttypc   Feb  8 07:09   (gator.netcom.com)
richg     ttype   Feb  8 05:37   (CALNet-pa1.netco)
kemnitz   ttypf   Feb  8 06:38   (CALNet-sj3.netco)
silver    ttyq0   Feb  8 06:39   (CALNet-sj3.netco)
```

9-4
If you'd like a chat, Netcom will tell you who's on when you are.

Choose 5 to get the USENET newsfeeds. The real fun of Netcom is the USENET. You can set up your default file to choose one of several news readers:

rn   The simplest, lets you read the articles in the order they were received in Netcom.

trn   A bit trickier, but sorts the articles into "threads"; that is, articles are in reply order starting with the original.

nn   This narrows down the ones you view: you decide which to "subscribe" to, and forget the rest.

vnews   Based on rn, but with a CRT-oriented interface.

Option 6 is for posting your responses, starting a topic, participating in the USENET.

Choose 7 and you are at the Netcom prompt. If you know how to use UNIX, you're now in the big playground. If you don't, type EXIT quickly!

Choose 8 for a quick roundup of where you stand with Netcom.

Choose 9 for file transfers. Unlike many other commercial nets we have noted, Netcom can be telnetted to and from; FTP and archives work; you can try out your archie skills here.

Using FTP is much like logging into UNIX here but with a limited set of commands; you have to use Netcomsv to use it. To use FTP, have handy the Internet name of the site you want to copy from and the path name of the file you need to get. This sample, from the "Netcom User's Guide", shows how to get the file foobar.tar from the site *nowhere.edu*.

```
$cd /usr/hack/ftp/tmp
```
[This changes you to your own directory, with a filename tmp.]
```
$ftp nowhere.edu
```
[This gets you to your foreign site.]
Connected to nowhere.edu
220 nowhere FTP server (Version # Date Time Year) ready
name (nowhere.edu:user): anonymous
331 Guest login ok, send ident as password
Password `yourid@netcom.com` *[This is not going to echo]*
230 Guest login ok, access restrictions apply.
ftp> `get foobar.tar`
200 PORT command successful
150 Opening ASCII mode data connection for foobar.tar (4558 bytes)

226 Transfer complete.
local: foobar.tar remote:foobar.tar
*X*number bytes received in *X* seconds
ftp> `bye`
221 goodbye
$

[The $ means you are back in Netcom.]

If you have problems, read the "Netcom User's Guide" or post a question on the USENET to netcom.com users. See FIG. 9-5.

Now if you are totally confused online and need help, type `help`; you'll get what's in FIG. 9-6.

```
USENET Administration):
> In article <1992Jan13.010828.13877onymouse@netcom.COM> onymouse@netcom.COM (Jo

hn Debert) writes:
>>
>> Is uucp to netcom somehow possible? It certainly is possible for
>> sending file via uucp.
>
> You cannot UUCP to the machine 'netcom' itself, but you can copy to
> netcomsv!/usr/hack/tmp, which is NFS mounted to netcom as well.

So that should mean that I can just cd to netcom's /usr/hack/tmp
to see whatever I sent?

(It would be nice to be able to uucp stuff from home to my netcom-home,
though... I'm beginningto hate XMODEM, etc.)

jd

--
jd
onymouse@netcom.COM

End of article 53 (of 53)--what next? [npq]
```

9-5
There's a special forum for Netcom users.

```
{Netcom:19} help
Before you send mail asking for help,  please read the following.  If you
do not follow these guide lines,  you may not get a response.

     o     Accounting questions should be in the form of an E-mail
           message addressed to accounting.  For a quick response
           call (408) 554-UNIX Monday thru Friday 8:00-11:30 or
           1:00-5:00.    All accounting questions sent to the
           support account will not be answered.

     o     Question concerning news accounts, policy,  or system
           problems should be addressed to bobr.

     o     Questions concerning Netnews or mail should be addressed
           to user netnews.

     o     If you have a "how do I do this" or "where is this"
           type question,  please use the man command and try
           to answer your own question by reading the on-line
           documentation.  If you have exhausted all resources
           and still can not get an answer,  you can send an
           E-Mail message to the support account.
```

9-6
When you need help, this is what you get.

If you can't find what you need that way, you can report problems to the following mailboxes:

postmaster   e-mail bounces, uucp
support   Support & system utilities
bobr   Anything about your account
accounting   What you owe, what you've paid
netnews   Usenet news problems

How busy is Netcom? Well, you can get the latest statistics off the news reader. FIG. 9-7 is a typical sample.

```
NNTP peer article transfers

Article Reception (they contact us)
System               Offered   Took   Toss  Fail Toss   Elapsed        CPU  Pct
192.100.100.50             4      4      0     0   0%    0:00:12    0:00:02  21%
130.43.2.2               594    577     17     0   3%    0:41:47    0:09:49  24%
16.1.0.19                731    190    541     0  74%    0:17:34    0:03:12  18%
darkstar.ucsc.edu         32     32      0     0   0%    0:04:13    0:00:57  23%
uucp-gw-2.pa.dec.com   28466   8138  20327     1  71%    8:48:11    1:12:25  14%
apple.com              27181  21749   5432     0  20%   25:54:43    5:44:48  22%

TOTALS                 57008  30690  26317     1  46%   35:46:42    7:11:15  20%

Article Transmission (we contact them)
System               Offrd    Took   Toss  Fail  Pct   Elapsed        CPU  Pct
nntp-gw.pa.dec.com    1116     249    769     0  69%    1:36:20    0:01:29   2%
darkstar.ucsc.edu        5       5      0     0   0%    0:01:23    0:00:01   1%
apple.com              658     559     99     4  15%    1:19:22    0:01:06   1%
delfin.com           26805   26805      0     0   0%   23:04:36    0:13:36   1%

TOTALS                28584  27618    868     4   3%   26:01:43    0:16:13   1%
```

9-7
Netcom statistics are available anytime.

Well, that depends on where you are, how you got there, what happened three moves before, and other factors I never really figured out. FIG. 9-8 shows a sample.

How to sign off

The no carrier occurred when I got REALLY frustrated and hit disconnect. I think the problem was I had stumbled into the wrong shell and couldn't see my way out.

But if you want full Internet and USENET access (even to the Bitnet!) and live in the Bay Area, you might want to travel to Netcom. It's a nice place to visit, and some people even live there!

```
Program terminated by libbi
{Netcom:2} bye
bye: Command not found.
{Netcom:3} off
off: Command not found.
{Netcom:4} out
out: Command not found.
{Netcom:5} logoff
logoff: Command not found.
{Netcom:6} logout
yj ,n}
NO CARRIER
```

9-8
Sometimes logging out is a problem.

10 *Powerful, personal Portal*

E-mail	*cs@cup.portal.com*
U.S. Mail	20863 Stevens Creek Blvd., Suite #260
	Cupertino, CA 95014
Phone	(408) 973-9111 [voice]
Hours	24 hours a day, but long-distance charges not included.
Basic rate	$19.95 start-up; $13.95 per month plus disk storage charges.
Notes	USENET feeds. Internet mail connect. Major archive site of Internet files. E-mail and chat. No telnet, no direct FTP.

This is a special place. It's friendly as the local coffee shop, big as your mall. It's got old-timers and brand new cybercitizens; and it's geared to both.

"Our president [John Little] is good about seeing the various possibilities and responding," said Carol Johnson, Portal's public relations person. "We are growing rapidly. John Little is one of the original hackers and goes to the Hacker Conference [sponsored by Whole Earth] every year. One of the EFF organizational meetings was held at his house.

"We were a little service that grew into a multi-faceted community. This started as a small friendly group. Now that electronic communication is growing we're growing with it," she said.

How to dial . . . how to log on

Portal is on Telenet, SprintNet (C PORTAL), PCI (PORTAL), SprintNet's PC Pursuit, or direct access. For International access, first you get on a public data network, then use the Portal DTE address:

311040800264

You can also reach them from Hawaii, Guam, Saipan and other Pacific Rim locations on PCI (PORTAL).

Their direct dial numbers/modems are

(408) 725-0561   [300-2499 bps]
(408) 725-1724   [USR HST]
(408) 725-1763   [Telebit PEP]

You'll want your settings at 8 bits, no parity, and 1 stop bit. Though various terminals are listed under the SET command, VT100 gives the least headaches. Be warned, however, that ASCII captures in VT100 will give you garbage. Better to transfer anything you want to save. More on that later.

When you connect to Portal, the first two prompts ask your name and password. Your name is not case-sensitive: type it in any way you want. But your password is *very* case-sensitive. Be careful with your typing here.

Rates

Account Startup is $19.95. Regular monthly use is $13.95 per month, plus whatever your connection charge is, be it long distance or another provider. SprintNet charges are put directly toward your Portal Account. Others will bill you separately.

You pay an extra $4 per month for the Clarinet News service; 4 cents per month for every kilobyte of information you store in your personal folders; $2 an hour for high-speed modems and $5 if you lose or forget your password and have to change it.

For the basic rate, you can subscribe to hundreds of the USENET newsgroups, plus participate in Portal-only activities. For example, in 1989, they held a contest to see who could upload the most useful public domain program. The prizes were $1024, $512 and $256. You can subscribe to any of the electronically published periodicals, the discussions on newsgroups, and any other USENET text. They're proud of being very accessible to the Internet.

Information on Portal comes in three levels. You have directories, which list the different "conferences." Within the conferences, you'll find "collections," which would be called threads in other systems. Under the collections, you'll find "articles," which are a series of messages on various subjects that have to do with the conference.

You subscribe to one by choosing either Computer Groups or Special Interest Groups and browsing around until you find an interesting one. Then type subscribe, and the system remembers that you want to read that conference every time. After that, type go subs and then read or scan through your subscriptions. You can also transfer your subscriptions, or mail, or programs, for use when offline. See FIG. 10-1.

Flavor

There's no front-end software; you log into a Unix-based system that's all text. Graphics are downloadable, but not viewable online. However, this is one of the least painful Unix systems for the non-Unix user I have found. The Help actually helps, listing the things you can do in non-jargon language. That's not to say there's no learning curve here; but it's certainly no more difficult than CompuServe, and much easier than some systems that assume your mother read you Unix manuals in the cradle.

```
 ◆  File  Edit  Setup  Connect  Fax              VT100   2400-8-N-1
No help for this topic
Command: help subscriptions

Help
Help/Subscribe
Lines 1 to 12 of 37 (32%)
-----
0  -  Examples
-----
Subscriptions Overview

Subscriptions are a convenient way to keep up to date on the activity in
selected Portal conferences.  You can subscribe to those conferences that
interest you, then read just the new articles that have arrived in them.
Portal keeps track of which articles you have read, so you don't see the same
article twice.

Starting subscriptions

There are two ways to start a subscription to a conference.  The first is two
use the 'edit' command from the main subscription form.  This will give you a
-----
page edit transfer mail help top logout set go done
Command:
```

10-1

Portal subscriptions tell the system what you like to read.

You cannot TELNET over Portal. "We can't overcome the security risks that presents," said Johnson. "And real FTP takes place over the lines in real time. We have 'fake' FTP: you put in your request, and it's processed later and then you get it back. We're working on becoming the largest archive site anywhere. That way you eventually won't have to FTP to get files; we'll have them right here."

Type go ftp to get help on how to do it. Really, it's pretty simple: you send the request just as you do on other systems. The request goes out "in the dark" to you and comes back pretty quickly. There's an excellent example by Online-Bear in that directory. Transfer it and read it offline. Then, you'll be ready.

How do you transfer? That's a little confusing at first. If your command line says "transfer" where you are, then type that. You'll get a menu that looks like FIG. 10-2.

```
 ◆  File  Edit  Setup  Connect  Fax       Alt-H for help   VT100   2400-8-N-1
Command: transfer 0-1

Transfer spec
-----
Download from Portal to you using xmodem
0  -  Download from Portal to you
1  -  Upload from you to Portal
2  -  Append to existing data
3  -  Overwrite existing data
4  -  Ascii
5  -  Xmodem
6  -  Zmodem
-----
mail help try_again top logout set go quit ok
Command:
-----
```

10-2

Portal's transfer menu tells you what will happen and what you can change.

Notice the first line of this menu tells you what will happen if you say "ok": The file will go from Portal to you in xmodem. If you want any of that to change, type the number of what is not to your liking, adjust it, and continue until it says what you want in that first line.

You can transfer from you to Portal, too, and that's convenient for offline mail writing. Save your letter in ASCII, while offline. When you get onto Portal, type `mail send`, then start your letter. When you are to "Get Letter Body," hit Ctrl-C and then "transfer." Choose from you to Portal and your preferred protocol. Send the body of the letter, then Ctrl-C, and "ok."

Busiest times are non-prime time in the Pacific Time Zone, when it's about 7 p.m. to 6 a.m. there, as well as on weekends. Saturdays and Sundays, I noticed both a lag in response time and garbage characters inserting themselves at will. I don't know whether that had to do with the phone connection, the number of people online, the SprintNet, or what.

Your first screen when you sign on is a list of what's new and how to get to it. Then, comes a list of any meetings and chats scheduled. Or you can go to the Portal Activity screen and see the stuff listed in FIG. 10-3.

```
◆  File  Edit  Setup  Connect  Fax              VT100   2400-8-N-1
Collection menu
/Portal Activities at a Glance/SIG News
14606.3
─────
0    -    ============================================================ [collection]
1    -    **                  What's Happening!                        [collection]
2    -    **            THE Place for PORTAL* SIG News                  [collection]
3    -    ============================================================ [collection]
4    -    **                                                           [collection]
5    %H:!Qis PORTAL* SIG News?                        [collection]
6    -    Entrepreneurs: GO GETTERS to the Entrepreneurs' SIG          [collection]
7    -    Family: ***** The Family Forum *****                         [collection]
8    -    GAMES on Portal! What's New!                                 [collection]
9    -    Games: Multi-User Game Project <go mug> needs YOU!!          [collection]
10   -    IBM: PC Bear's Workshop News                                 [collection]
11   -    PORTAL* Pals: New User Orientation - Type: 'go pals'         [collection]
12   -    Online: Whats New at Online Services                        [collection]
13   -    Poetry Update                                               [collection]
14   -    Radio: What's New & Exciting in Havana Moon's "Los Numero   [collection]
15   -    Singles SIG                                                  [collection]
─────
page mail help top logout set go done add_collection scan read subscribe
unsubscribe
Command:
```

10-3
Portal activities are updated regularly.

To get around, you type `go` and either the name of the conference or place, or its menu number. The menu number appears at the top of the conference menu, like what's in FIG. 10-4:

To get to this subscription from the home menu, type `go 13853`. Mail is pretty easy here. You type `mail read` and you're there. Type `mail send` and you're prompted for header information. Enter that, then "ok" or "try_again" if you goofed. Then you enter your text, typing Ctrl-C to signal that you're done; "ok" tells the system to send it on. It's really quite simple. Your Internet address on Portal is *your_full_name@cup.portal.com.*

Anytime you feel lost, type `top` and you're back at the main menu. Anytime you feel alone on Portal, check out the meetings (`go chat`). Anytime you feel lost *and*

```
 ◆  File  Edit  Setup  Connect  Fax                    VT100   2400-8-N-1
Article menu
.../* Computer Underground Digest
13853.3.29
-----
0   -   11/11 1989   0    HM: ============================================
1   -   11/30 1989   0    HM:    **        The Computer Underground        *
2   -   11/11 1989   0    HM: ============================================
3   -   3/15  1990   120  ckp: The Legion Of Doom --==>> What's Ahead For BBS
4   -   3/25  1990   388  TELECOM Moderator <telecom@eec: TELECOM Digest Spec
5   -   3/21  1990   1761 C0144%CSUOHIO.BITNET%CORNELLC.: Recent Internet Hac
6   -   3/23  1990   4656 gam@dawg.cvedc.prime.com (Greg: Re: Recent Internet
7   -   3/24  1990   638  POO%CUNYVMS1.BITNET@cunyvm.cun: hacking debate
8   -   3/28  1990   1195 CuD                           : ComUndDig 1.00
9   -   3/31  1990   649  ckp@cup.portal.com: Computer Underground Digest #1.
10  -   3/31  1990   447  TELECOM Moderator <telecom@eec: TELECOM Digest Spec
11  -   4/3   1990   434  sun!UICVM.uic.edu!TK0JUT2%NIU.: Computer Undergroun
12  -   4/5   1990   47   ckp@cup.portal.com: 2600 Address
13  -   4/9   1990   627  sun!UICVM.uic.edu!TK0JUT2%NIU.: C-u-D, #1.03
14  -   4/10  1990   454  sun!UICVM.uic.edu!TK0JUT2%NIU.: C-u-D 1.04 (a)
15  -   4/10  1990   541  sun!UICVM.uic.edu!TK0JUT2%NIU.: C-u-D #1.04 (b)
-----
page mail help top logout set go done add_article scan read subscribe
unsubscribe transfer move
Command:
```

10-4

At the top of the conference menu is the number for that area. You can go 13853 to get here directly.

alone on Portal, send a message to customer service (*cs@portal.com*). Before you do that, though, check out go 16224.3.1 for a treatise on how to report problems, or go 9850.1 for common questions and answers about Portal. There's also Portal Pals online, which we'll cover later.

"The User's Guide", which comes when you're all signed up, has all this, by the way. Reading it offline helps; I kept it close by my side for the first dozen sessions.

Sights

When People Link (known as Plink) disappeared from the market, Portal managed to snap up one of their most popular SIGs: the Amiga Zone. It's still one of the most active areas on Portal, with a conference almost every night. (See FIG. 10-5.)

```
 ◆  File  Edit  Setup  Connect  Fax                    VT100   2400-8-N-1
* PORTAL is a service mark of Portal Communications Company.

Enter name, NEW, INFO, or HELP: elizabeth crowe
Enter password:

                More newsgroups added!  Type "Go CHANGES"
_____
-RADIO   - GO *PIRATES*PIRATES*PIRATES*PIRATES*PIRATES*PIRATES*PIRATES*

-AMIGA   - Fish disks 1-610 are now online!  Type "Go AMIGAFISH"

-BOOKS   - Buy unix books with your Portal account!  Type "Go SHOPPING"

-GAMES   - Live games in General Meetings with DeafyDuck!
_____
                    ** Thursday's Activities  **

-  7:00 PM PT - AMIGA ZONE Hardware in SIG Meetings - "Go AMIGA"
-  7:00 PM PT - Duck Trivia in General Meetings
----                                                               ----
Remember, this is an open system where you are responsible for what you
say and how you use it.  Please report problems to "CS".  408/973-9111
Portal Communications 20863 Stevens Creek Blvd. Suite #200 Cupertino, CA 95014
Press <RETURN> to continue
```

10-5

The Amiga Zone is always busy.

Another coup for Portal is snagging Spartan. Spartan is Rich MacKinnon (*Spartan@cup.portal.com*). He's sort of famous and infamous on the net.

"I got a modem with my first computer," he says diffidently. "The guy said, 'You want a modem with that?' and I said, 'Uh, yeah.' So I went home with a 1200-baud modem. I never intended to get into it." That night in 1987, he signed onto the Shark's Head BBS, a local board, and chose as his handle the school mascot, Spartan. And he's been calling some network, bulletin board, or system every day ever since.

If you've traveled anywhere with a modem, you've probably seen Spartan's messages. The net oldtimers call him Sparty. "I really didn't realize choosing that handle would have such an impact on my life," he says. "For a long time, some people call me Sparty even after they've met me face to face and know my real name."

In fact, it has set the course for his life: He was hired as Portal's customer service department, "sight unseen" as he puts it, based on his work as a volunteer administrator on the system. MacKinnon himself says his first day on the job, he was Sparty to everyone on the Portal staff. Carol Johnson says some people got upset when MacKinnon used his real name for work, Portal's customer service, and Spartan when telecomputing on his own time. They felt betrayed, somehow, that he was "incognito" when they talked to him on the phone; it was a minor controversy on Portal for a time.

Which is one factor that led to MacKinnon's current project: he is going for his doctorate in political science. "My dissertation is studying the evolving forms of governance within computer networks," he says. "When most people think of government they think of institutions, but I'm talking about how these self-organized groups govern themselves. What types of structures do they use, and what are they modeled after? And why: a set of ideals, or just what the strongest person in the group can get away with? And I'm also studying the lack of government in some groups."

He's had ample opportunity to get firsthand experience in this: when PC Pursuit had no cap on time you were hooked on, as long as you paid your monthly minimum, Spartan was everywhere—BIX, GEnie, CompuServe, Boston Computer Society, around the globe. He's articulate and witty, and soon had correspondents everywhere. And he proselytized: at one point his whole family was traveling electronically together. Now, after his parents have divorced, he travels alone, but still enjoys it. One of his favorite spots (besides Portal, of course!) is FreeNet, which is modeled after National Public Radio. "They call themselves National Public Teleputing Network," he says. The nodes are local calls in Youngstown, Cleveland, and other large cities.

His advice for the neophyte electronic traveler is: "Look for the magazines where you bought your modem, like *InfoWorld* or *Computer Shopper*. Start by calling the local boards listed in the classifieds there. Ask folks on the local board about other boards they like. Go visit those. Ask again. See what happens. That's what I did." A few hours after talking to Rich McKinnon, I found this letter from Sparty in my Portal mailbox:

Hiya Libby!!

I don't know about you . . . but git the feelin' that you ended up interviewin' Rich about Sparty . . . so now's yer opportunity to rap with the real modem surfer hisself :-)

I got my start on Portal as a chatline host . . . sort of a radio talk show host. The show was called "Saturday Mourning" and was on from Friday midnight to 1 a.m. The target market wuz those who were either crawlin' back from the bar scene or who never made it out of the house. In those daze, I had no idea if there was anyone in the room with me unless they lemme know.

It was hard work . . . just typin' away into oblivion . . . but I kept at it until I was able to trade fer a better time slot. I think it was Wednesday nights at 7. I changed the format to the Spartan Saloon. It was a sort of Cyberspace Western hideout with a long bar. People would mosey in with hats and boots and we'd <sllllliiiiiiiddddeee . . . . . . > the sasparillies down the bar to 'em. Had lots a good fights. We had a good time and the Saloon had a good number of regulars until we all got tired of each other :-)

On the community service side, I started Portal Partners. Actually the idea was suggested to me by "Bubba" my bouncer. I think he's still online as WestWEM. The idea of Partners was to match new users with experienced ones . . . a sort of new-user orientation. Well, it worked! Partners ended up bein' a kind of shadow Customer Service. And that experience led to my hirin' on at Portal CS. Partners is still around. I gave it to my lieutenant, Lynlee. The program is called Portal Pals now (I guess some people thot it was some sort of dating thang, so we changed the name). Type go pals.

Ever notice that I talk phunny? Yep. Cuz way back when when I was on Shark's Head (SHBBS), someone in chat said "Gee, are you an adult? You write so formally." Well that last thang that I wanted to be was an adult. But the important point was made. In a werld where werds are everythang, we can't all be writin' in perfeckt grammer or else we'd all end up lookin' alike. So Spartytalk or Spartydrawl was born. Now you know that Rich don't talk like this . . . and it don't matter. The drawl adds to Sparty's character . . . it conjures up an image beyond the handle itself. It helps give Sparty an identity and fleshes him out.

There I go talkin' about mysef in third person agin . . . ain't skitso, really!

Lissen, Libby . . . . tanx fer writtin' about me . . . who knows, mebbe yer plug of my research will help me git a grant someday!

Sparty

The information on the Portal Pals line goes like this:

Read article (text) . . ./ ¦ >* WELCOME to PORTAL PALS Read-2 *< ¦
9853.3.2.1 Portal Partners Program Description
11/27/88 16:33 37/1584 Spartan
Lines 1 to 10 of 37 (27%)
- - - - -

You are reading a text article. Use <RETURN> or 'page' to move through the text ('help page' for details). Type 'add_article' to reply, 'forward' to move to the next article, and 'done' to stop.

PORTAL PARTNERS

Portal Partners is a system orientation program that matches new users with experienced ones. Portal Partners is especially effective because all the participants are voluntary and are either willing to help or willing to learn.

After completing a short application, new users become Junior Partners and can select their Senior Partner from among those that are available. The new user is encouraged to send e-mail to as many people on the availability list as possible. After making contact, both partners decide whether or not they should become matched. In most cases, each Senior Partner will be matched with only one Junior Partner.

Portal Partners is always looking for experienced Portal users to participate as Senior Partners. Senior Partner candidates *should note that they are experienced* on their application. Unless stated otherwise, all applicants are assumed to be new users.

Portal Partners operates its own conference located at "go partners." The Partners Conference is designed especially for handling new user-related problems. It also gives Junior Partners the opportunity to ask questions of all the Portal Partners.

From time to time, Portal Partners will hold online meetings affording participants the opportunity to gather in a private, interactive setting.

If you want to join us in the Portal Partners Program, please visit us in our conference at "go partners".

Spartan
Portal Partners Program, Coordinator

Carol Johnson has lots of stories about interesting people online at Portal: Keith Henson, for instance, started a fund online at Portal to help with the legal defense of Craig Neirdorf (see the appendix on EFF).

"We have a member in Guam who is trying to save the last few birds of an almost extinct species. Portal is his main contact with the outside world," she said. And "One member, about 16 years old, has been on 5 or 6 years now, already uploading useful programs. You could say he's growing up here on Portal."

Portal allows you to go by your given name or by a handle, which is a pseudonym you make up. You can use this as your logon name and as your e-mail address (in which case your e-mail address becomes *handle@cup.portal.com*).

"The whole thing about handles is interesting. You have people creating basically alter egos, and it's a fascinating psychological process," Carol Johnson says. This process is particularly evident on chats, she said.

And, things get organized on Portal:

"We've been in contact with a new group that's starting up that might use Portal as its official network," Johnson said. "The group is International Women in Technology. The International Women in Technology group (WITI) is still in the formative stages. All the women here at Portal attended their first meeting, which was jam-packed with high-powered businesswomen. You can still get membership info from Carolyn Leighton. Just e-mail her through Portal at 'witi.'"

That's just a sampling of Portal; it's got lots of other groups. Some are USENET reflections, some are unique to Portal. Exploring them all would take a long time!

How to sign off

Type logout. And it does.

11 The slick "PSILink" & "PSINet"

E-mail	*all-info@psi.com*
U.S. Mail	11800 Sunrise Valley Dr.
	Reston, VA 22091
Phone	(703) 620-6651 [voice]
Hours	24 hrs
Basic rate	From $75 to $900 per quarter, plus registration fee.
Notes	Emphasis on e-mail, and FTP. No chat, no telnet, no discussions.

Performance Systems International, Inc.'s message and information service is called PSIlink. This is a turnkey service package giving you the power to link directly to the Internet wide area network system for batch-style and real-time applications, just like the colleges. Well, maybe better than the colleges, because the front-end software is really fun to use. This is a great system for busy, White Rabbit types. Many organizations and individuals who cannot afford the expense of installing a separate Internet gateway are using PSI's services to connect to Internet.

Once, links to PSINet or the Internet required use of a computer using the UNIX operating system. Now, you need feel left out no more because of a PC or MAC. PSILink represents a novel option for folks wanting to use easy electronic messaging. Think you're chained to your PC for e-mail and messages? Nope. PSIlink has access to text pagers and radio modems with this service. Now there is no hiding!

You can get electronic versions of their information packages by sending a null electronic mail message to *info@psi.com*.

PSI bills itself as a value-added internetworking services provider. It does have a wide spectrum of services for the individual and corporate user of electronic information, ranging from electronic mail products to turnkey integration of local area networks into the PSINet wide area network system and the Internet. PSINet has local nodes in major cities throughout the U.S. (See FIG. 11-1.)

PSI is one of six commercial providers that have direct links to Internet, and they formed an organization to directly connect these commercial systems. This

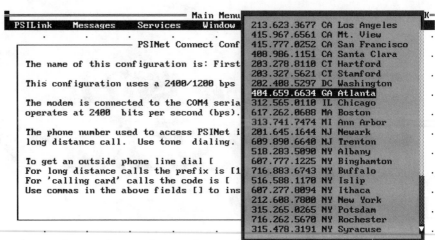

```
                                        Main Menu                              K=
  PSILink    Messages    Services     Window       213.623.3677 CA Los Angeles
                                                    415.967.6561 CA Mt. View
      ●         ●          ●            ●           415.777.0252 CA San Francisco
                      PSINet Connect Conf          408.986.1151 CA Santa Clara
                                                    203.278.8110 CT Hartford
    The name of this configuration is: First       203.327.5621 CT Stamford
                                                    202.408.5297 DC Washington
    This configuration uses a 2400/1200 bps        404.659.6634 GA Atlanta
                                                    312.565.8110 IL Chicago
    The modem is connected to the COM4 seria       617.262.0688 MA Boston
    operates at 2400  bits per second (bps).       313.741.7474 MI Ann Arbor
                                                    201.645.1644 NJ Newark
    The phone number used to access PSINet i       609.890.6640 NJ Trenton
    long distance call.  Use tone  dialing.        518.283.5090 NY Albany
                                                    607.777.1225 NY Binghamton
    To get an outside phone line dial [            716.883.6743 NY Buffalo
    For  long distance calls the prefix is [1      516.588.1170 NY Islip
    For 'calling card' calls the code is [         607.277.8894 NY Ithaca
    Use commas in the above fields [] to ins       212.608.7800 NY New York
                                                    315.265.0265 NY Potsdam
                                                    716.262.5670 NY Rochester
                                                    315.478.3191 NY Syracuse

Press TAB for phone number completion.
```

11-1

Part of the configuration is choosing the closest connect city. This is just part of the list.

connection of commercial network service providers is called the Commercial Internet Exchange (CIX). More on that later.

By linking through a company like PSI, ordinary people and businesses can access the Internet directly and benefit from discussions on it. Further, using PSI, or one of its CIX partners, you may send commercially oriented messages to other members of the same system. The dreaded taint of profit will not rub off on those parts of the Internet funded by tax dollars, ensuring free and fair competition. O:-}

PSI was incorporated in the spring of 1989. It is privately held, so dollar figures are not available; but we do know it went from 220 customers at the end of 1990 to 1100 at the end of 1991. This is a happy sign that they are meeting a need.

Today there are more than 1000 organizations on PSINet; that's thousands of individuals. The volume of daily news traffic, according to marketing specialist Kimberly Brown, is approximately 50 megabytes per day of new articles. The busiest hours of traffic flow: 4:00 p.m.–7:00 p.m. EST.

How to dial . . . how to log on

First you send your money to the Virginia office, specifying which version you need. Then you sign the forms included with the software, sending in your payment for the first month, as instructed. (You can even fax in all the information, credit card and all.) Soon, you will receive your account number and your password. Now your account number will be used as part of your Internet address as follows:

pl9999@mail.psi.net

where *9999* is the number assigned to you. There, you are now officially part of the Internet!

The PSILink software package developed is easy to install, set up and use, and help windows abound. On my system, with an internal modem on COM4, it took a little fiddling and a white lie to the program about the interrupt to use—then it worked great. I chose the Atlanta number as the gateway closest to me. With the newest version of PSILink, Macintosh users also can dial up to the local PSI gateway and have complete access to the Internet at a single monthly fee payable to PSI. (See FIGS. 11-2, 11-3, 11-4, and 11-5.)

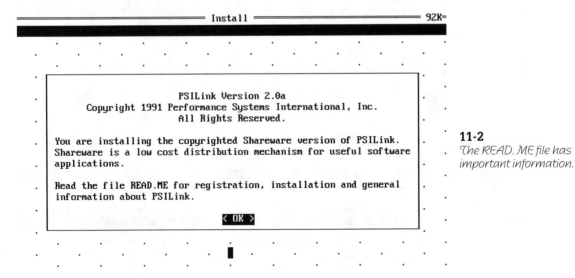

```
=========================== Install =========================== 92K=


   .     .     .     .     .     .     .     .     .     .     .
      .     .     .     .     .     .     .     .     .     .
   .  ┌─────────────────────────────────────────────────────┐  .
      │                                                     │
   .  │              PSILink Version 2.0a                   │  .
      │   Copyright 1991 Performance Systems International, Inc.  │
   .  │            All Rights Reserved.                     │  .
      │                                                     │
   .  │  You are installing the copyrighted Shareware version of PSILink.  │  .
      │  Shareware is a low cost distribution mechanism for useful software  │
   .  │  applications.                                       │  .
      │                                                     │
   .  │  Read the file READ.ME for registration, installation and general  │  .
      │  information about PSILink.                          │
   .  │                  < OK >                             │  .
      └─────────────────────────────────────────────────────┘
   .     .     .     .     .     .     .     .     .     .     .
      .     .     .     .     .  ▮  .     .     .     .     .

Press ENTER to continue.
```

11-2
The READ.ME file has important information.

```
============================ Main Menu ============================
 PSILink    Messages    Services    Window    Help                 ▼

   .     .     .     .     .     .     .     .     .     .     .
      .     .     .     .     .     .     .     .     .     .
   .           ┌──────── PSILink:Setup ────────┐            .
      .        │                               │        .
   .           │         Your full name:       │            .
               │ The name of your organization:│
   .           │ Your time zone (F1 for Help): -0600 │       .
               │ The name of your PSILink account: ▉▉▉▉▉ │
   .           │              < Cancel >  < OK > │            .
               └───────────────────────────────┘
   .     .     .     .     .     .     .     .     .     .     .
      .     .     .     .     .  ▮  .     .     .     .     .

Enter your PSILink account name.
```

11-3
Setting up PSILink is easy with the menus.

After everything is set up, you can write your mail while offline, with simple menu-guided steps. The screens guide you to put everything in its proper place and allow you to store aliases of people you know in a special file. Help is just two keystrokes away: Tab and F1. (See FIGS. 11-6, 11-7, and 11-8.)

```
─────────────── Help for Services:Paging in Main Menu ───────────────
A service provider can provide you with a 'paging' address.  Messages sent to
this address can be sent to a variety of devices.  The most common are
alphanumeric pagers.  Using this mechanism you can monitor your incoming mail
in real time.

To turn paging on or off you must select 'on' or 'off', press the < OK >
button and then connect to PSINet.  When paging has been changed you will
recieve a notification in your PSILink mailbox.

                                        ◆
```

11-4

You can even set up the system to send messages to your pager.

```
Press ESC to back up, ALT+x to quit immediately, TAB and then F1 for more Help
```

```
════════════════════════════ Main Menu ═══════════════════ 1:05   50K=
   PSILink     Messages     Services     Window     Help                ▼
           ──────────────── PSINet Connect Configuration ────────────────
           The name of this configuration is: First

           This configuration uses a 2400/1200 bps Hayes Compatible modem.

           The modem is connected to the ▓COM4▓ serial port.  The serial port
           operates at 2400  bits per second (bps).  The speaker should be on.

           The phone number used to access PSINet is 404.659.6634.  This is a
           long distance call.  Use tone  dialing.

           To get an outside phone line dial [                    ].
           For long distance calls the prefix is [1,                   ].
           For 'calling card' calls the code is [                        ].
           Use commas in the above fields [] to insert any required delays.

                                      <Cancel>   <Expert>   < OK >
```

11-5

The program tries to remind you of all parameters. The Expert selection lets you set the COM and IRQ if you need to.

```
Press SPACE to toggle.
```

You can also get files FTP, again, all menu-guided. (See FIG. 11-9.)

Saving all these to the out box, then you choose CONNECT, and you get the screen shown in FIG. 11-10. Saving your password to a file is optional; you can choose to type it in yourself each time.

Briefly, this screen lets you choose whether to get or send mail. The system then dials, shows you how things are progressing, and signs off. And if you do it wrong? (See FIG. 11-11.)

There's no telnetting to Furry here . . . it all happens quickly, and you go on to doing something productive! However, the FTP service is easy to use. Simply click on services, the batch FTP. The screen explains it all. (Look back at FIG. 11-9.)

When you click on connect, you have a choice of send out mail, get your waiting mail, or both. FTP requests count as sending out mail. Then you click on OK (or hit

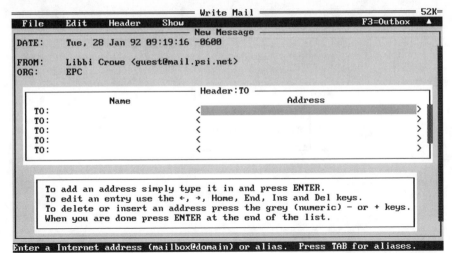

═══════════════════ Write Mail ═════════════════ 52K═
File   Edit   Header   Show   F3=Outbox ▲
─────────────────── New Message ───────────────────
DATE: Tue, 28 Jan 92 09:19:16 -0600

FROM: Libbi Crowe <guest@mail.psi.net>
ORG: EPC
┌──────────────────── Header:TO ────────────────────┐
│   Name   Address   │
│ TO: <███████████████████████████████> │
│ TO: <   > │
│ TO: <   > │
│ TO: <   > │
│ TO: <   > │
└──┘
┌──┐
│ To add an address simply type it in and press ENTER.│
│ To edit an entry use the ←, →, Home, End, Ins and Del keys.│
│ To delete or insert an address press the grey (numeric) - or + keys.│
│ When you are done press ENTER at the end of the list.│
└──┘
Enter a Internet address (mailbox@domain) or alias. Press TAB for aliases.

11-6
Frequent correspondents can be stored in an address book.

═══════════════════ Write Mail ═════════════════
File   Edit   Header   Show   F3=Outbox ▲
─────────────────── New Message ───────────────────
DATE: Tue, 11 Feb 92 08:39:43 -0600

FROM: Elizabeth P. Crowe <p10165@mail.psi.net>
ORG: EPC
┌──────────────────── Header:TO ────────────────────┐
│   Name   Address   │
│ TO: <brown@psi.com███████████████████> │
│ TO: <   > │
│ TO: <   > │
│ TO: <   > │
│ TO: <   > │
└──┘
┌──┐
│ To add an address simply type it in and press ENTER.│
│ To edit an entry use the ←, →, Home, End, Ins and Del keys.│
│ To delete or insert an address press the grey (numeric) - or + keys.│
│ When you are done press ENTER at the end of the list.│
└──┘
Enter a Internet address (mailbox@domain) or alias. Press TAB for aliases.

11-7
Just type in the addresses you want; it's that easy.

return for your rodentless ones). The program takes over, dials, connects, tells you how good your line connection is, and hangs up when all is done. Then you can read your messages offline, freeing up your phone.

The software comes as part of the service registration fee, which is $35 for a version running under Windows 3.0 or DOS, with some additional cost for MacIntosh software.

The services are provided at a flat fee for two flavors and two speed options: E-mail only at 300/1200/2400 baud is $19 per month, with 9600 baud costing $29 per month. Basic service, including unlimited messaging, USENET NEWS, and anonymous FTP, is $29 per month using up to 2400-baud modems and $39 per month using V.32/9600-baud modems, with monthly news and FTP data transfer over 100 megabytes incurring additional fees of $1 per meg.

Special deals, subscription information

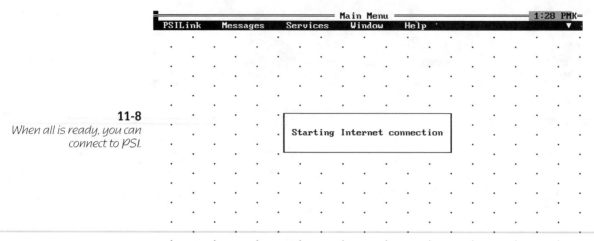

11-8

When all is ready, you can connect to PSI.

Starting Internet connection

Press ESC to cancel.

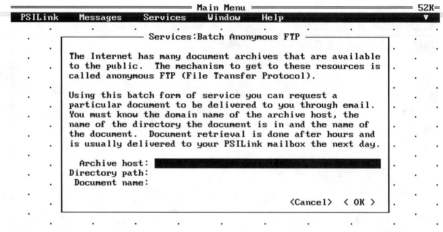

11-9

You can also get files FTP; the process is all menu-guided.

Enter the Internet address (domain) of the FTP archive.

The company has over 35 separate nodes in major cities around the U.S. Privacy is good on this system; they do not send your mail through a university's system, so there are no restrictions on use and no one to check on you.

For organizational services of PSI, they will handle the registration and assigning of a domain name (like a fictitious name when starting a business) for you.

One such service, called UUPSI, provides access to electronic mail, USENET NEWS, and ClariNet, a business information service. UUFTP, their anonymous FTP service that is built on UUPSI, costs $1 per megabyte, minimum $25 per month (there's a one-time $75 fee to sign up). There's an online list of Select Internet Archives included on this service that they update regularly.

One-way delivery of text messages from electronic mail networks to pagers nationwide is available now, and PSILink was the first commercial package to

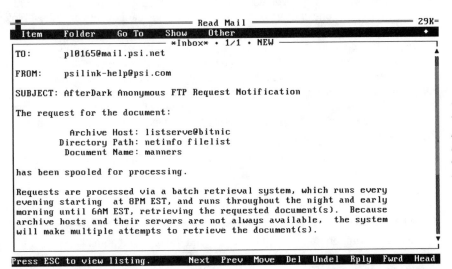

PSILink   Messages   Services   Window   Help   ▼
·   ·   ·   ·   ·   ·   ·   ·
·   ·   ·   ·   ·   ·   ·
┌──────────────── PSILink:Connect ────────────────┐
·   Choose a configuration to connect to PSINet, enter your PSILink   ·
    password (make sure your CAPS LOCK is off) and then select < OK >.

·   To enter a new or edit an existing configuration, type in the name   ·
    (use the TAB key to check spelling) and then select <Edit>.

·   Configuration name: ▓▓▓▓▓▓▓▓▓▓▓▓▓▓▓▓▓▓▓▓▓▓▓▓▓▓▓▓   ·
              Password:

·   Send Mail [√] Receive Mail [√]   <Cancel> <Edit> < OK >   ·
└───┘

11-10
You can enter your password manually or store it in a configuration file.

Press TAB for name completion.

Item   Folder   Go To   Show   Other   ◆
─────────────── *Inbox* · 1/1 · NEW ───────────────
TO: p10165@mail.psi.net

FROM: psilink-help@psi.com

SUBJECT: AfterDark Anonymous FTP Request Notification

The request for the document:

          Archive Host: listserve@bitnic
          Directory Path: netinfo filelist
          Document Name: manners

has been spooled for processing.

Requests are processed via a batch retrieval system, which runs every
evening starting at 8PM EST, and runs throughout the night and early
morning until 6AM EST, retrieving the requested document(s). Because
archive hosts and their servers are not always available, the system
will make multiple attempts to retrieve the document(s).

Press ESC to view listing.   Next Prev Move Del Undel Rply Fwrd Head

11-11
The system sends you a message about what will happen when you request an FTP. This is not real-time FTP.

integrate with systems like those provided by SkyTel®/SkyWord® and PACTEL. Two-way services providing transparent communication between wired electronic mail systems and two-way data radio networks, such as RAM Mobile Data's, were available in the second quarter of 1992. With two-way systems, you have totally wireless e-mail. They do it with mirrors . . .

The operating system is as simple as yours. The staff is kind and helpful, and respond to questions posted to *psilink-help@psi.com* very quickly.

Flavor

Sights

The entire Internet and USENET are available here. The PSI White Pages are famous as an attempt at a usable system of name and address storage, comparable to the AT&T phone book. In July of 1989, the NYSERNet network sponsored a White Pages Pilot

Project. This service, the largest pilot project to use the OSI Directory standard (X.500), is now available throughout PSINet. This service, which includes several international connections, represents the first large-scale use of OSI services in the Internet.

The software that makes up computer networks allow users to interact in many ways. Like the telephone system, it can allow a simple transfer of messages. Or it can be used in more complex ways such as sharing data for research or allowing a group to share the same information. We can send text messages, whole articles, and even just chit-chat. Unlike the telephone system, the internet lacks a standard place to store addresses and their owners.

Most network services assume you the user can find the infrastructural information you need to get your stuff where you want it to go. If you are using an electronic mail service, for example, it's assumed you can supply addressing information for all the intended recipients. Finding the addresses is your job. And in some systems, the attitude of the operators is that if you don't know the proper address already, you don't need to!

This model works fine in small groups, where you all know each other and the addresses in the group might even be in print somewhere. The problem gets geometrically complex when you add people to get a medium or large environment. If a network has millions of users belonging to thousands of organizations, the job of memorizing all the addresses on it would be impossible. Besides, even if you did, the information changes frequently, as people and resources move around. The goal of a white pages service is to provide, on a voluntary basis, the necessary information, and to make the complexity of the infrastructural information seem invisible. This is a grass roots effort, both to understand the white pages service users need and to understand the limitations of the OSI Directory in providing those services. Organizations can store information about their network and personnel there, and are urged to maintain their part of the directory there.

For resource constrained members of PSINet, PSI will offer maintenance service just as it does for the Domain Name System (DNS). Eventually, the goal of the Pilot Project is to use the same programs and tools to access both global and local white pages information. As a part of this, new applications that might make use of the white pages service, such as private mail, will be encouraged.

PSI gives software running the OSI Directory, and the user and administrator guides. Anyone can download the software on PSI's service host, *uu.psi.com*; simply use anonymous FTP and retrieve the file, pilot/src/pilot-ps.tar.Z in BINARY mode. This is a compressed tar image containing the documentation for the service, and it contains the Administrator's Guide: details on how to retrieve the software and join the project.

For further information, write to *wpp-manager@psi.com*. A user interface called fred was developed and established as a publicly available service on *wp.psi.com*. fred emulates, as closely as possible, the existing WHOIS name service. fred is not just an imitator, but also a translator: it provides a somewhat simple syntax to the user and then translates the user's commands into complex directives for the OSI Directory. The OSI Directory offers more functionality than the older WHOIS service, so fred allows a user to give more powerful directives.

Suppose you're on some other system, and want to try out PSINet's White pages. Here's what it will look like:

```
% telnet wp1.psi.net
Trying 192.33.4.21 . . .
Connected to wp1.psi.net.
Escape character is '^]'.

SunOS UNIX (wp1.psi.net)

login: fred
    Last login: Wed Mar 11 10:00:27 from HILLEBRANDT.MDC.
    SunOS Release 4.0.3c (WP_PSI_BOOTBOX) #2: Tue Dec 17
    12:20:46
    EST 1991

Welcome to the PSI White Pages Pilot Project

Try "help" for a list of commands
"whois" for information on how to find people
"manual" for detailed documentation
"report" to send a report to the white pages manager

To find out about participating organizations, try

    "whois -org *"

accessing service, please wait. . .

fred> whois brown -org psi
    Trying @c=US@o=Performance Systems International . . .
Kimberly Brown (2)       brown@psi.com

Marketing and Communications Specialist
    PSI Inc.
    165 Jordan Rd.
    Troy, NY 12180
    USA

Telephone: +1 518-283-8860 x103

Mailbox information:
    internet: brown@nisc.psi.net

Locality: Troy, New York

Picture: (No display process defined)

Name: Kimberly Brown, Sales,
Performance Systems International,
US (2)
Modified: Tue Sep 25 16:13:23 1990
by: Manager, US (3)

fred> quit
Connection closed by foreign host.
%
```

These examples show how any host that supports telnet can login to *wp1.psi.net* as fred and look up information on participating organizations. Suppose a user is interested in finding information about someone called "brown" at some place called "stony". The user invokes an interface to the "white pages" (fred), and issues the query:

```
whois brown -org stony
```

fred determines which organizations have "stony" in their name. Depending on user-options, this might use simple wildcards or a complex Soundex (phonetic) algorithm for matching. In this example, only one organization is found. The user-interface then focuses its search on this organization asking about someone named "brown." Again, depending on user-options, various matching algorithms might be used. The box shows fred found 13 people with "brown" in their names. So, the user specifies an abbreviation for the desired person ("4"), and fred expands that entry.

So fred shows the name of the person ("Edward J Jr Brown") with an abbreviation for the person's handle ("4"), and Edward J Brown's Internet mailbox. After this, any other names for the person pop up. After this, the usual postal, telecommunications, and e-mail addressing information come up. Finally, the date and time of the last change to the entry give the user an idea of how current the information is. You should know that only some information is textual. Often, the attributes are complex binary structures and it's up to your interface to display this information in a pleasing, or even intelligible, fashion.

Besides the fred interface, they have an interface based on the X Window System, called xwp. The X Window System is a trademark of the Massachusetts Institute of Technology. It supports interactive queries, and browsing for easy-to-use examination of the White Pages; simply click on a line displayed by xwp and additional information comes up. Besides providing a window-based interface to the fred model of searching, xwp incorporates "user-friendly naming" in which naming information is entered as it might be found on a business card, e.g.,

Wengyik Yeong, PSI
kille, cs, ucl, gb
L. Eagle, "Sue, Grabbit, and Runn," Oxford

This user-friendly naming scheme uses imprecise matching and assigns "goodness" levels to matches, querying you for assistance on questionable matches, the better to find your intended target. Again, suppose you want to find information about someone called "brown" at some place called "stony." You click on the WHOIS button and enter

```
brown, stony
```

You will get several possibilities. Clicking on any of these will yield additional information. xwp is available via the PSI Software Source Distribution package. Contact *ssd-info@psi.com* or 1-800-82PSI82 for further details.

As of February 1992, the White Pages contained approximately 250,000 entries, distributed over 98 sites. To find out which sites are participating, use fred and enter the query:

```
whois -org *
```

Besides all that, PSI has information about its various services online; you can browse through them if you want. These mailboxes run automatically; PSI human staff rarely deal with them. To get these automatic mailboxes to respond to you, simply send a mail message to that address. For example, at your prompt, type

```
mail all-info@psi.com
```

Then hit Enter . The "Subject" line will appear; type

```
Send Info
```

and Enter. In the body of the message, just put a short message like, "Please send me information." After you send the message, an automatically generated message will be sent back to you with the information from that mailbox.

Each service can be ordered by following the instructions given in the responses. Each mailbox is available *@psi.com* (example *ccs-info@psi.com*). The mailboxes are

PERSONAL DIALUP SERVICES

Mailbox Name	Description
gds-info	Information on PSI's Global Dialup Service (GDS) that provides telnet/rlogin access to the Internet at 300–2400 baud 24hours/day via local dialups for a flat fee of $39/month.
psilink-info	Information on PSI's personal network service that provides flat fee e-mail and other Internet and communication services on a dialup basis.

ORGANIZATIONAL DIALUP SERVICES

Mailbox Name	Description
host-dial-info	Information specific to HOST-DIAL, and HOST-DIAL+, which provide V.32 and V.32bis dialup SLIP access for a single host
host-dial-questions	Questions most often asked about HOST-DIAL.
host-dial-x25	Information on International HOST-DIAL access.
lan-dial-info	Information specific to LAN-DIAL and LAN-DIAL+, which provide V.32 and V.32bis dialup PPP access for an entire LAN
lan-dial-questions	Questions most often asked about LAN-DIAL.
uupsi-info	PSI's UUCP fixed price UUCP Mail and/or USENET News service through local phone numbers.
uupsi-brochure	The ASCII text of the marketing brochure for UUPSI.
clarinet-info	Information on CLARINET services available through UUPSI.
x25-dialups-info	Information on International dialup access to PSINet and the Internet.

ORGANIZATIONAL LEASED LINE SERVICES

Mailbox Name	Description
bcs-info	PSI's Basic Connection Service (BCS), the basic (and inexpensive) leased line PSINet/Internet access service from PSI.
ccs-info	PSI's Customer Connection Service (CCS), a leased lined service to PSINet/Internet, with dozens of value added capabilities; however, the customer provides the router.

scs-info	PSI's Standard Connection Service (SCS), a leased line turnkey service to PSINet/Internet, with dozens of value added capabilities, with PSI responsible for everything including the router at the customer's site.
scs-brochure	The ASCII text of the marketing brochure for SCS.

OTHER INFORMATION

Mailbox Name	Description
hardware-info	Hardware (Routers, modems, etc) that PSI sells to its customers
map-info	A Postscript file of the PSINet Topology map.
numbers-info	Provides the actual local phone numbers for IDS and UUPSI.
pop-info	A listing of PSI's Points-of-Presence (POP) in major cities throughout the US.
snmp-info	Information on PSI's source code implementation of SNMP for agents and network managers is available here.
software-info	A listing of commercial software products compatible with PSI services and available for purchase through PSI.
ssd-info	Information on licensing X.500 and Z39.50 source code technology is available here.
tutorial-info	Information on PSI's TCP/IP and OSI Internetworking tutorials that are free to CCS, SCS, LAN-DIAL and HOST-DIAL customers.
wp-info	Information on the PSINet/Internet WhitePages (WP) service using X.500.
wp-brochure	The ASCII text of the information brochure for WP.

Finally, some information is available via anonymous FTP on *uu.psi.com* (*136.161.128.3*) that includes:

Press Releases	in	/press.releases
Newsletters	in	/newsletter

If you'd like to communicate with a human for more detailed questions, send e-mail to

`info@psi.com`

Strength in numbers

I promised that I'd tell you about CIX. In February, 1991, the first Commercial Internet Exchange (CIX) Association was formed. It now consists of

PSINet (founder)
CERFnet (founder)
AlterNet (founder)
BARRNet
NEARNet
US Sprint

Anyone else who wants to join the CIX Association (Trade Association 506c) must join the CIX to participate/route in the network. Among the members of this organization, there are no restrictions on usage and no settlement costs between members. You might say the CIX came about by popular demand: it resulted from requests by commercial customers of these network providers. The interconnection uses redundant T1 facilities of the networking firms and will provide service even if there's a complete failure of the NSFNET backbone. So no matter how the political winds might blow, or how tied up the government nets get, the CIX will get the mail through . . . for their customers.

This is one face of the commercialization of the Internet we mentioned in Chapter 2.

The CIX agreement provides for all customers of AlterNet, CERFnet and PSINet to exchange Internet traffic directly, despite which network the customer obtains service from, and at no additional cost. These competing firms provide most of the commercial TCP/IP-OSI internetworking services in the United States. They are not subject to government-mandated "acceptable use" restrictions on their traffic. The CIX will allow firms or individuals connected to one network, such as CERFnet, to communicate with firms connected to AlterNet or PSINet without traversing the government restricted backbones, such as the NSFNET (National Science Foundation Network). This allows you to get high-speed access throughout the AlterNet/PSINet/CERFnet interconnected T1 network systems without violating government imposed restrictions on parts of the Internet.

12 WELL connected

E-mail	*support@well.sf.ca.us*
U.S. Mail	27 Gate Five Rd.
	Sausalito, CA 94965
Phone	(415) 332-6106 [voice]
Hours	24 hours a day
Basic rate	$10.00 per month plus $2.00 per hour. Additional fee for disk storage above 500K.
Notes	No FTP or telnet. Chat and e-mail. Very discussion-oriented.

No glitzy graphics here. No homogenized news feeds. No prefab events. The WELL is very personal, personable and personality-rich.

"It's a very social-oriented system," says Matisse Enzer, one of the very supportive support people at the Whole Earth 'Lectronic Link. "It's full of personal relationships, some of them close. This is a social connection. Most of the users, I'd say about 60%, are in the SF bay area. The rest are spread out across the continental US and the world. About 200 people are internationally connected.

"What's neat about it is these are real people. You can't be anonymous here. And we build real relationships between people," Matisse continued.

"We have 200 public discussion areas called conferences. They have from 20–200 topics in each. Anyone can start a topic in any conference. Conferences are run by hosts, and the administration can move or replace a host, though I don't think we ever have.

He noted that traffic varies by conference. Some post one message a week, some 30 messages a day.

"On January 1, [1992] we became an Internet site. We expect the Internet connection will bring us more connections from around the world," Matisse noted proudly. The WELL's Internet address is *userid@WELL.sf.ca.us*, and the IP number is *192.132.30.2*. It gives access to e-mail. If you need help you can write *support@WELL.sf.ca.us.* If you need information on the WELL, you can write *info@WELL.sf.ca.us.*

When Matisse tried to list the conferences of note on the WELL, it was like trying to list all the things that might possibly interest men and women. It includes:

East Coast
Virtual Reality
Politics
Writers
Star Trek
Gardening
Pacific Rim
Mucho Media
Future
Books
Transportation
Apple
Artificial Intelligence
Various computer makes
Jewish

In addition, you have Misc and Unclear for topics that just don't fit anywhere else.

Private conferences are available at no extra charge for small groups, families, etc. One example is a French university where students get MBAs. The WELL is how the students, faculty, and alumni all over the world keep in touch. Some stay strictly in that conference, while others cruise the whole WELL.

"The WELL is unique. It has a rich community of good people. Social action is very important here," Matisse said. "They tend to be more than just computer professionals. A lot are self-employed, or consider themselves to be, in a variety of ways. We have carpenters, musicians, writers, consultants. And of course, they are all comfortable expressing themselves with words, which is the medium we use. That's an easily overlooked but ever present factor in our environment."

WELL is very social, and conferences can range from the frivolous (WEIRD is a conference where you can go just to be goofy) to the highly dry and technical.

And some people use the WELL to get their work done. The Electronic Frontier Foundation was born here. The founders—Mitchell Kapor, of Lotus and visicalc fame, President (*mkapor@eff.org*), and John Perry Barlow, of Corelsay and Grateful Dead fame, (*barlow@eff.org*)—met each other here. The WELL was the EFF's first electronic home; now, of course, they have their own Internet site and are leaders in the field of political action for privacy and fair use of electronic networks. But it started here, and there is still an active EFF conference.

The WELL hosted the Network Association Convention in 1990.

"We offer a variety of services," Matisse says. "We have a USENET connection, though we are not cost effective if that's all you want. You can TELNET or RLOGIN to the WELL but not out. By August, we expect to have FTP capability; as long as you sign an agreement to live by the guidelines, you can use the WELL like any other Internet connection.

WELL, it's a deep subject . . sometimes you get water . . .

"We don't have much software here, that's not what we're about. We're conversationally based. Still, anyone can upload or download; we're not against it!"

How to log on

In Europe, people connect the WELL with the X.25 network. In London, that's $14 per hour; in Japan, $18 per hour; and in Australia, $26 per hour. Most people in the US can get onto a connection for about $4 an hour; that's in addition to your WELL subscription. The details are below, in the signon procedure.

To sign on, you can dial directly at (415) 332-6106. Or you can connect to the Well over CompuServe's Packet Network (CPN). This is accomplished by dialing your local CIS connect number, and at the HOST: prompt, typing WELL. From most places in the Continental U.S., it's $4.00 an hour this way, charged to your credit card (see later comments).

To get there after work hours, a cheaper alternative is PC Pursuit; You call (800) 736-1130 and set up an account with them; it will be billed separately from your WELL account billing. Connect-USA also provides a separately-billed, low-cost alternative to connect to the WELL. The charge is around $3.00 an hour any time of day, but it is limited to certain major cities in the US. Their number is (505) 255-2553.

Or you can TELNET on an Internet connection.

No matter how you go about it, when you connect to the WELL for the first time, you'll get some opening screens telling you about the system and its 200 conferences (discussion groups). Then you choose your terminal; "Dumb" usually works well. You input your name, address, and phone number; and then you'll get a description of the charges.

Charges (billed by calendar month)

Monthly membership	$15 every month
Hourly usage	$2/hour regardless of time of day, 1200/2400 baud
CompuServe Packet Net	$4/hour (300/1200/2400/9600-baud access). Call (800) 848-8980 for local access number.

The WELL also charges for file storage. Each user is allowed 512K of free disk space. Each 1024K above 512K is charged at $20/month prorated.

Then you choose your billing method. Charge cards are accepted.

Then you choose your online name, called the "login id." This login id can be 2–8 characters long and doesn't have to reflect anything about your real name (unless you want it to).

Now you choose a password. The password *must* have 7 or 8 characters and must not be a dictionary word or name. It should be a unique combination of letters, numbers, and other characters. It *must* have at least one *uppercase* character, as well as a numeral or special character like one of these:

!@#$%^&*(){}[]'";:?><\/

The program will reject any password you enter that does not fit this criteria.

Next, you answer a questionnaire about how you heard of the WELL and get some information on ordering manuals. Then, if you like, you can enter an online biography introducing yourself to the others on the system. Finally, the system logs you off. After a few days to verify your payment method, you'll be allowed back on with your new ID and password.

Get—and keep close by your side—the *WELL Power User's Card*. The commands are similar to other systems but differ just enough to get you in trouble.

For instance, to get to the mail area, type `MAIL`. On many other systems, you can add the word `READ` in order to read your mail. On the WELL, first type `MAIL`, then wait for the list of letters in your "mailbox," choose one by number, and then read it.

Don't do as I did and type `MAIL READ`. It seemed that nothing happened. But what *did* happen was that the WELL member whose userid happens to be "READ" got a blank message from me.

He finally wrote to ask me why I was sending him blank letters—or, in one case, a letter with a "?" in it (I was typing "?" to get help on my options . . . and instead was typing a letter with a question mark in it!) At first I was altogether puzzled, and then I noticed his userid in the header. The light came on, and I apologized profusely. As I never heard back from him, I can only imagine he shook his head and muttered about the technologically illiterate among us.

The discussions are fascinating, and addictive. Some examples:

A recent, long topic about the ins and outs of being blind brought out that while many books for the blind are available, they tend to be less than current (never a bestseller while it's on the bestseller list) and very, very tame (as in, you won't find cyberpunk SF). The WELL users decided that both those things could be fixed. The discussion resulted in several WELL users volunteering to read current novels on tape for blind WELL users. One blind member said that choosing the first book was like being a kid in a candy store: where to begin?

Another discussion about parties gave this new user insight into the famous WOPs: Well Office Parties. Monthly, those who live near enough to attend get together face to face (in WELL jargon, F2F) with the staff at WOPs. They sound quite fascinating.

But this led to a long discussion about what makes a good party, some voting for no more than two or three people for a really good party, others recalling the Bad Old Days when a party meant smoking and drinking too much, and believing you were having a good time.

Another fascinating topic was Stump the Well, where one of the online hosts asked users to post any question to see whether someone on the WELL knew the answer. Thus, "Who is the mayor of a small Mid-West town?" etc . . .

Right after the new year began, another host asked, "What have you just done for the first time?" The answers ranged from the profound to the deliciously mundane.

I won't quote any of the actual conversations for two reasons. One is that they are still there, and you'll have fun reading them online yourself. The other is the opening screen shown in FIG. 12-1. And I don't want to be challenged!

In fact, when I posted a message asking for comments for the book, it was swiftly pointed out to me how close a community the WELL is, and that asking questions for personal profit was not in the spirit of the place. Despite the fact that I was a

```
This is The WELL

DYNIX(R) V3.1.0  (well)
Type your userid or    newuser    to register
login: lib
Password:
Last login: Mon Feb 24 11:47:25 on ttyxb
DYNIX(R) V3.1.0 NFS  #33 (): Wed Feb  5 15:01:47 PST 1992


    You have reached the WELL (Whole Earth Lectronic Link).

    You own your own words.  This means that you are responsible for the
    words that you post on the WELL and that reproduction of those words
    without your permission in any medium outside of the WELL's conferencing
    system may be challenged by you, the author.


    _____

You have new mail.
```

12-1

The WELL is up front and personal about their rules.

newcomer, and not really part of the in crowd, I did get several gracious replies to "What do you like best about the WELL?":

Topic 466: Totally nonscientific poll
3: (bbraasch) Mon, Feb 24, '92 (18:26) 17 lines

The unpredictability of it all. I thought downtime correlated to high tides when I first got here. Made sense when I found out that the phone lines terminate at sea level somewhere very close to the Pacific Ocean. Then it turned out to have nothing to do with high tides, but was because we ran out of disk space. Made sense because data always gets bigger over time. Then it turned out to be hung modems. Maybe so, but then again, maybe it's just too many users at once. Or maybe too many long distance users. Or maybe too much mail.

Reminds me of the first television set my family had. Whenever it broke, my dad just hit the side of it with the flat of his hand and the picture cleared up. Until the time he hit it and the picture went away forever.

We just need to know where to slap it and it'll all clear up. Or it'll go away and never come back.

Quote it if you want.

Topic 466: Totally nonscientific poll
4: well's cargo (dlee) Mon, Feb 24, '92 (21:40) 5 lines

Like John, I've had the opportunity here to meet numerous fine folks that I wouldn't have otherwise, and it's a milieu quite unlike my normal workaday one. It has addressed some very real needs in my life, and allows me to expose and explore sides of myself that I otherwise have much less opportunity to show and see.

Topic 466: Totally nonscientific poll
5: Eric Rawlins (woodman) Mon, Feb 24, '92 (22:24) 4 lines

I've spent 20+ years working in places full of people I feel "different" from. It's nice to have a place where I feel at home. Rather a frightening thought, considering some of the characters who hang out here, but there it is. :-)

Topic 466: Totally nonscientific poll
6: katharine mackaye (kvkm) Mon, Feb 24, '92 (23:19) 2 lines

The laughing out loud. Right now my mind is flashing back to an interviewer in "Doonesbury."

Topic 466: Totally nonscientific poll
7: Design Propeller-Head (pk) Tue, Feb 25, '92 (00:16) 3 lines

The WELL is "The Diary That Talks Back" for many of us. (This quote is stolen already, so feel free.)

Topic 466: Totally nonscientific poll
8: Fan mail from a blender? (gail) Tue, Feb 25, '92 (00:51) 13 lines

I like a way to do group improvisation.

Whether crafted, edited, typo-ed spontaneously or second guessed, there's no way to know how what will happen next.

And I like to talk about issues and ideas with people who have concrete experiences or thought-out philosophies that are new for me, to swap brains with an assortment of lively verbal people. The way we talk about our lives is very moving to me.

All of us are much smarter than any of us. (Of course, it can be argued that all of us are stupider than any of us, too, but that's seldom my experience.)

Topic 466: Totally nonscientific poll
10: Constantly surprised by people . . . (wndrwmn) Tue, Feb 25, '92 (08:36) 4 lines

I also have come to the WELL to meet people that I ordinarily wouldn't have. It is purely a social occasion for me, unlike many others whom I know use the WELL for business/research, etc. . . . And it works for me. Quote me if you want . . .

Topic 466: Totally nonscientific poll
11: well's cargo (dlee) Tue, Feb 25, '92 (23:37) 3 lines

Along the lines of Gail's comment, nana told me that (for her) logging on was "plugging into my brain." This comment has made more and more sense to me as time passes.

Topic 466: Totally nonscientific poll
12: The Man With The Million Dollar Dander (phanson) Wed, Feb 26, '92 (01:57) 6 lines

Add me to the list of people who come here to meet folks they otherwise would never have met. That wasn't my intention when I joined The WELL, and I had very few regular correspondents here until relatively recently. Since last summer, The WELL has been my chief way of meeting people, and I'm happy to say it has led to several friendships I cherish and want to preserve.

Topic 466: Totally nonscientific poll
18: Hopelessly addicted to romance (susanf) Thu, Feb 27, '92 (21:53) 5 lines

Here's what I like best about the WELL: The opportunity to know, and be known by, such a diverse group of people, on levels that would not be possible any other way. Having just begun to work for myself, that sense of an "extended virtual family" is invaluable, I find. (If you have use for such a convoluted sentence, feel free to quote!

;-)

Topic 466: Totally nonscientific poll

\# 20: Junk Food for Thought (campbell) Fri, Feb 28, '92 (18:49) 46 lines

The Well gives me a way to meet and carry on day-to-day social relationships with dozens of interesting, articulate, talented and intelligent people who I would never have met, otherwise. Having such contact available, day-in, day-out is wonderful, fun, and sanity-preserving. I would not otherwise have so much human interaction on a daily basis (I work at home and know few people living locally.)

I can walk into this ongoing myriad of conversations at any time, day or night, and never miss a thing that went on while I wasn't around. I can chime in without fear of interrupting or of being interrupted. If what I say has value or is of interest, it will be heard. And I can listen to dozens of discussions and "rewind" if I need to ponder something someone has said. I can take my time and hear what people are saying without worrying about how I will react or what I will say in response. I need not even respond, if I have nothing to say.

The Well also provides a fantastic resource for information about anything you'd care to name—a living, breathing reference library.

As you can tell, the WELL has a very real sense of "place." The WELL is all words, but you can almost see the different "areas" as you move from conference to conference.

Some flaming goes on, and gets quite feisty and irascible at times. This is especially true when a host is seen as falling down on the job.

Other times, the genuine love and caring the conference members have for each other is palpable just from reading their words. It's an extraordinary experience to feel the connection here. The main complaint is that it's so addicting, you can easily rack up vast bills sitting around this electronic watering hole!

Part three
Villages of the electronic underground

We visit some one-man shows, some mom-and-pop shops, and some places just about to make the big time.

Chapter 13 *Bulletin board systems: Tales of 1,001 bytes.* An overview of how an online system gets started.

Chapter 14 *Canada's Remote Systems: A center of activity.* The little system that grew in Canada, with something for everyone.

Chapter 15 *Channel 1 carries on.* Mom and Pop keep filing away, capitalizing on networks and users' expertise.

Chapter 16 *Exec-PC: Hometown boy makes good.* They don't do nets, but man, those files!

Chapter 17 *Here, Fido! FidoNet.* A grassroots, freewheeling connection of independent bulletin board systems. Anarchists welcome!

Chapter 18 *The oasis of civility: ILINK.* A message-based community where courtesy is not just expected—it's mandated.

Chapter 19 *New Parents Network: Bulletin boards for baby.* Because babies don't come with manuals, this online community is there with information for you.

Chapter 20 *RIME rings the world.* A psychologist wanted to talk things over with a few friends. A decidedly non-techie, highly personal mail echo resulted.

13 Bulletin Board Systems

Tales of the 1001 bytes

The cities and towns of the electronic underground are fun places, and they tend to be stable and reliable. Now let's go for a smaller feeling, with a bit more adventure. In the villages are the hidden treasures of the electronic underground: Bulletin Board Systems, known by their affectionate nickname BBS. Here, things pop along pretty quickly. Some of the BBSs, like Brigadoon, are only around sometimes; some BBSs, though, have become serious business concerns.

As the cartoon in FIG. 13-1 suggests, many people enjoy many different BBS, displaying different personality characteristics on each system. That's part of the fun for a few people: hiding behind the modem, expressing things they'd never say in person.

13-1 *Messages on bulletin board systems can reveal—or conceal—personalities. Reprinted with special permission of King Features Syndicate.*

What is a BBS?

Prosaically, it is an entity comprised of one or more computers, modems, and various styles of disk drives programmed to accept and disseminate information—not unlike the setups we've seen before but usually much smaller.

Poetically, it's a meeting place, like a tavern or a small pub, with a personality as distinct as the sysop who runs it. You might call it a byte club.

One description of a BBS follows:

> "Press a few keys and the unbelievable power of the machine is unleashed. A glowing window opens onto a new vista. A parallel universe, until now invisible, is revealed, right there on a desktop. Mopping his brow nervously, adjusting the pith helmet on his head, the explorer braces himself to step through the gateway his tinkering has opened.
>
> "Whoops! Got a little carried away there."
> —Dennis Fowler, *Computer Shopper*, August 1992, v12 n8 p705(3).

Yeah, it is a lot like that. Note that you can almost see the fanatic gleam in the author's eyes: *that's* BBS fever, and it's contagious.

They come in many flavors

A bulletin board system is usually self-contained, in one place, run by one person. Thousands fit this description. Some of them connect to more than one "network." A bulletin board network is a system whereby BBS call up other BBS to exchange messages and files, usually at a certain time every night or in the wee hours of the morning, in a round-robin affair that can reach around the globe. It gives you more people to talk to, more subjects to read about, and—on certain BBS networks—more files to get.

But despite the existence of BBS networks, a BBS is different from one of the Big Three in three ways. One, it often concentrates on aspects of one particular topic, such as Windows, or publishing, or genealogy, although this is not a hard and fast rule. Two, it is usually started by one person, although reinforcements are frequently called in quickly, and generally from the original sysop's own family. And finally, at least in the beginning, it is a volunteer, just-for-the-fun-of-it, nonprofit-with-a-vengeance operation. Later on it might make money, but rarely at the outset.

To find a bulletin board near you, pick up *Computer Shopper* at your local grocery store and look under the Bulletin Boards listings. These are updated for each issue; because BBS come and go so quickly, or change numbers as they get busier, or change their emphasis, CS only lists boards that have recently sent in a card with the latest information, including how to reach the sysop by voice.

Another good source is Jack Rickard's *Boardwatch* magazine, which traces not only the worthy BBS but the trends and issues currently important to the sysops and their users. *Boardwatch* is usually available at newstands, as well as in computer stores where modems are sold.

Finally, look for bulletin boards first in your own town. If modems are sold in your town, it's almost certain someone has started a user's group of one sort or another. Ask at your nearest store about meetings.

Most BBS run a particular software program. It might be called RBBS, or Wildcat, or PCBoard, or some other name. The differences are in format, not function. The average BBS will have menus to let you deal with these things:

- Messages. Sometimes this is called Mail. If you are interested in lots of messages, there might be a "mail door." When you enter any door, the BBS software stops running and the door software takes over to let you do what you need to. Often these doors will let you define the messages you are interested in, letting you ignore all the rest. Other doors allow you to automate your session; for example, you might be able to tell the door to always first get your replies to previous messages, then download your new messages, then log you off.
- Files. Most BBS exist because the sysop has programs or text files to share and likes to collect them as well. Files will be listed in some way. Uploading and downloading will be in one of the protocols: xmodem, ymodem, zmodem, kermit, etc. Most files will also be compressed in some way: ZIP, or ARC or some other version. Generally, the sysop will pick one compression format for DOS, one for MACs, and allow you to download the program that will restore the file to original form.
- Games. Again, usually a door must be used to play a game. Some are solitaire, while others are multi-player. As in the case of any door, when the door software stops, the BBS software starts again.
- Bulletins. These are short text files of what the sysop thinks you need to know. Some can be downloaded to be read later; some must be read while you are connected.
- News. These are short items of interest about the board itself.
- Environment. This goes by many names but basically allows you to set the BBS to give you color or graphics or neither, choose the protocol and doors you like best, decide whether your commands need an Enter key to execute, and so on.

A horse of a different color

A bulletin board is a more exclusive, sometimes more intimate, version of the online services we looked at in the first part of the book. Many started out as a place for computer nerds, or for hardware and software junkies of various flavors of commercial products. Today, they are more eclectic by far. Some of them are populated by people who think no more of their computers than they do of their sewing machines or their lawn mowers.

An example is SeniorNet, a San Francisco board with over 4000 users and connections at senior centers as well as private homes. It's a place for those who might feel their children and grandchildren have left them behind in the technology; or just want to download information from local social services, doctors, and other agencies serving the elderly population.

Another example would be FreeNets, which started in Cleveland. This is the idea of National Public Radio or PBS adapted to the online experience. As of February 92, Communications Week reported 10 were in operation across the US.

For additional information on NPTN and Freenet activities or programs, you can write to

Dr. Tom Grundner, President NPTN
Box 1987
Cleveland, OH 44106
(216) 368-2733 [voice]
(216) 368-5436 [fax]

By e-mail, you can write him at Internet: *aa001@cleveland.freeneg.edu* or CompuServe: *72135,1536.*

Supported by volunteers, corporations, and sometimes quasi-governmental agencies, FreeNets are for everything from support groups to hobby groups. AIDS information and guinea pig raising, community events and private friendships abound on these.

Some BBS are restricted, though. In Alabama, a statewide network gives the law enforcement professionals their own conference. Every level from township to state can log on, upload information about a crime, and download similar information, thus coordinating their investigations. However, the moderator makes sure that only sworn law enforcement officers and officers of the court receive the messages, which could be explicit descriptions of the latest homemade bomb or critical clues in a murder. This conference never uploads to a backbone (i.e., national hubs) as an added security measure. This is a big point: If your conference of choice is on the backbone, it is a public, nonsecure facility; if it is not, then it is private and restricted.

If your tastes are more cosmopolitan, or at least international, consider ALINE, a service to connect you to France's online services. The first practical application of videotext in homes, it's something to see. ALINE is expensive, though.

Other boards are more businesslike because that's what they're for. Many computer product dealers run a BBS for their customers and employees. On the customer side, it's used to support the product, allow users to give feedback, and get tips for the best way to use the product. On the employee side, it can be used to communicate internal memos, hold discussions without a meeting, and perform other management functions.

A good vendor-run BBS is the DAK customer board. If you buy hardware or software from the DAK catalog, the documentation from DAK will have this BBS number on the inside back cover. Besides having technical questions answered and getting advance notice of DAK's new products and prices, there are public domain programs and helpful tips to download. And of course, if you have something you think will help other DAK customers, you're free to upload that. The only cost is that of the phone call.

Settling in

Visit a board a few times before you decide to join. Some are raunchy as a biker's bar. Some are so narrowly focused you won't be interested (there's one just for dog breeders. Other topics, even horse or cat breeding, are verboten). Some are places for preaching to the choir; if you don't agree with the sermon of choice, they don't want you.

But other places are open and friendly. Topics abound and wander from subject to subject. Some are very local in focus, with a connection to one or more echo mail networks to bring in messages from other parts of the state or region.

Some of the bulletin board systems and networks you will hear about but not be able to use, such as the Alabama law enforcement board mentioned earlier. But it's nice to know that they exist.

Be prepared

There are some dangers out there, as we've mentioned before.

One person, who shall remain nameless because he really did know better than to do this, used exactly the same password on every system he signed onto. From CompuServe to Fred's Pretty Good BBS and everything in between, he used precisely the same series of characters to identify himself as the proper user of that account at that online place.

Anon, in the course of being amiable, he left his ID numbers for some of these other systems he subscribed to in messages on BBS, so folks he met online could meet him in another place, so to speak. It was sort of like saying "Meet me at the corner pub, and ask for Charlie."

Now, the electronic traveller must understand that *some* BBS are run by those with morals and discretion not yet fully developed. And a system's operator (known as the sysop) is all-powerful on his own BBS; he can look up any information deposited on his board, even passwords.

Someone less than ethical had decided to try that online ID number in a message with the password from the BBS "secret' files, just to see if it worked. It did. Every place where Charlie had an account. Pretty soon old Charlie Nameless found himself paying for other people's joyrides on some of the more expensive online services.

Learn from his costly mistake: your password should be unique on every system. It should never be something easy to guess such as your maiden name or your birthday. It should not even make much sense to anyone but you. And to make it truly secure, which is the whole point of a password anyway, combine numbers, letters and punctuation marks. !m55d19y3# cannot be guessed by someone trying every word in a 40,000 word dictionary to break into your account.

Another danger is viruses. The smaller, less commercial, and cozier the BBS, the greater the likelihood of finding a virus there. This danger stems from the sneakiness of virus writers, the amateur (that is to say, innocent, maybe even naive) status of the sysop of smaller boards, and the smaller chance of being detected in an out-of-the-way place. In my humble opinion, a virus writer is on the same plane as a rapist, with similar modus operandi and motivation.

But even the big guys get a virus now and then. To prevent that from being fatal, they get inoculated. Various commercial, shareware, and freeware virus protection programs are on the boards for downloading and at your favorite computer store. Don't leave home (via your modem) without them.

Now, just how will you get there?

Conveyances

In looking at PSI, Portal, the WELL, and other services, we noted that we dial a certain number, usually local, and get connected to someplace nonlocal, even foreign. This is not done with mirrors. It is done with packet-switching networks, which are also known as public data networks or PDNs.

The point of these systems is cost. These PDNs allow you to connect via modem (not voice) for as low as a dollar an hour. This is better, no?

Some major players follow . . .

CPN

CompuServe's Packet Network is how you dial up CIS locally. But it's not the only place you can go on CPN, and you do not have to be a CIS member to dial other boards. For information on where you can dial, call (800) 848-8199 [voice] and ask.

BT Tymnet

Originally an American rival to the GTE telnet, Tymnet was purchased by British Tymnet some years ago. For information and local access numbers, call (800) 937-2862 [voice] or (215) 666-1770 [voice].

To look up access numbers by modem, dial a local access number, hit the Enter key and a, and then enter information at the "Please log in :" prompt.

PC Pursuit (SprintNet)

PC Pursuit may be used to call a modem in any of 44 major metro areas in the US from local access numbers around the country. For information and registration, call (800) 736-1130 [voice] or 1-800-877-2006 [data]. More information is also available on the PC Pursuit support BBS (see later).

To look up access numbers by modem, dial 1-800-546-1000, hit the Enter key three times at 1200 baud or '@' with two hits on the Enter key at 2400 baud. Enter MAIL at the "@" prompt, then PHONES at the "USER NAME:" prompt, and PHONES at the "PASSWORD:" prompt.

The PC Pursuit support BBS provides a deluge of information about PC Pursuit, including rates, terms and conditions, local numbers, etc. To access the PC Pursuit support BBS, first set your modem parameters to 8 bits, No parity, 1 stop bit. Then dial a local access number and hit D1 and the Enter key at 1200 baud or '@D' and hit the Enter key at 2400 baud. Enter C PURSUIT at the "@" prompt. The opening screen will tell you how to log on as a new user.

13-2
The opening screen when checking out PC Pursuit.

```
US Sprint's THE NET-EXCHANGE, home of PC Pursuit!
   Reston, Virginia

The following limits are in effect:
   Max Kbytes: 382 +/- bytes (daily)    Usage time: 60 minutes +/- dt
   Login time: 5 minuTe$              Response time: 5 minutes

**********************************************************
*                      WARNING!                         *
*  You are being billed for this call if you used       *
*  "C PURSUIT,id,pw" to get here.  Please, only         *
*  use "C PURSUIT" to access this system!               *
**********************************************************

New users should use the name: Sprint Guest
            with a password of: outdial
REMEMBER:   -- passwords are case sensitive!
            -- For a New PC Pursuit user, it is required to logon as
               a regular Sprint Guest, ane0then fill out the "new_user"
               questionnaire to get registered with this BBS.
On at Mon Mar  8 14:12:37 1993


Enter your first name ( or first and last )    ==>
```

PC Pursuit costs $30 per month. This gives you 30 hours of "free" calls per month between the hours of 6 p.m. and 7 a.m., your local time. There are special rates for disabled persons, too. They offer their service over the Telenet international network. For more info, call their voice number: (800) 736-1130 or (703) 689-6400.

EXEC-LINK from Computer Productions, Inc.

This is a public data network supporting 1200-, 2400-, 9600-bps connections. It provides local call access in many cities. It is one new low-cost way to reach Exec-PC from 800 cities worldwide. Running on the CompuServe network wired directly to the Exec-PC hardware on a leased line, it was designed exclusively for callers to Exec-PC. EXEC-LINK offers 300–2400 baud connections in over 800 cities, and 9600 V.32 support in over 150 cities.

EXEC-LINK has varied payment options. The best part is there are no calling time restrictions. Call in the middle of the day during the week, call at night. The price is the same: $15 for 15 hours per month, anytime day or night or $30 for 30 hours per month, anytime day or night. Hours over the monthly limit are $4.80 per hour, day or night. For more info, call their voice numbers: (800) 947-0936 or (818) 358-0936.

These are just some of the options available; your local phone company might also have reduced-rate plans. So let's see a small sampling of what's out there.

Others

14 Canada Remote Systems
A center of activity

Snail Mail	Canada Remote Systems
	Unit D, 1331 Crestlawn Dr.
	Mississauga, Ontario L4W 2P9 CAN
Modem	BBS Demonstration Lines 300-16.8K, including HST, V.32/V.32bis:
	(416) 629-7000
	(416) 629-7044
Voice phones	(416) 620-1439, Toronto
	(800) 465-6443, Canada WATS line
	(800) 465-7562, USA WATS line
Tech. support	(416) 620-1571, open 1–7 p.m. every weekday.
	(416) 629-0771 [fax]
Hours	24 hours, 7 days a week. Busiest at night.
Basic rate	$13 per month for messages, etc. Can add on features such as "Adult" for extra charges.

Figure 14-1 shows the screen that will greet you when you enter Canada Remote Systems.

Canada Remote Systems is not your mom-and-pop byte shop. With 143 lines operating on an MS-DOS 80486 with 19,000Mb running PCBoard 14.5/X199 with US Robotics at up to 19,200 bps, we are talking the big time here. It was started in May of 1991; now you can be a member with payment of a $130 annual fee. Billing itself as North America's largest PCBoard installation, it includes 10 international mail networks, 250,000+ files, and pays close attention to not just IBMs and MACS but CP/M, Amiga and other orphans. Access for U.S. users is through Detroit.

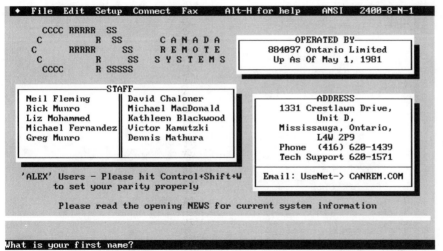

14-1
The Canada Remote Systems Welcoming Screen.

CRS runs three BBS: the PC-Board system, which this chapter will cover extensively. Also available are a chat board, called CITYLINK, and a UNIX-based system for USENET UUCP e-mail and newsgroup.

As a new member, one of the first files you see is this:

CANADA REMOTE SYSTEMS: MEMBERSHIP PRICING

Monthly Plan	Annual	Pre-authorized Payments (PAP)*
Personal Membership: Includes 2 hrs/2 Mb a day, all files (except adult areas), all conferences (except adult & info services), CRSEasyLink, international echo-mail, & much more . . .	$129.95	$12.95
Business Memberships: Include 6 hrs & 6 Mb a day, corporate identification, all extra options, & all of the benefits of a Personal Membership.		
* Single Access Account	$395.00	$39.95
* Three Separate Access Accounts	$495.00	$49.95
Extra Options—Please see Item #18 for a full description of each extra option. These add-ons are an extra cost in addition to the basic personal membership.		
* Information Services - stock market results, news feeds & CD-ROMs.	$39.95	$3.95
* Extra Time & Bytes - increases daily limit to 4 hrs/day & 4Mb/day.	$49.95	$4.95
* Adult Services - largest collection of online adult material in Canada.	$59.95	$5.95

* CITYLINK membership	$39.95	$3.95
- 200 hours of unlimited online time & downloading.		
* Commercial Advertising	$99.95	$9.95
- Advertise your business/commercial endeavors online.		

** DISCOUNTS **

For Multiple Add-ons:	Annual	Monthly PAP
One Add-on:	No discount	No discount
Two Add-ons:	$10.00/discount	$1.00/discount
Three Add-ons:	$20.00/discount	$2.00/discount
Four Add-ons:	$30.00/discount	$3.00/discount
All Add-ons:	$40.00/discount	$4.00/discount

** Maximum possible discount is $40.00 annually or $4.00 monthly when all add-ons are taken.

What the file doesn't mention is that you can sign up for a 90-day trial membership for about $60.

I signed on for the first time in the middle of the day. Turned out that was a lucky choice; David Chaloner of Marketing told me later, "If you had signed on at night, you might have found all 140 lines busy." Yes, this is a BBS big enough for a marketing department, 1-800 phone lines, and their own homegrown front-end software. If it weren't for the physical resemblance to the Sound of Music's installation of PCBoard, it might have been CI$ in the early days.

The connect screen is the same whether you are new or registered, as shown in FIG. 14-2.

```
AT&FE1V1X4&C1&D2S0=0S7=60
OK

CONNECT 2400/NONE
CONNECT 2400 / 12-10-92 (11:41:31)

CRS Premium Bulletin Board - USR 16.8K Dual Standard
PCBoard (R) v14.5a/350 - Node 94 - TFE721C3322

Operational Languages Available:

1 - English Operations (Default)
2 - Operation Francaise
3 - Standard PCB Prompts
4 - Canadian - Eh?

6 - CRSEasyLink Version 1.25 - (Not Available Yet!)

Enter Language # to use (Enter)=no change?
```

14-2

The Canada Remote connect screen. The Missing option "5" is for front-end users. You can't choose it if you aren't using it.

When you register as a new user, a special screen comes up (see FIG. 14-3).

The new user information is extensive, and takes most of the 30 minutes allotted to the electronic tourist to read it. I finally just downloaded it all, deciding to read it when the long distance clock wasn't ticking and use the information later.

```
                    CANADA REMOTE SYSTEMS
                    NEW USER INFORMATION

  Thank you for your interest in Canada Remote Systems.  On this demonstration,
  you'll have 30 minutes to look around and see what is available to you.

  30 Minutes is hardly long enough to see everything, but we'll give you the
  flavour of our systems.

  You've been taken automatically into our NEWUSER section.  Please review our
  catalog of info, take a tour of the system, and then (if you like what you
  see), join us.

  * Once you have entered the bulletin board, you have some options *

  To View this information again, type  F V NEWUSER
  To Download this information,    type  D NEWUSER
  To Join Canada Remote Systems,   type  S <cr> 1    or CALL (416) 620-1439

            Thanks for having a look at Canada Remote
Press (Enter) to continue
```

14-3
The New User Screen. The new user bulletins are best read off-line if you're calling long distance.

Subsequently, when I realized just how busy and popular this place is, I realized that's also the courteous thing to do. Some nights it's awfully hard to log on.

In an interview with Neil Fleming, the CEO of CRS, I learned some of the history of the board:

Neil Fleming, owner

"Canada Remote Systems, Ltd., started out as a one-line BBS in 1981 on a single computer—running CP/M," he said. "In August of 1990, the CRS Ltd. had 72 lines, 8 gigabytes of storage, and 5000 members.

"The old owners of the mom-and-pop-type organization kinda got hyperextended a little bit, trying to run about 4 businesses at once. When the recession started hitting, it kinda went boom," Fleming said. "At the end of August 1990, I put together a group of people to acquire the assets of CRS Ltd. and started up a new firm. Today we have annual sales of a good 1.6 to 1.8 million dollars."

So today the setup has 215 lines, 35 gigabytes of disk space, and members upload 40 megabytes of files per night. The e-mail is mind-boggling: 5000 message conferences on 10 e-mail nets bring in about 350,000 messages per week. The current physical setup is 7 files servers running Novell, on 215 nodes, CDROMS as well as the aforementioned gigabytes, and USR dual speed modems.

The staff includes, but is not limited to, Neil—owner, chief cook and bottle washer; systems operator Rick Monroe, chief sysop, who has been working on computers for decades, and was sysop of his own BBS in the past; Mike McDonald, who does software research and development; and Victor Komisky and Greg Monroe, who both work under Rick. Marketing and Sales are done by David Chaloner.

Who's there

"We sell membership services. Basic memberships, and few add-ons with information services. Corporate memberships, BBS within BBS, and we also sell modems," Fleming said. "So we have narrowed the focus of CRS.

"We have several hundred thousand files online, messages and technical help and support, hotlines, drop in online sessions with experts. That's what we have now. Long-term vision wise, I envision a global network of low-cost entry points into this network. The people who will do well will be the low-cost providers who emphasize customer service, technical support, and ease of use, and that's us."

A new front-end program called CRSEASY is supposed to help with that. We'll visit that later.

Asked what is CRS' best feature, Fleming said, "That's tough to say. Initially, 80% of our members join to get files and programs. After a few months, they get tired of collecting all these shareware programs and they start participating in the messaging. So it's messaging and information services that keep them here in the long run, but files that attract them in the meantime. We do all three of them very well. We have as many or more files as anyone else. We have as many or more message forums as anyone else. And we do a darn good job of technical support.

A few years ago, CRS bought out another BBS in Canada called CityLink. I asked how that was working out.

"It's working out only fair. I'd say not well. It's a case of the tail wagging the dog and not having the time to really properly pay it attention. It's a chat system based on TBBS and it's very nice. But I think we're finding that we don't have the time to pay it the attention it deserves. We're debating about what to do about that at this point. If you have a 10,000 user BBS on one side and 300–400 user BBS on the other, which gets the attention?"

Fleming said the company is continually working to improve: striving to be easier to use, offering strong technical support, continuing to add more information services. "We are, for example, the only BBS that has Reuters and UPI online. We're going to have more CDROMS and more services. We are in the process of reorganizing and reclassifying our main file area so we do a better job on that," he said. "We're very connected. You can reach 30 million people through the nets we have."

The buy and sell area is the most active local conference, he said. "It's pretty tough to say [what's the busiest] in the files area. It's pretty widely spread. The busiest files area would be the new files, nightly downloads. People like to peruse the categories they like."

Asked about the type of people there, he said "We have smatterings of individuals from all over the world, Germany, Australia."

While CRS is on several PDNs, such as Datapac, etc., they all tack on a fairly steep cross-border surcharge. Dialing CRS from out of Canada is hefty no matter how you go.

Signing on   The first time you sign on, unless you mailed in a check to the above address and received the new front-end software, you will get a typical BBS-type logon:

How to Speed up Your Logon

If you'd like this type of display	Type This at the Prompt Below
MONO DISPLAY, and NO WELCOME SCREEN:	N Q or N;Q
COLOR DISPLAY, and NO WELCOME SCREEN:	Y Q or Y;Q
FULL WELCOME DISPLAY in MONO mode:	a carriage return [ENTER]
FULL WELCOME DISPLAY in COLOR mode:	Y and a carriage return

Then—WHEN PROMPTED FOR YOUR NAME—type both your first AND last names together—to speed up your logon! If you've already registered and have a password, type it in, too. If this is your FIRST call, DO NOT ENTER A PASSWORD UNTIL YOU'RE ASKED FOR ONE!

NEW USER Example: Kevin Costner
REGISTERED USER Example: Kevin Costner wolves

FOR EVEN FASTER SIGNONS—CHOOSE LANGUAGE 3 when prompted for a language!

Do you want graphics (Enter)=no? y

I truly did enjoy the demo, and downloaded the bulletins for future reference.

We're still in the manual mode here: we'll look at CRSEASY in a minute.

The Main Menu, in FIG. 14-4, shows most of what you can do online.

Movin' around

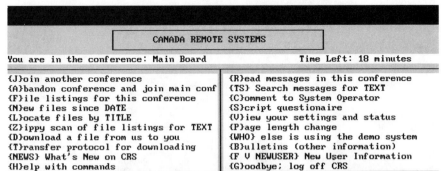

```
                    ┌──────────────────────────────────┐
                    │      CANADA REMOTE SYSTEMS        │
                    └──────────────────────────────────┘
You are in the conference: Main Board              Time Left: 18 minutes

{J}oin another conference          {R}ead messages in this conference
{A}bandon conference and join main conf  {TS} Search messages for TEXT
{F}ile listings for this conference  {C}omment to System Operator
{N}ew files since DATE             {S}cript questionaire
{L}ocate files by TITLE            {V}iew your settings and status
{Z}ippy scan of file listings for TEXT  {P}age length change
{D}ownload a file from us to you   {WHO} else is using the demo system
{T}ransfer protocol for downloading  {B}ulletins (other information)
{NEWS} What's New on CRS           {F V NEWUSER} New User Information
{H}elp with commands               {G}oodbye; log off CRS

Files are available for non-members only from file areas 1 and 2.  Use the
{F 1} or {F 2} command to see files available for downloading by non-members!

JOIN CANADA REMOTE by completing Script #1 at any time during your demo session
                    today on Canada Remote
(Node 94/18 min left), (H)elp,(CR)more,(N)o More?
```

14-4
The Main Menu from the Main Board or conference.

Message bases

Getting your messages isn't quite so easy on CRS as on some smaller systems. There's just so much to choose from, it's practically an embarrassment of riches.

The main mail door is QM4, which I've used elsewhere but seemed to work differently here. I wanted to flag any conference to do with "WRITERS." With all those different e-mail nets, that should have been easy. It was frustrating, and took me over an hour (long distance from the U.S.). QMAIL lets you select by number or by name. Now, with the network offering over 5000 conferences, selecting by number would be impossible for the new—and ignorant—user. (Whatever you do, *DON'T* select "ALL"! For the next thirty minutes, the program will refuse to be interrupted as it marks all 5000 conferences, 45 at a time.)

So I typed WRITERS and got one conference flagged. On other systems on which I have used QMAIL, typing WRITERS again would simply take me to the next instance of the string, whether it stood alone or as part of I-WRITERS, R-WRITERS, S-WRITERS, or whatever. Not on CRS. It would instead DESELECT the writer's conference I had just selected. Frustrating.

I never had a successful mail download from CRS, but don't let that worry you: it turns out at the time I was trying all this, CRS discovered a bug in DOS 3.3 (that's the operating systems CRS was using at that moment) that was causing the problems I had. The bug, according to a news bulletin in January, 1992, was fixed.

So peruse the new member's manual carefully, and you will find what you need. Precisely note the numbers of the conferences that sound interesting while you are offline. Once signed on, enter those numbers from the QMAIL Select conferences menu by typing SELECT ##.

For instance, say you need technical support. CRS' message conferences for support include

```
Qmail Support........ 24
Usenet Gateway.......8
Technical/Help.........9
```

Other conferences include, but are by no means limited to:

GENERAL CONFERENCES

A.I. Discussion	47	CAD	21	EDPAA/ISSA	72
BBS Ads	75	Comics/Cards	341	Genealogy	336
BWI - U.S.	3397	DOS 5.0	80	ITIS	112
Business/Finance	30	Diplomacy	99	International	40
Buy & Sell Ads	34	Disabled	25	KLM Computers	3451
Medical Topics	55	Paradox	48	System EX-10 Supt	53
Microsoft Dev	111	Parents	77	TPUG	74
Midi	100	Pascal	58	Tandy	79
Missing	89	Pers. Com Club-Tor	81	Tax/Accounting	69
NANET—Comments/Sug	70	Psychic	83	Technical Support	60
NANET—Moderators	90	Qmail Support	24	Technical/Help	9
Networks	16	Robocomm	351	Telix Support	59
The Unknown	334	Vendor Support	4	Word Processing	94
Toronto Computes	31	Ventura	92	WordPerfect	68
Toronto Star	122	Videos/Films	335	Work at Home	76
Travel	57	Virus Discussion	51	Writers	61
USRobotics HST	26	Vision 2000	3392	Zoo (The)	50

You will also find that many conferences are supported directly by shareware authors and/or manufacturers. In these supported conferences, you're dealing with the experts affiliated with that particular product. This resource can be invaluable when a difficulty you have is unraveled by someone in one of CRS' conferences.

Files Files are all over the place in CRS. There are up-to-the minute news files from news services to stock quotes. And, for the student, CDROMS: CIA Factbook, On-Line Hotline News, The Complete Works of Shakespeare, Monarch Notes, Family Doctor, and more.

Then, for an extra fee and your driver's license number, there's the "adult" collection. Why people with arrested adolescent prurient interests insist on that label for their hobby, I'll never understand . . . But on to the interesting stuff.

With over 500,000 files, you should find something for your system. Conferences have files, especially the computer brand name conferences. From the Main Menu, you type J to join the conference you're interested in:

Amiga 5
Apple II 14
Atari 6
Commodore 64/128 13
IBM-type PCs 2
MacIntosh 1
NeXt 105
UNIX 18

Then choose among the commands: N for newest files, L for title, Z or TS for a certain text in the name or description, or F to simply list. The files list menu looks like FIG. 14-5.

```
════════ IBM FILE AREAS ════════              20/07/92

A.  GENERAL INFORMATION - All Computer Types

Information on CRS.................1   Catalogs and Lists.................2
Byte Listings.....................3   PC/MacTutor Magazine Listings.......4
Computer Language/AI Listings.......5   Unclassified......................6

B.  USER GROUP DISKS - User Group Software is more nicely cataloged than
    Topical Software, but may not be as complete or as current.

PCSIG is on CD-ROM,                   PCBlue (NYACC) is on CD-ROM,
Type OPEN 70 to download..........351   Type OPEN 71 to download.........352

C.  TOPICAL SOFTWARE - Software in the following areas is arranged by topic.
    You may find considerable duplication and older versions, so exercise
    some caution when looking in these areas.  New software always resides
    in areas 394 to 399.


       ARTIFICIAL INTELLIGENCE          BULLETIN BOARD SYSTEM SOFTWARE
LISP programs.....................17   BBS News.........................27
Updates/Text files................19   BBS Listings/Information..........26
(Node 151/87 min left), (H)elp,(CR)more,(N)o More?
```

14-5
For IBM files, the list is categorized. You can use other commands to search for specifics.

If you are viewing a list of files from one of the other commands, you get one screenful at a time. Figure 14-6 had the help response should you be overwhelmed.

Downloading software supports every protocol you ever heard of, batch and single file, so to speak.

CRS, it should be clear by now, would like to be in the same league with Prodigy, only with better customer service. To that end, they have developed CRSEASY, a self-installing front end that knows the commands and makes log on easy. But beyond that, it seems to get in the way.

CRSEASY

Pulling up CRSEASY, you get the screen in FIG. 14-7. As you configure the program, you can choose from all the two dozen or so possible phone numbers; after that, CRSEASY remembers for you.

14-6

*Paging through a list of files,
you can flag some for batch
download.*

```
                        Definitions And References (More Advanced
                        Than Ctags). Now Supports References, Auto-
                        Next, And Dos & Os/2. (1-9-91).
GEOUTIL.ZIP   19826  11-22-91   (CRS) 3 Utilities For Geoworks Ensemble A
                        Real Ruler For Geodraw, A Grid Pattern, And A
                        Bunch Of Arrows For Clip Art
IOVIEW.ZIP     6680  08-02-91   (CRS) This Excellent Util Allows You To
                        Monitor Io Ports Great For Debugging When
                        You'Re Trying To See If The Port You Think Is
                        Getting Hit Really Is!
KBHAND20.ZIP  39008  01-04-92   (CRS) The Layer Handler V2.0: Easy To Use
                        Standalone Util That Allows You To Edit The
                        Layer Names And Their Corresponding Linetypes
                        And Color Codes Via Dxf Files For Autocad,
                        Etc.; 12/10/91; K.B. Synectics.
(85 min left), (H)elp, (V)iew, (F)lag, More? ?
       (Enter) continues on with display
       (Y) yes, continue on with display
       (N) no, stop displaying this text
       (NS) continue reading in non-stop mode
       (V) View a file, then continue displaying files
       (F) Flag a file for later download, then continue displaying files

(85 min left), (H)elp, (V)iew, (F)lag, More?
```

14-7

*CRSEASY's first screen.
Punch the button and signon begins.*

```
Canada Remote Systems EasyLink - A PCBoard Navigator (VERSION 1.01)
(C) 1991,1992  884097 Ontario Ltd. o/a Canada Remote Systems.


        =[ Dialing Menu ]=

          CCCCC RRRRR   SS  Canada
          CC       RR   SS  Remote            ┌─────────┐
          CC       RR   SS  Systems           │ C A L L │
          CC    RRRRR   SS                     └─────────┘
          CC       RR      SS
          CC       RR      SS                 ┌─────────┐
          CCCCC    RR   SSSSS                 │ E X I T │
                                              └─────────┘

<F1=Help> <F2=About>                                        CRSEasyLink
```

If you don't get a busy number, the program signs you on, requiring only an Enter
key from you to send your password. If you get a busy signal, it simply keeps dialing
the numbers you installed until you tell it to quit.

Now, when you sign on, the BBS software tells you whether you have any
messages, and if so, in which conferences. *Keep a pencil and paper nearby.* That
message will scroll off, CRSEASY will enter a door to update itself whether it needs
it or not, and you'll not have a chance to go read the mail for another minute or two.
(That going off into the bushes at international rates makes me nervous.) So,
without a photographic memory, you're not likely to find your mail.

When CRSEASY gets done with all that, you have the screen shown in FIG. 14-8.

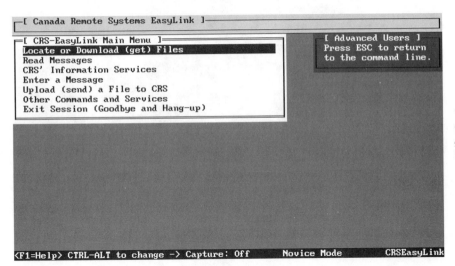

14-8
CRSEASY's main menu. If you know precisely what you want to do, this is a help.

So, say you choose "read messages" and "select conferences," but if after that, all you remember is that you had one message in genealogy and one in writers', you are up a creek. See FIG. 14-9.

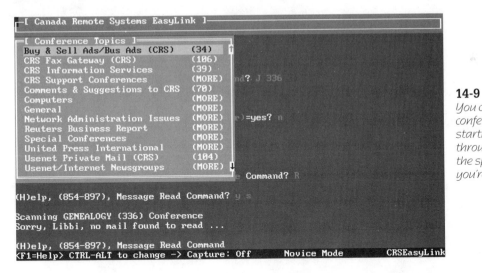

14-9
You can choose to read conferences one by one, starting with this menu. Step through several levels to find the specific one you want. If you're lucky.

First you have to figure out that "genealogy" is hidden under General in this menu, and Hobbies in the next. Then you have to remember WHICH genealogy conference has your message in it. Of the two I found that way, neither of those had a message to me, so there must be some genealogy conferences under some other description. If there's a way to retrieve that original sign-on "you have a message" information, I never found it.

You can, from the "read message" menu, choose "advanced options," which lets you set up your favorite conferences. Again, here, write down what you want first, because the screens are too numerous to page through. See FIG. 14-10.

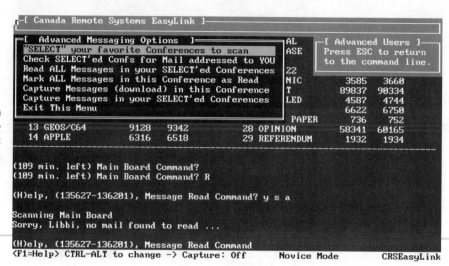

14-10
You can select your favorite message conferences from here.

Using CRSEASY to download files is only slightly easier than doing it from the command line. Where the program really makes life on CRS simpler is in the information services. To get stock quotes, news from UPI, or the CDROMs, it's just a few keystrokes.

The capture session function works well, except when you enter a door, such as QMAIL4. Then the capture suspends, and if you wanted to know what went wrong with the session, you won't have a record of it.

In short, if you have studied the CRS manual and know precisely what you want to do but don't know the BBS software PCBoard well enough to do it, CRSEASY will help.

The CRS shop

You might have noticed a mention of selling modems earlier. This is the only sideline Fleming is allowing at the moment. The company has special offers on membership/modem deals, as well as the most advanced products on the market to sell. Usually, your signoff message will have something about the latest prices and deals. Some have been real honeys: free upgrades of hardware and software, or a deep discount on a yearly subscription to CRS. It changes all the time, so keep your eyes open for the latest deal.

Conclusion

CRS is on its way to competing with the "pay by the minute" services, as they call them. It's worth checking out, especially if you are north of the US border.

Channel 1 carries on

E-mail	*channel1.com*
U.S. Mail	P.O. Box 338
	Cambridge, MA 02238
Hours	24 hours a day
Basic rate	$20 for three months or 150 file downloads (45 minutes a day, maximum) or $60 for one year or 600 file downloads (70 minutes per day maximum. Other flavors of membership available including Internet Access add-on for $25 for three months, $80 for one year. Corporate plan. Special deals for software authors and uploaders, but this is not a pirate board.
Notes	FILES are the main emphasis here. There's e-mail and Internet and games and stuff but the main claim to fame is FILES.
Phones	(617) 354-7077 [modem, 2400/1200 baud]
	(617) 354-5776 [modem, 14,400 v.32/v.32bis]
	(617) 354-3136 [modem, 16,800 HST]
	(617) 354-0479 [modem, Telebit]
	(617) 354-4443 [modem, CompuCom]
	(617) 864-0100 [voice]

Want to feel really connected? Try Channel 1.

One of the ways to connect to the Internet/USENET universe is to subscribe to a BBS that has a connection. The only way to tie into one of the major bulletin board nets is to subscribe to a BBS on that net.

Channel 1 of Boston must be a good option for all of that, because it certainly is one of the largest BBS in the world. It's connected to the USENET and the Internet. Sometime in 1993 they plan to be a commercial Internet TELNET and FTP site. BBS nets included are USENET, RIME, SmartNet, ILINK, and FidoNet (See FIG. 15-1).

In using the board, I found this both blessing and bane. The blessing: instead of trying to get onto the three local, forever busy boards which carry RIME, ILink, and FidoNet (SmartNet isn't anywhere in my state), I could dial Channel 1 and find

15-1

The networks available on Channel 1

messages for me from all three at once. One call, one download, and all my favorite conferences were right there . . . in one 350K zip format file.

The bane: it's a long distance call to Channel 1 (though it is available on PC Pursuit and that cuts the cost.) And I found it was harder to keep straight which network I was reading at the moment. It helps that some of the conference names have identifiers tagged on the end (S for SmartNet, I for ILink, R for RIME), but not all of them do. And at any rate, when you're on more than one net at a time, it's hard to remember what you've answered, what you posted, where, and to whom.

All in all, that's the only problem with Channel 1. There's just too much there to cover in one lifetime!

But that's easy to put up with. Because just about everybody you ever met online is on Channel 1 sooner or later. It's sort of the courthouse steps of cyberspace.

The staff is gracious and helpful; I once forgot my password when trying to log on. This is easy for me to do, as I have always made up a new password for every new place I log on. It's hard, until you can write a logon script, to keep them straight.

Well, when you have a name the system recognizes but you cannot logon with the proper password, PCBoard lets you leave a message for the sysop. I did, explaining my plight, and leaving my number to be called voice. Then I disconnected. Within 5 minutes, a sysop called to say, "Your password is . . . . . "

And they're willing to let you try them 30 minutes a day for 30 days, with no fee. There's even a file you can download listing the files especially for the freebie user.

Who are "they," you ask?

Mom & Pop

Running this watering hole of the phone wires are Brian Miller and his wife Tess Heder. Right after Brian got his first PC and 1200-baud modem, he discovered the electronic underground (and was one of BIX's first users), color BBS, and e-mail. Discovering the reality (which at that time was really rather limited) excited him to the possibilities. Noting the dearth of reliable, high-end, slick, and fancy boards in his area, he and Tess decided to start a two-line, professionally run system. The first goal was to grow as fast as possible, and sure enough, within three years, they were the third largest in the business.

They designed their system to be self-supporting, bait the hook with free access with pay options once the user bit, and to always have the fastest, most flexible hardware and software available at the moment. The point was to have fun and make money. Not a bad idea, really.

For you hardware freaks, here's the goodies on this system: U.S. Robotics HST 9600, 14400, Microcom 9600, V.32, V.32 bits; V.32 HST Dual Standard; CompuCom CSM; and Telebit T2500 V.32/PEP. 70 ports. Each caller gets his own 386 workstation.

Many of the connoisseurs and virtuosos of the electronic underground consider Channel 1 a good place to go for software. The sales brochure proudly quotes no less a pontificator than John Dvorak as saying "Channel 1 gets the most and the best daily new file uploads of any system in the U.S."

"We're trying to be the biggest, best general BBS system in the country," says Brian. "Diversity, depth and professional quality."

When you look at the diversity online, you might feel he's definitely within range. The board has programs for many different computer flavors, utilities and applications, and games. Something for almost everyone.

There are many numbers to Channel 1. The management recommends you enter TWO Channel 1 access numbers in your communications program. Choose from:

Signing on

2400 baud/1200 baud	(617) 354-8873
	(617) 354-7077
	(617) 354-6155
V.32bis 14.4	(617) 354-5776
	(617) 354-3230
	(617) 354-2317
HST 16.8/V.32bis	(617) 354-3137
Dual Stand	(617) 354-2505
	(617) 354-4128
Telebit	(617) 354-0470
	(617) 354-0784

Dialing one of the many numbers, you can log on as a new user and take a tour.

Figure 15-2 is the opening screen. Many people oooh and ahh over the pretty way the menus are displayed. A warning though: those with MACS will have a less resplendent view.

15-2
Channel 1's opening logo.

As one reviewer of BBS observed, those partial to perusing a polyglot of choices should be happy from the first set of selections on Channel 1, which is shown in FIG. 15-3.

```
Channel 1(R) Communications [ATI 2400 v.42]
PCBoard (R) v14.5a/100 - Node 12 - PFE78E76F779

Operational Languages Available:

1 - English [Default]
2 - Standard Prompts [Robocomm]
3 - Deutsch
4 - Español
5 - Français
6 - Norwegian
7 - Portuguese
8 - Brazilien
9 - Italian
10 - Finnish
11 - Dutch
12 - Serbian
13 - Slovenian
14 - Slovenian - req country.sys/codepage 852
15 - Esperanto
16 - Startrek

Enter Language # to use (Enter)=no change?
```

15-3

A plethora of languages to choose from is your first menu on Channel 1.

Flavor

I like the opening screen. It offers several "language" choices, some just for fun. Star Trek will give you prompts in trekkie language (Hit communicator badge to continue). Glitz gives you colorful, ANSI-studded prompts. Of course, the German, French, and so forth choices are for real. On my first time on, in a little less than half an hour, I logged 115K in my text buffer. The interface is very friendly, open and comely, and things go fast. You'll also see a list of useful instructions for getting around, getting files, etc.

Your first time on, I highly recommend you Join the Free conference and download CHAN1HLP.ZIP, get off, unzip it and read it. It's a big file [107K zipped!] but reading it OFFLINE will save you a lot on your phone bill. Also, be aware that, as a public service, anyone can log onto Channel 1 and download latest versions of the virus scanners. Other files in the "free" area (that is, it costs nothing against your allotted time online) are shareware communications programs, the PKZ110.EXE (pretty much the standard in compression programs), and various mail readers.

Who's on

"There's a lot of features all in one place here," Brian observes, "and the personality of the board is broad and diverse. Users range from 8-year-old girls to retired grandfathers, and you'll find messages where they're helping each other. No one single community comes here; it cuts across the boundaries. Housewives, auto shop owners, retirees, and computer programmers all come here."

The quickest way to learn any bulletin board is to read the bulletins (makes sense). Figures 15-4 and 15-5 show the bulletin menus.

The list of conferences is enormous. Besides those of only Channel 1 users, there are more than 2000 from Internet and USENET. To keep up with who's saying what on any of these, you read the index of the conferences and at a command prompt

```
                  =[ Bulletin Listings ]=

    1] Channel 1 System/Access Information   11] Usenet Access Information
    2] User Agreement                        12] BoardWatch Magazine
    3] Channel 1 Membership Information       13] Telecomputing Magazine
    4] McGraw-Hill Online Bookstore          14] Hot Files
    5] * Disks and Tapes by Mail *           15] Top Uploaders
    6] How to Use Channel 1                  16] Directory Totals Report
    7] How to Read Messages                  17] Your Account Information
    8] How to Download                       18] System Info News
    9] How to Use DOORS                      19] Channel 1 Modem and Node Info
   10] How to Use Conferences/Echoes         20] Channel 1 Commands Reference

   21] Channel 1 Store - Computer Products   28] Daily Stock Markets Summary
   22] Channel 1 - Info about Advertising    29] Financial News of the Day
   23] Game Master Journal - new!            30] Weekly Financial Markers
   24] Datanet Computer News                 31]
   25] EEEKbits -- fun!                      32]
   26] ASP Shareware                         33] Real-Time NE Weather
   27] Electronic Frontier Foundation News   34] Sunrise/Sunset Times

                  =[ Enter --> more ]=
Help, NS, N=Stop, (Enter)=More?
```

15-4
The first Channel 1 Bulletin menu . . .

```
                  =[ Bulletin Listings ]=

   35] Channel 1 System Configuration       53] Internet/Usenet Mail
   36] Node 1 graphic stats                 54] Overview of networks
   37] Channel 1 total system stats         55] Usenet newsgroup list
   38] Channel 1 daily message flow         56] Internetworking Guide
   39]                                      57] Rules for posting
   40] ILink Users Guide                    58] Usenet Community Primer
   41] RIME SITEID/SITENUMBER list          59] Getting network information
   42] RIME last transfer time              60] Active newsgroups
   43] RIME last transfer by conference     61] ALT news hierarchies
   44] RIME previous transfer               62] SOCial newsgroups
   45] RIME Exported msgs totals            63] Style
   46] Info for prospective RIME nodes      64] Frequently Asked Questions
   47] *NEW* Ch1 Conference Changes         65] CH1 Usenet activity report
   48] Numerical list of all C1 Cnfs        66] CH1 Internet Confs Sorted
   49] Non-Internet CH1 Cnfs Sorted         =! Internet Info !=
   50] ALL Ch1 Conferences Sorted           67] How to use Lookup
   51] PC-Pursuit tips                      68] Ansi music: Yellow Submarine
   52] Unix .tar file pointers              69] Voter Door Results

                  =[ Channel 1 ]=
(H)elp, (1-70), Bulletin List Command?
```

15-5
And the next . . .

type J and the number of the conference. For instance, to join the RIME genealogy conference ROOTS, type J 123. Then the program will show you the messages and let you post to that conference. Figure 15-6 is just one of a dozen screens of topics from which you may choose. You can also search by keyword to find a topic discussing your interest.

But if any board ever proved the value of offline readers, Channel 1 is it. Each offline reader has something going for it, and discussions on the "best" abound in every conference, regardless of purported topic. But basically, without a .QWK compatible reader, your phone will stay so busy for so long, your friends will wonder what's become of you!

You should also consider that using an offline reader is a politeness to the others who want to log onto the same board. When you download your messages and desired files and then get off to peruse them at leisure, then someone else can get on.

```
┌──────────────────────────────────────────────────────────────┐
│              C H A N N E L   1   C O N F E R E N C E S          │
├──────────────────────────────────────────────────────────────┤
│        >>  J oin conferences from the main prompt   <<         │
├──────────────────────────────────────────────────────────────┤
│  *40 Common (pvt msgs )   +53 Business      +66 DSZ            │
│  *41 Doors                *54 Stocks        *67 Handicap       │
│  +42 Beyond               *55 Con_Echo      +68 Qmodem         │
│  *43 Medical              +56 Francais      %69 Hayes          │
│  *44 Spanish              *57 XYWrite       +70 C-Lang         │
│  *45 OOPS                 %58 LegalNet      +71 Pascal         │
│  *46 RlyUsers             *59 Deadhead      +72 QBasic         │
│  *47 Telix                *60 Windows       +73 AI             │
│  *48 USR\HST              *61 Robocomm      *74 EZReader       │
│  +49 PKware               *62 Cuisine       +75 Astronomy      │
│  %50 Desqview             *63 UpLink        *76 Engineers      │
│  *51 Comp_Gen             +64 Qmail         +77 Writers        │
│  *52 Finance              +65 Database      +78 Netusers       │
├──────────────────────────────────────────────────────────────┤
│   = Private       * RIME        % Smartnet       + ILink      │
└──────────────────────────────────────────────────────────────┘

Help, NS, N=Stop, (Enter)=More?
```

15-6

You can page through more than a dozen of these menus, or search for a keyword from the main menu.

Offline readers that will allow you to download the new files list, the newest bulletins, and flag the conferences you want to add and delete also save you online time. Also look for a reader that will allow you to search for a certain string of text in the hundreds of messages you download a day. It saves you the time of reading the uninteresting ones.

End of sermon. Let's see what else is on Channel 1.

Looking around

To test out this board, I decide to play some games. The games menu is more than one screenful, but FIG. 15-7 gives you a good idea of the choices.

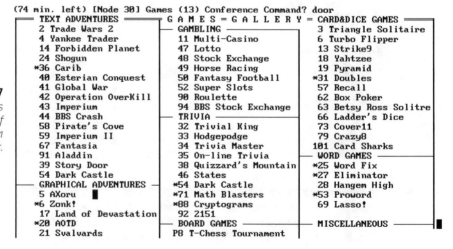

```
(74 min. left) [Node 30] Games (13) Conference Command? door
┌── TEXT ADVENTURES ──┬── G A M E S = G A L L E R Y = CARD&DICE GAMES ──┐
│  2 Trade Wars 2     │  ── GAMBLING ──         │  3 Triangle Solitaire │
│  4 Yankee Trader    │  11 Multi-Casino        │  6 Turbo Flipper      │
│ 14 Forbidden Planet │  47 Lotto               │ 13 Strike9            │
│ 24 Shogun           │  48 Stock Exchange      │ 18 Yahtzee            │
│*36 Carib            │  49 Horse Racing        │ 19 Pyramid            │
│ 40 Esterian Conquest│  50 Fantasy Football    │*31 Doubles            │
│ 41 Global War       │  52 Super Slots         │ 57 Recall             │
│ 42 Operation OverKill│ 90 Roulette            │ 62 Box Poker          │
│ 43 Imperium         │  94 BBS Stock Exchange  │ 63 Betsy Ross Solitre │
│ 44 BBS Crash        │  ── TRIVIA ──           │ 66 Ladder's Dice      │
│ 58 Pirate's Cove    │  32 Trivial King        │ 73 Cover11            │
│ 59 Imperium II      │  33 Hodgepodge          │ 79 Crazy8             │
│ 67 Fantasia         │  34 Trivia Master       │101 Card Sharks        │
│ 91 Aladdin          │  35 On-line Trivia      │ ── WORD GAMES ──      │
│ 39 Story Door       │  38 Quizzard's Mountain │*25 Word Fix           │
│ 54 Dark Castle      │  46 States              │*27 Eliminator         │
│ ── GRAPHICAL ADVENTURES ─│*54 Dark Castle     │ 28 Hangem High        │
│  5 AXoru            │ *71 Math Blasters       │*53 Proword            │
│ *6 Zonk!            │ *88 Cryptograms         │ 69 Lasso!             │
│ 17 Land of Devastation│ 92 2151               │ ── MISCELLANEOUS ──   │
│*20 AOTD             │  ── BOARD GAMES ──      │                       │
│ 21 Svalvards        │  P8 T-Chess Tournament  │                       │
└─────────────────────┴─────────────────────────┴───────────────────────┘
```

15-7

The games menu continues the Channel 1 tradition of more choices than you can shake a stick at.

The lemonade stand game was a simple one about making enough lemonade to suit the weather conditions and pricing it according to anticipated demand. I went bust in five minutes, but it was fun.

One of the nicest areas is the Doors, which are programs you run while logged on.

Not only are there a selection of mail readers but also some searchable databases. Figure 15-8 shows the Doors menu. Because Channel 1 runs PCBoard, you can type OPEN 7 from the main menu and go straight to door 7, the QMAIL program.

```
=======================================[ DOORS ]=========================================

     1]  ZDoor:          ZModem Transfer Door
     2]  ProDoor:        Extended Protocol/Archive Utility Door
     3]  Info:           CH1 tutorial/Bulletin reader/Microbytes
     4]  Deposit:        Deposit - Time Bank (30+ security req.)
     5]  RIMElist        RIME/PCRelay HUB/NODE search door
     6]  WhoDoor:        Find Out Who Uploaded That File
     7]  Qmail 4.0:      Qmail - upload & download your messages
     8]  MarkMail 2.0:   MarkMail - upload & download your messages
     9]  Voter Door:     Voter -- Vote on topics/create your own
    10]  BBSQBase:       Search for international, national, or local BBSs
    11]  Users' Bios:    Enter your biography and read others' of Channel 1!
    12]  Horoscope:      Your personalized daily fortune!
    13]  Good Book DB:   Get suggestions for books you may enjoy reading!
    14]  Cam-Mail        Cam-Mail -- upload and download your messages
    15]  Secdoor:        Security level update door for uploaders
    16]  Places:         Search database of New England Lodging
    20]  PowerList:      Choose any of Channel 1's directories to download
    21]  AbleData:       Products for the disabled [requires Doorway mode]

At The  XT:             Determine how long a file will take to download
Help, NS, N=Stop, (Enter)=More?
```

Notice you have the choice of three mail doors. These are three of the most popular, and you can try each one to see which makes you happy. My favorite is QMAIL 4.0. First, you can select the conferences by name OR the number. Second, you can configure it while you are offline by using a QWK mail reader and sending a "reply" that says ADD 27 or DELETE 93, and the next time you upload replies, these conferences are so configured. Finally, when packing it seems to go a little faster. But maybe that's selective perception.

Other doors let you do the following:

- "Bank" your unused time for later use (members only).
- Search RIME/PCRelay's list of hubs and nodes for one near you
- Search for who's uploaded files this month. Look for your favorite software author!
- Cast your vote in opinion polls on topics.
- Search a database of BBS by location, software used, or topic of interest. You can also upload to this if you have new information.
- Search for or enter your own biography. A new way to get to know those online.
- Check out your horoscope.
- Chat with others who are online at the same time.

But as we said earlier, Brian and Tess are proudest of their files. No doubt about it, they get more uploads daily than the average BBS gets in a week, and more than some smaller ones will get in a year.

FILES!!!!!!

A warning, though. The files menu appears to be a dead end—that is, once you're there, your choices are to do file things or get off. I could not get back to the main menu with any command I tried; I had to sign off and get back on.

When you first logon, you'll see this:

* J FREE at the Channel 1 Command? prompt.

There you can download immediately CHAN1HLP.ZIP, the Channel 1 file lists, Internet access information, basic communications programs, other programs, and the latest 4DOS 4.0 files. The daily financial market summary is available in Bulletin 28.

Download the latest Microsoft Systems/Windows Journal files by entering J MS at the Channel 1 Command? prompt.

You will be able to browse the system (conferences and files directories), read all the Bulletins including the Channel 1 Store, Bulletin 21 and the McGraw-Hill Online Bookstore, Bulletin 4.

And you can purchase items of your choice online.

Now, with so many files, it's probably impossible to just thumb through, so to speak, and find what you like. Never fear. The board has a neat program to search for you, called PowerList.

You give it a keyword to search for, and it goes off into the bushes for a while. On the keyword INTERNET on ALL file directories, the search took 14 minutes. The resulting list had more than 400 text files in it.

But then comes the beauty of this program. You can have the program pack the findings in ZIP format, download the result, then read the list offline. Then later you can sign on, get into the files area, and download the files you want in a batch.

To get to PowerList, use these keystrokes. From the main menu type Open 20. Then the menu gives you these choices:

(C)hoose by directory
(T)ext search all directories
(S)can for files by date
(D)ownload your power list
(H)elp with power list
(K)Hot Keys on/off
(Q)uit back to the BBS
(G)oodbye / log off

I used (T)ext search, but if you know which directory is likely to have your desired file, (C)hoose by directory will be faster. When the search is finished, choose (D)ownload your Power List, which will be sent to you in ZIP format. Of course, as this is a PCBoard BBS, you can use Z for Zippy search and look for New Files since a certain date, all from the main menu, and so on. But PowerList was the neatest list of files program I have seen.

If you don't want to check out ALL directories as I did, choose from this list:

[Channel 1 File Directories]

1] Archive	33] Science & Eng.1	65] DTP/Clipart
2] Communications 1	34] Science & Eng. 2	66] Fonts
3] Communications 2	35] Lottery/Gambling	67] GraphicsApp/Viewer
4] E-Mail	36] CAD	68] Reserved
5] BBS	37] Geoworks	69] Printer
6] PCBoard	38] Sound/Music Prgms	70] Laser

7] Internet/USENET	39] Sound/MIDI files 1:	71] Virus/Security
8] Database(s) 1	40] Sound/MIDI files 2:	72] Language: ASM
9] Database(s) 2	41] Textfiles 1	73] Language: Basic
10] Clipper	42] Textfiles 2	74] Language: C 1
11] Reserved	43] Periodicals	75] Language: C 2
12] Finance/Business 1	44] Periodicals	76] Language: C++
13] Finance/Business 2	45] Shareware Reviews	77] Language: Pascal
14] Stocks/Trading	46] Bible	78] Language: Other
15] Reserved	47] Genealogy	79] AI/Neural Nets
16] Spreadsheet	48] Legal	80] Programmers' Tools
17] Professional 1	49] Disk Utilities	81] Demos 1
18] Professional 2	50] Files/Dirs	82] Demos 2
19] Desk Utilities 1	51] Batch	83] Unprotects
20] Desk Utilities 2	52] Shells/Menus	84] Games 1
21] Maillist/Managers	53] Screen Utilities	85] Games 2
22] Words/Editors 1	54] DOS/System 1	86] Games Adjuncts
23] Words/Editors 2	55] DOS/System 2	87] Golf 2
24] WordPerfect	56] DOS/System 3	88] Chess
25] HyperText	57] Windows 1	89] SVGA GIFs 1
26] Multitasking	58] Windows 2	90] SVGA GIFs
27] Education 1	59] Windows Adjuncts	91] GIFs
28] Education 2	60] OS/2	92] Animations
29] Reserved	61] LAN/Novell	93] Other pictures
30] Ham Radio	62] Unix 1	94] Fractals
31] Food	63] Unix 2	95] Miscellaneous
32] Health/Medical	64] GNU	96] Uploads

There are also files in these conference directories: TeX, Amiga, Mac, and Adult. But you must be a member and J those conferences from the Main Menu to list those files.

If you want to save money on your telephone bill or just don't have time to babysit a download, you can order any (or ALL!) of the public domain and shareware software on disks or tape. Disks cost from $5 to $11 each depending on size of disk and number of disks ordered, but there's no additional shipping or handling charge. Or if you're a software glutton, you can order a 40 to 120 megabyte tape with an entire directory's files, for $150 to $275.

If files are what you're after, a Channel 1 subscription would be worth it. You'll soon find enough to fill your hard drive and any floppies you have lying around!

Fill 'er up

16 Exec-PC Hometown boy makes good

U.S. Mail	Exec-PC
	PO Box 57
	Elm Grove, WI 53122
Phone	(414) 789-4210 [modem]
	(414) 789-4400 [CHAT]
	(414) 789-4200 [voice]
Hours	24 hours a day
Basic rate	$25 for 3 months; $75 for one year; free in Demo mode for up to three months.
Notes	The cutting edge of BBS: the newest in hardware and software and the people who make them happen are here.

Lots of people start up a bulletin board system. Most of them want to run the most useful and friendly BBS they can manage. Some of them get quite elaborate with it; sometimes it turns into a sideline business. But the Mahoneys have taken the BBS to the maximum expression of the form. Bob's managed to turn his little hobby into a full-time family business. It's become the largest BBS in the U.S., and so large and complex it's really not a BBS anymore.

Back in November 1983, with one CP/M computer and one modem, Mahoney opened his BBS to the public. The fact that he ruined the family's Thanksgiving celebration by running upstairs every few minutes to check on the new "baby" was the first clue that this was not just another hobby like bridge or bowling.

By the end of 1985, Exec-PC had six lines, and both NASA and General Mills had installations of the EXEC-PC software. Early in 1986, Bob's wife Tracey quit her job as an interior designer to handle the paperwork of the subscriptions, then running at about $35 per year.

On January 19, 1988, the one millionth caller logged on. The two millionth call was in August 1989, as the BBS was about to be moved out of the house (the buzzing of the power lines and 100 phone lines was keeping up the neighbors at night!). The three millionth call came just after midnight October 19, 1990; the four millionth, September 1991, from Sweden! The pace continues at about one million calls every seven months.

What's drawing all these callers? Software, for one thing. Shareware authors, upon registration and verification, are granted unlimited free access for as long as they continue to upload their latest releases. There are programs for MS-DOS, Windows, Amiga, Macintosh, Atari, and Unix computers. There are picture files, clip art, and yes, "adult" files. With more than 650,000 files (quite a few on CD ROM), that draws a lot of users like you and me, who are eager to get those latest releases.

The accessibility is another big draw. First of all, as an unregistered user, you are still granted a demo version of the board, some limited download privileges, and some other features, for free.

Exec-PC has several alternative connection plans (see later) to make connecting as painless as possible. The BBS handles 250 callers at once. It averages around 200,000 local (not networked) messages on the board at one time, there's a separate line for real-time chatting, and Bob Mahoney prides himself on being on the cutting edge with the modems he has answering the phones.

And that spirit of innovation is another big draw. Mahoney pioneered, according to one bulletin on the system,

- Generous time and byte credit for file uploads and public message posts.
- Time allocation by the week, not by the day.
- One computer per phone line (processor per user)—pioneered in 1983.
- No consistent busy signal problems since rapid expansion began in 1983.
- Hyperscan™ file search feature invented and trademarked by Exec-PC— Searches 20,000 files in 2 seconds.
- ISDN direct connection for downloads at 50K characters per second.
- Entire PC-SIG California file collection online for download at all times, plus other collections. Check out the Apogee games!
- Full file menu capabilities at pause of file listing.
- Direct connect to packet networks for low-cost long distance calls—first to SprintNet, then Connect-USA, now Exec-Link via CompuServe network.
- Autodownloading, invented and trademarked by Exec-PC.

And he's done all this not in Boston, near MIT, nor in Silicon Valley, nor in any other highly touted hi-tech corridor, but in Elm Grove, Wisconsin.

Who's there

According to Mahoney, a large portion of his callers are either sysops of smaller other bulletin boards or shareware distributors. The rest are average BBS users with a yen for files. Mahoney's famous philosophy: "We do not have silly 1-hour-per-day time limits or silly limits on the total number of files you can download. Some systems stand in the way of your fun with these ridiculous limits.

"A few other reasons to call here," Mahoney says, "[include] our large system size eliminates busy signals. At the same time, we have maintained that friendly, small system ambience. Exec-PC has a philosophy of easy, direct menus. Although we have full graphics, color and music capability, we don't overdo it—we only use color and graphics to guide your eye when necessary. Music from a BBS is annoying—we will not use it. We want to make your call to this system as efficient as possible. You will notice our user interface is logical in its layout and does not waste your time with lots of rules and warnings. We want you to get what you came here for: lots of files, lots of messages."

The rules

Although the Mahoneys feel that Exec-PC's users are a mature and self-guiding bunch, the inevitable disagreements about proper conduct on the BBS do surface from time to time. As delineated in one of the bulletins, these are the guidelines:

First and foremost, Exec-PC is a business and copyrights the materials there except for files downloaded from the file collection. Various other individuals might or might not have copyrights on that material. But cross-posting things from Exec-PC to other BBS without Exec-PC's permission is forbidden.

Similarly, Exec-PC doesn't want any copyrighted, commercial software uploaded. Public domain, shareware, freeware, and demos are all fine. If you are in doubt as to which is which, you need to read "What is Legal for Distribution on a BBS," under the <h>elp system.

Other files not accepted: any advertisements or files lists for other BBS; or sorted copies of Exec-PC's files lists (they consider their search system adequate).

When you are sure your upload is allowed, put it in the appropriate file area. Picture files go in the Picture collection; PC and Compatible (except pictures) go in the Mahoney collection; MAC, Amiga and Atari go in the germane collections.

On the message system, the rules are what you'd expect. First, stay on-topic, unless the topic leader (conference sysop) says it's OK. Disputes are to be settled by the topic leader, if possible, and then by the Sysop. Flaming simply won't be tolerated here, especially racist, sexist (see later), or insults aimed at nationality or ethnic groups.

Second, follow up to any message you post that will gather replies. When you ask a question, or place an ad, be sure to check daily for responses. Exec-PC is considered a family board: no profanity, and keep the lewdness in the "adult" area.

Refreshingly, Exec-PC has a specific rule on sexism: "Avoid sexism! The male-to-female ratio on this BBS is sadly out of balance. Let's not insult each other on gender-related topics. I don't just mean the men should not pick on the women—I have seen some pretty good men-bashing going on too! I admit that some of it is fun when it starts out as mild teasing, but it usually gets out of hand and someone gets hurt, leaves the system in a huff, and might not ever come back!"

Getting there

Exec-PC has aggressively pursued package deals and information on how users can call long distance cheaply. Some of the ways are listed here.

PC Pursuit from Telenet costs $30 per month. This gives you 30 hours of calls per month from 6 p.m. to 7 a.m., your local time. They offer their service over the Telenet international network. For more information, call their voice numbers: (800) 736-1130 or (703) 689-6400.

EXEC-LINK from Computer Productions, Inc., offers 1200-, 2400-, and 9600-bps connections. Local call access from 800 cities, running on the CompuServe network wired directly to the Exec-PC hardware on a leased line, and designed exclusively for callers to Exec-PC. EXEC-LINK offers 300–2400 baud connections in over 800 cities, and 9600 V.32 support in over 150 cities.

EXEC-LINK has a few different payment plans; none have calling time restrictions. Whether you call in the middle of the day during the week or call at night, the price is the same: $15 for 15 hours per month, or $30 for 30 hours per month. Hours over the monthly limit are $4.80 per hour, day or night. For more information, call their voice number: (800) 947-0936.

In June 1992, Exec-PC announced a "long-distance association" deal with U.S. Sprint. Rates for this package are 15 cents per minute daytime, 12 cents per minute evening, night, or weekend. To apply, call (800) 998-3932, and be prepared to answer these questions:

- Do you want a business and/or personal account?
- Business name and address (or residential), and a listing of all phone numbers and a company or personal contact person.
- Type of service—i.e., outbound only, 800, travel cards, etc.
- Credit and bank reference.

Choosing your method of transport, dial them up. If you're sure you want to join, have your credit card ready, and you can do so online. Otherwise, feel free to use the demo mode.

Logging on

Your first logon, you'll be asked for a password. After your password is recorded, you can speed up your logon by stringing together your name and password with semicolons (no spaces.) The opening screen is shown in FIG. 16-1.

```
(NODE# 70, 2400bps)

  Exec-PC(tm) BBS  Copyright (c) 1980-1992 Exec-PC, Inc.
            EXEC-PC (R) Reg. U.S. Pat. and Tm. Off.
  _____
              Exec-PC - The Business Knowledge Exchange
                         ASP Approved BBS
      ---- 250 PHONE LINES- LARGEST AND MOST POPULAR BBS IN THE WORLD ----
      The largest LAN-and-microcomputer-based online service in the World!
                     5.8 million callers since 1982
          100+ uploads per day!  650,000 files in compressed files
                  200,000+ active messages online
                      4,500+ callers per day
         Home of Hyperscan(tm), searches through 20,000 files in 2 seconds!
  _____
  Via: Exec-Link,PC-Pursuit,V.32bis,HST,V.42bis,MNP,CompuCom,9600 V-series

  >> IMPORTANT NOTE:   YOUR COMMUNICATIONS PARAMETERS MUST BE SET TO 8,N,1 <<


                    !------------------!
  What is your FIRST name ->
```

16-1
The opening screen to Exec-PC. When you are registered, you can string together your logon: FirstName; LastName;Password.

The next screen gives you more phone numbers to call, as well as the bulletins and mail you need to read. (See FIG. 16-2.)

Then you are in the top menu. From anywhere in the system, typing the carat sign (^) will get you back here. (See FIG. 16-3.)

Let's look at all these options. Two of them are simply toggles: <A>nsi/color will turn on or off color and graphics for this session on the BBS; <X>pert toggles expert mode (short or long menus). For permanent changes to these and other settings,

Press any key to continue ->

```
Node 70 cpu    speed rating... 1        Logon at:  11:30 am, 01/23/93
Node 70 modem speed rating... 1

Good morning, Libbi, you are caller number 5,927,577.
<SYSOP (SYStem OPerator): Bob Mahoney    Main system number: 414-789-4210>
<  This system will be down for maintenance every Thursday 2pm-6pm CDT  >
<       Standard 2400 bps modems on all lines (except as noted below)   >
<       V.32bis, V.32 (14400, 9600) ................ 414-789-4360       >
<       US Robotics HST 9600 and MNP5 ............. 414-789-4337        >
<       US Robotics HST 14400 ..................... 414-789-4352        >
<       CompuCom Speedmodem 9600 ................. 414-789-4450         >
<       Hayes 9600B V-series, 9600bps only(non-V.32).. 414-789-4315     >

You haven't read the following messages addressed to you:
0    messages found.  (More detail - use <S> in Message Conf menu, or)
                      (                <M> in Environment menu        )

[>> No system bulletins have been updated since your last read. <<]
```

16-2

The second screen. You might want to have capture set to "on" to refer to this later.

Press any key to continue ->

```
YOU ARE ON NODE# : 70           SUBSCRIPTION LEFT: 0 (You have never subscribed.)
CALLER NUMBER    : 5,927,577
YOUR LAST ACCESS : Saturday, 01/23/93
YOUR TOTAL CALLS : 10
YOUR UPLOADS     : 0              YOUR DOWNLOADS: 2
DOWNLOAD LIMIT   : 1,000,000 characters per day (0 used today)
SECURITY LEVEL   : 5
--------------------------------    >>Demo Mode, Some Limits<<
Exec-PC  T O P   M E N U
<?>help ....... Help with this menu
<S>ubscribe ... Subscribe or Renew for Exec-PC full access
<B>ulletins ... Info about this BBS
<H>elp ........ Help on the most often asked questions
<R>ead mail ... Read all pending messages addressed to me
<F>ile ........ File Collections
<M>essage ..... Message system
<W>ho ......... Who is on the system right now?
<E>nvironment . Change my password, address, prompts, etc.
<A>nsi/color .. Turn on/off color and graphics from BBS
<L>ist-user ... Find names of other users of this BBS
<X>pert ....... Toggle expert mode (short or long menus)
<G>oodbye ..... Log off system (hang up)

(47 minutes left) >>Demo Mode, Some Limits<< TOP (SBHFMREALWXG, ?=HELP) ->
```

16-3

The Top Menu of Exec-PC. The carat sign (^) will get you here quickly.

choose <E>nvironment. There you can change your password, billing address, how your prompts look, favorite transmission protocol, and more.

The two "help" options can either describe specific commands here, or answer the question most new users have. <W>ho will tell you not only who is on the system right now, but also what they are doing, in this format:

Node# Time   DL UL Current Activity Name & Location 01/16/93 10:56:43
----
81   10:50 0   0 Whoison   LIBBI CROWE HUNTSVILLE AL

<L>ist-user will help you find names of other users of this BBS, should you want to correspond or chat with someone. <G>oodbye, the logoff system command, works from most menus.

The rest of the commands lead you to other menus. As a demo user, you have full access to the menus under <S>ubscribe and <B>ulletins.

The Subscribe menu simply leads you through signing up as a paying member either by mailing a check or using your credit card online. In each case, it will take a few days for you to be officially recognized as a paying member at logon. Your daily logon update will show you when your subscription is about to run out.

The bulletins are informative and updated regularly; unfortunately there's no function for downloading them at all so that you can read them offline (i.e., cheaply). You have to page through each one separately.

For reading messages, you have two choices: <R>ead mail to display all the messages addressed to you, and <M>essage for looking at the entire message system. I saw no offline mail door; under these commands, you have only three choices.

"Y" will make the BBS pause after displaying each message, allowing you to <D>elete the message if you sent it, <R>eply to the message, go <B>ack to the previous message, or follow the <T>hread, and so on. "N" tells the BBS to NOT pause after each message. This is similar to the Turboread™ option listed below, but it still allows these options.

"T" Stands for Turboread. You can only choose this when you are doing a <N>ew or <D>ate read. It works like NO pausing, but faster. The messages will not display color in the messages; you will not be able to use the <B>ack, <R>eply, and other commands. The only keys you can use during a Turboread™ are "P" to pause, or "S" to stop the read altogether. Turboread™ is designed for people who want to capture all the messages as quickly as possible. It's not a mail door, but it helps. As far as I can tell, you can upload a pretyped reply as text from the message menu, however.

As an unregistered user, you can read messages in the WANT ADS, MS-DOS, COMMENTS, and anything addressed to you in the topic e-mail, conference Private. But the only e-mail you can send is a message to the sysops.

<F>ile takes you to the File Collections, where you can download even as an unregistered user, in certain collections. The menu is in FIG. 16-4. Choosing one of the collections takes you to a menu like the one in FIG. 16-5.

```
(47 minutes left) >>Demo Mode, Some Limits<< TOP (SBHFMREALWXG, ?=HELP) -> F
?C O L L E C T I O N   S E L E C T I O N   >>Demo Mode, Some Limits<<

     DU File Collection Description        DU File Collection Description
     -- ------------------------------     -- ------------------------------
<A>     Mahoney IBM Compatible MS-DOS    <M>     CoCo RSDOS & OS9 Collection
<B> D   FREE! - DOWNLOAD LISTS           <N>     Mainframe and Midrange Files
<C> D   FREE! - UTILITIES AND VARIETY    <O> D   FREE ATA Digital Data Standard
<D>     MS Windows                       <P> D   FREE! Apogee Games Collection
<E>     OS/2                             <R>     UNIX / XENIX
<F>     FREE! OS/2 Serv. PAK and BETA!   <S>     FREE! UNIX LINUX full system!
<G>     Adult Pictures & Files PG,R,X    <T>     CD-ROM PC-SIG 11th Edition
<H>     Picture files (.GIF,.PIC,etc)    <U>     CD-ROM So Much Shareware
<I> D   FREE! Apple Copyright Software   <V>     CD-ROM So Much Shareware II
<J>     Macintosh Collection             <W>     CD-ROM So Much Screenware GIFs
<K>     Amiga Collection                 <X>     CD-ROM So Much STareware ADULT
<L>     Atari ST Collection              <Y>     CD-ROM STORM-1 Adult

(In the "DU" column:
  "D" you may Download in this file collection, "U" you may Upload.)

COLLECTION SELECTION (ABCDEFGHIJKLMNOPRSTUVWXY^Q?, Q=QUIT, ?=HELP)->
```

16-4
The Files menu. Some collections are open to unregistered, first-time users, especially virus scanners.

```
Exec-PC  F I L E  S Y S T E M
FREE! - UTILITIES AND VARIETY
<?>help         HELP with this menu
<C>hange        Collection selection
<L>ist          Directory of files
<N>ew           Files since your last call
<U>pload        Transmit file(s) from YOU to BBS
<D>ownload      Transmit file(s) from BBS to YOU
<S>can          Hyperscan(tm) search for text phrases in file list
<A>ccess        Access a .ZIP or .ARC file (view dir, read, download members)
<T>ype          Type out the contents of an ascii file
<W>ho           Who uploaded that file & what else did they upload
<E>xtra         Extra detailed info about a file
<Z>recover      Resume an aborted Zmodem upload
<F>iddle        Delete files, modify descriptions
<P>rotocol      Set default transfer Protocol
<Q>uit          Quit this menu
<G>oodbye       Log off System (hang up)
CPS=0, 1,000,000 bytes left, >>Demo Mode, Some Limits<<
(52 minutes left) FILE MENU (CLNUDSAT^WEZFPXQG,?=HELP) ->
```

16-5

The Collection Selection menu, this one for "Utilities" from the menu in Fig. 16-4. Fiddle (change your options) and Zrecover are Exec-PC innovations.

Conclusion

Exec-PC tries to be the epitome of what a BBS system should be and attempts to help sysops of smaller systems aspire to their standards. With all the files and local messages, it's definitely worth a visit.

17 Here, Fido!

E-mail	Your local Fido BBS's
Phone	Your local Fido BBS's
Hours	Your local Fido BBS's
Basic rate	Your local Fido BBS's
Notes	Fido is the grassroots, freewheeling BBS network. When you know Fido, you know the basics about BBS networks. Also the basics of anarchy.

You might have noticed that the biggest fad in computing so far in the 90s is connectivity. Hooking up various computers into a network, locally all the way through internationally, is all the rage.

But almost as long as bulletin boards have been around, and long before the current craze for interconnecting local area networks to share data and electronic mail, there was Fido. Fido was designed to hook together the multitudes at their individual PCs, MACs, and other breeds of computers.

This has always been a distinct kind of wide area network. The hardware matters somewhat, of course, but the basis for Fido is software. Hobbyists and software authors needed utilities to automatically share files, messages, and e-mail among various BBS. So they wrote them.

The first Fido software was written by two guys living on opposite coasts—Ken Kaplan and Tom Jennings. The idea was to have a good program for hobbyists who wanted to run a local BBS. These authors required an easy way to swap updates across the continent. The best idea seemed to be to have the computers and modems do it at night, when rates were cheap. (This was before public data networks.) So the programs were set up to "fetch" the needed data. Legend, in the form to Thom Henderson, has it that this program was concocted from three different programs. The comment was made "that's a real mongrel" and so the name Fido was born. Soon what was at first a software program to run a BBS became an automated wide area network program as well.

Fido, fetch the mail

& that puppy grew . . .

Of course, they weren't the only ones who needed this capability, and it seemed that the logical next step was to permit the traffic of private mail messages, called NetMail, between the sysops of various boards along the way. So the program grew to include routing through hubs, leaving off and picking up messages, either private or public, and then the routine would continue down the line. Thus we now have EchoMail, or the ability to have a message on a local BBS echoed across several, or even thousands, of other boards.

It got so big that, according to Thom Henderson, the users decided that maybe they needed a framework to manage this system. Thus the FidoNet Association was born.

"But," says Henderson, who was the last chairman of the last board of directors of this group, "it was shut down. The members had decided they like to be more loose knit than that." Henderson, author of the ARC programs, said that the organization was just too formal for the sysops on FidoNet. Deep in their hearts, the FidoNet sysops are basically anarchists.

Fido today

Let's look at how Fido works today.

Jim McCullars is systems manager of Computer Services at the University of Alabama in Huntsville (UAH). He is also SYSOP of ACCESS, a bulletin board operated by UAH, and a Huntsville hub for FidoNet.

In FidoNet terms, he said, node and host are almost synonymous. "A node is a site made of hosts. Where you're sitting is a host. Someone can remotely log into a host. So your local BBS can be a host."

Explaining further, he said a node is a gateway. "If you look in the dictionary it says a node is a point of concentration; a central point. The people who invented a lot of these network terms were biologists; and a lot of these terms are from biology."

FidoNet is a means to an end, McCullars said, the end being communication among the computer hobbyists. Hobbyists can talk to one another about anything. To do this, FidoNet uses echo mail. Whether to be part of FidoNet is a choice of the owner of a BBS.

"Echo mail is like a conference," he said. "With access through a local BBS you can leave a message to people all over the country. If you leave a message for FidoNet, you assign it to a certain interest group, say legal or Windows. That night, the BBS operator has his computer dial a regional hub and upload all messages. The hub knows where the packet came from and will send it to all other BBS in the region according to which BBS accepts messages on which topics. It also sends it to national hub, which sends it to every national hub plus every regional hub except the one it received the packet from. The regional hubs also distribute according to what echoes the BBS asks for."

In this processing, the echo mail can go anywhere. The backbone knows where it came from and it bundles and sends the messages everywhere except where they came from, he said. Before you post an echo mail message, you must ask your SYSOP which topics he covers, and how much geography.

Unless the BBS sysop charges a fee for signing on (some do, some don't, some charge by the message) this looks "free" to you the user. Yet someone, somewhere, is paying that long-distance charge. It could be the BBS sysop, who pays the hub sysop, or the university sponsoring a hub, or even your tax dollars if you've used a gate to the Internet. This is why it is so important to stay *on topic* of the group to which your message is posted. The guns group does not want their time and long-distance calls wasted on messages about sewing!

Figure 17-1 is a simplified version of what McCullars drew for me on his office white board.

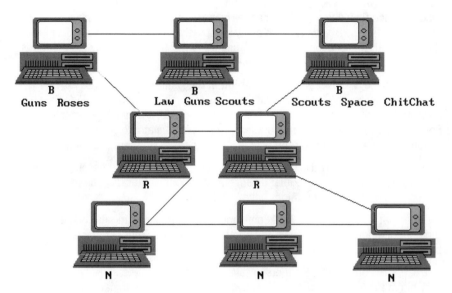

17-1
How messages are echoed across the network.

B represents a local BBS. The words below it represent the topics the BBS SYSOP has chosen to accept messages about. H represents a local host for several BBS. R represents a regional hub for several Hosts. N represents the pieces of the "backbone," the national hubs. All traffic on the lines goes both ways. The B's might or might not be connected: sysops call other boards all the time, to chat with friends, check on the "competition," and exchange locally interesting mail that won't go on to an H or R or N.

Any message on any B can wind up on ANY other B if the connection goes all the way to the backbone, and the SYSOP there accepts messages on that topic. Alabama Echo goes only to Hosts in Alabama, limiting the distribution.

"The personality of the echo depends on the moderator of the echo," McCullars said. Each echo is required to have at least one moderator, he explained; and while this is often a BBS sysop, it is not always. The moderator is required to check that messages are on topic and will often chastise senders who do not adhere to the rule.

Each echo will also have its own rules on language. Again, it is the moderator's job to monitor and control this. For instance, SCOUTER, see later, is very strict about clean language. Some echoes, aimed at adults only, are rife with obscene language. Others might allow an occasional outburst but will draw a line somewhere.

Be aware that you basically have no privacy on FidoNet, even if a message is sent as "private." There's no encoding on Fido; the only security is your accepting or not accepting a certain echo's messages. Generally, on most BBS, if you are not cleared by the Moderator and the Sysop to see the adults-only echoes, you will not be able to read those messages; but on some boards, everybody gets everything.

Some echoes become so busy that they split off to become another network. In 1992, GlobalNet became one of these. It truly is global in scope, and according to one of its founders, Howard Sucher (GC), "This fairly new network was created for those sysops who have had their share with the hassles of many other networks. There are many networks out in the BBS world, that many sysops don't know which one will work for them. GlobalNet has taken all the good qualities of these other networks to bring them into one GREAT network that a sysop will enjoy as well as the users of your BBS."

As you can see, FidoNet is for the amateur, in the sense of people who do something just for the love of it, whether it pays anything or not. The FidoNet folks love BBS for their own sake. As with all amateur efforts, it's hard to keep track of it. Some 10,000 BBS are on the net, and each might have claim to 500 users. But that doesn't really tell you how many people are on the net, Henderson says.

"People who call BBS call a lot of BBS," Henderson says. "And some call, register, and disappear. Others are regular users, but of the online files, not the message system. So, on the net, you might have 20,000 people."

But that's at any given time. BBS come and go with dizzying regularity, and a member of a defunct BBS has to find another board on the net before he can get back on the EchoMail line.

The sense of community, Henderson says, comes from the message system. It's very big in Europe and Australia, he says, where people love to carry on conversations in written form.

FidoNet, while growing, is not doubling every year anymore, Henderson notes. At first, the growth was so prodigious that the original program kept losing boards off its official node list. Seems a line in the program limited the number of nodes to 500, so registered boards kept "falling off the edge" so to speak, after Louisiana in the alphabetical file. Eventually that got fixed, though.

My dog has fleas

Asked what's FidoNet's biggest advantage, Henderson said, "It's free. You pay your phone bill, or a subscription to the local board sometimes to help with his phone bill, and you're in touch with the world. And that's with people on the leading edge. FidoNet people were the first to use protocols, the first to use top-of-the-line modems, the first to figure out how to squeeze every last bit of data into each packet down the line.

"You know some of these guys go to vendors' shows, and talk about device drivers to support 9600+ baud. The manufacturer rep says, 'But DOS doesn't do that.' And the sysop is saying, 'Oh, yes it does, if you know how. I do it all the time.' They know how to replace standard UARTS with something that'll go 38,000 baud or better. They'll do what they can to let the users download 1 megabyte in 10 minutes."

Asked what the biggest disadvantage is, Henderson said, "It's free. The sysops can be wonderful, but some can be not nice to deal with for the average user. A lot of them feel their boards are a public service and try to help the average user. Others feel it's their own baby, and 'I'll do it the way I want to.' To these guys, the users are at best unimportant and at worst a nuisance. Remember, these guys are tied into 1000 other boards, and they sometimes feel they don't need the local user so much."

So shop around your hometown and find a local FidoNet board. One way is to log onto CompuServe at the TELECOM forum, download the latest list of bulletin boards, and look for a Fido connection. Another way is to hang out at a local users' group and ask for a local Fido node. Then, after determining which flavor of sysop you have here (the helpful, public service flavor or the "it's my party and I'll do what I want to" flavor), jump in on the FidoNet EchoMail.

Every FidoNet BBS has to have the right Fido software to call the hub, or backbone if that be the sysop's job, to send this mail. Each Fido BBS sysop will choose a BBS program to suit the local conditions, the BBS hardware and so on. In fact, some BBS might have programs for detecting a call from a user (as opposed to a mail run), running the BBS itself, tossing the mail on the datbit truck, and several "door" programs. But to you, the user, that part is invisible. So learning to enter a message on FidoNet is learning how to use the local BBS.

The pack

How does a BBS get on FidoNet? McCullars explains.

"Anyone who runs a BBS can join FidoNet. The only requirement is that you run a FidoNet-compatible mailer during Zone Mail Hour," he said. This mailer program can be either a FidoNet-compatible BBS program like Fido or Opus, or you can be running PCBoard and have only a Fido front-end mailer program (like FrontDoor or BinkleyTerm). Just because it's easier, most FidoNet boards run their mailer program in the background 24 hours per day, but the BBS only has to be able to accept FidoNet mail only during ZMH.

"To join FidoNet, you actually apply for a node number within a network that is operating in your local calling area," McCullars said. If the area does not have net in place, the sysop can apply to the Region Coordinator (in North America, FidoNet is divided into 10 regions) for an independent node number within that region. "If at least three BBS's wish to form their own net, they may apply to the Region Coordinator for a net number. Within a given net, the Network Coordinator assigns the individual node numbers," he said.

"For example, suppose you start up a board in Huntsville and decide you want to join FidoNet so that you can carry some echoes of interest to you and your users. By calling some boards you know to be in FidoNet, you discover that there is an active net in town, and that it is Net 373. You get a copy of the nodelist and the FidoNet mailer of your choice, and now you are ready to apply for a node number. You configure your software with a 'dummy' node number (like 9999) of the net you want to join (like 373), so you would tell your mailer that you are address 1:373/9999. Then, you send a message to 373/0 telling him you wish to join Net 373. In the message, you include the following information:

BBS Name
Sysop Name
BBS Phone Number
Modem type and baud rate
Type of FidoNet mailer in use
Whether you run the mailer only during ZMH or 24 hours.

"The NC will then assign you a real node number, and send it back to you during ZMH (this way, he is sure that you are running a FidoNet-compatible mailer during that time). You then configure your software with your real address, and you are in. In the meantime, the NC has also sent an update for the following week's nodelist to reflect that there is a new node is his net," he concluded.

Now, you might be asking, how does the sysop's mailer program know the Network Coordinator's phone number to deliver the message? From the nodelist. When the sysop gets FidoNet software, it must include a current nodelist so that the BBS sysop can at least get a message through to the NC of the nearest net (or RC of the region, if the sysop wants to become an independent node). The node list is updated weekly and sent to all the coordinators on the net. So it seems you have to be able to find a FidoNet board in order to have your board join FidoNet, right?

"Unfortunately, that is about right. I don't know of any 'central number' you can call from anywhere to get information. There is a Zone Coordinator, but the person filling that position might change, or his BBS phone number might change (for whatever reason). Securing a current nodelist is an almost absolute necessity to be able to join FidoNet," McCullars said.

Fido's friends

You can soon learn how to send a message to the other users of your BBS, and the local area FidoNet. And generally one keystroke will send your message to everyone who gets that echo on the entire network.

Then, it's just beginning. For Fido has connections to the rest of the world, thanks to people like Tim Pozar. He has written UFGATE, a program to help e-mail move from one system to another, more specifically from Internet to FidoNet. Several other programs exist to hook up several other nets, but his is the most commonly used.

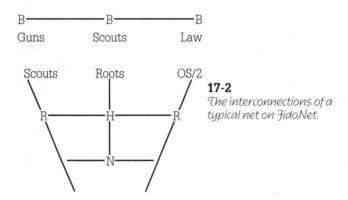

17-2
The interconnections of a typical net on FidoNet.

UFGATE runs on IBM-PC/XT/AT or PS/2 machines or compatibles. UFGATE will also work with MS-DOS or PC-DOS machines that are not 100% IBM-PC hardware compatible with an appropriate FOSSIL (a communications device driver). You can even use it with PC Pursuit.

The package will handle the importing and exporting of UUCP messages and will delete automatically old USENET newsgroup messages. UFGATE will also handle mail/newsgroups that have been either 12- or 16-bit compressed.

UFGATE can handle addresses in either UUCP bang-style, Internet domain style, or a hybrid of both. It can also handle aliases for individuals or machine names. Message forwarding is also built in. UFGATE can handle multiple hosts.

Message formatting, like the automatic appending of individual signature files, is supported. Detailed debugging is available, so setup is easier than it used to be.

The best part is that UFGATE is free to noncommercial, non-supported users. If you are interested in support, which includes updates for a year, the Late Night Software telephone support service, and a hard copy of the manual, a $35 fee is asked. If you are a commercial site, you will automatically get the support just described, and the manual for $195. Support is available to all users via the UFGATE echo on FidoNet.

You can download the UFGATE package from the Late Night Software BBS at

+1 415 695 0759

They have a USR Dual Standard (HST/v.32) modem. The time to transfer the file (UFGATE.ARC) at 9600 baud is 10 minutes, or at 2400 baud about 40 minutes.

UFGATE is also available via anonymous FTP from *zeus.ieee.org*. You want to grab ufg_103.arc from the directory /pub/fidonet/ufgate.

When you address a message on FidoNet, it looks like this: *1:105/302.0*. Usually the 1:(which means North America: Canada, Mexico and the U.S.) and .0 are left off, but they are there by default. (Europe is 2:, the Pacific Basin is 3:.) That address can be translated as "Zone 1, Net 105, FidoNode 302, Point 0."

Sniffing out the trail

To make that an Internet address, you reverse the order and put a letter in front of the numbers. According to Pozar, "That has two purposes. It makes it easier to parse out in case of errors, and there's a rule that you can't begin an Internet domain address with a number."

So our FidoNet address becomes *p0.f302.n105.z1*. But we're not through. You must add the FidoNet domain of *.fidonet.org* to the end of that, cut off the p0 (it is again, a default) and you have *f302.n105.z1.fidonet.org*—the "Fully Qualified Domain Name" of a FidoNode.

Now if the node in question has several points to it (that is, several different machines at that address), you don't chop off the p#. Should you have a FidoNet address *1:105/4.3* (zone 1, net 105, node 4 point 3), it would be written as *p3.f4.n105.z1.fidonet.org* (as there is a point number other than 0, we have to keep it in.) If the address were in Europe or the Pacific Basin, the z1 would become z2 or z3, respectively.

So, once you have the basics of addressing down, you can send this message to your nearest Fido/Internet gate. The local sysop should know or be able to find out where that is. At this point, hope fervently that you have chosen the helpful, friendly flavor of sysop.

FidoNet generally sets the pace for other BBS nets. The echoes are as amorphous as the number of boards on the net, and any list here would be out of date before I could send it to my publisher.

Leader of the pack

In general, though, several hundred echoes deal with product support for different brands of hardware and software. Especially in communications hardware and software, the inventors/authors/engineers might be found on various echoes on FidoNet.

Two interesting echoes are SCOUTER and SCOUTING. By definition, the first is for the child scouts, and often the messages are posted from local Boy Scouts of America and Girl Scouts of America BBS. The SCOUTING echo is defined as an exchange for the adult leaders. However, as in all things FidoNet, the crossover is considerable. (In FidoNet, rules are like the Apocrypha in Protestant doctrine: they are good for inspiration and instruction, but they're not Gospel.)

A recent enhancement of Fido is the ability to attach a program, picture file or other non-text file to a message, and route it to a particular person. Both SCOUTER and SCOUTING use this to send GIF files for troop newsletters, suggest "Scout's Own" projects, and so on.

Canadian Guides discuss winter camping with Scouts from Florida; boys from all over trade patches. The leaders exchange messages about what to do in situations from making the kids keep up with their own stuff and serious behavior problems to getting caught outdoors in severe weather.

There are many active genealogists on FidoNet. Echoes include Genealogy Data, where tafels are uploaded; Southeast Genealogy for searching in the lower right-hand corner of the US; Roots, a general query and answer echo; and Genealogy software, where the plethora of programs for family history are picked apart. Blessed is the genealogist who finds a local board with all four!

Other less tame conferences abound. The local Fido BBS won't carry every one because the volume would be prohibitive. But shop around. There are nearly 20 Fido boards in my hometown and each has a district collection of echoes.

But speaking of volume, especially with a FidoNet board, you need an offline reader. The Alabama Echo, a general chitchat conference, can have more than 200 messages A DAY. Even if you only download the ones to you and the ones addressed to ALL, that is too much to read while connected to the board, especially one with a 30-minute a day limit.

The tale wags the dog

All in all, FidoNet is still the most freewheelin' of the nets. It has few rules, which are sometimes ignored, and lots of users. The sysops are independent and cooperate, most of the time.

"I enjoy the FIDO network, [but] I consider myself a PCBoard sysop," says Conan Dickson, sysop of Occam's Razor in Huntsville. "FIDO is a mail network that carries many conferences."

18 ILink
The oasis of civility

E-mail	Your local ILink BBS
Phone	Your local ILink BBS
Hours	Your local ILink BBS's
Basic rate	Your local ILink BBS's
Notes	"Give InterLink a few minutes and it will bring you the world!" is their claim. Everything's an open forum, and there are no "addressing" nodes for directing private messages, and no files go over the net. Your local BBS may have text and program files; however, they will not be transferred among the BBS of ILink.

"InterLink is an electronic mail network that connects a large amount of PCBoard bulletin board systems across the United States, Canada, Europe and other locations worldwide," says a text file to be found on any ILink BBS. "InterLink transfers conference mail daily through our international hub system in Mount Vernon, New York, The Executive Network. Seven other major systems in the US and Canada, known as 'Super-Regionals,' feed mail directly to the ExecNet via the Qmail door. These SR systems in turn supply mail to other PCBoards that call them directly."

Jim Lee, ILink planning administrator (and in real life, a computer consultant/shepherd), said, "In 1987, a bunch of sysops got together and decided it would be fun to exchange e-mail. [These included Jim Pottkotter, Jim Key, Sparky Herring and Charles Grissmore]. Sparky Herring in Memphis had written a program to communicate with other boards. So with 6 or 7 other guys in Canada, the West Coast, New York, and other places, they began to exchange 6 or 7 echo mail conferences. Then it got out of hand . . ."

How it all began

The common thread here was that all the BBS involved were using PCBoard BBS software. And that is one requirement to being an ILink BBS to this day. Another is to use the Qmail door.

"Well, then they put out Qmail Doors, a program to read this mail quickly and efficiently, in April of 1988," Lee said. "Now it's being used all over the world. That informal beginning has spread to 230 boards, in 20 countries, exchanging 2000 messages in 150 conferences every day."

InterLink has been a distinct network since September 1988. In e-mail terms, that's venerable. The current Super-Regional sysops are some of the major movers and shakers in the development of electronic mail networks.

InterLink host systems were initial Alpha- and Beta-test sites for the Qmail door and were major participators in PCB ECHO, the first PCBoard electronic EchoMail network. PCB-ECHO disbanded in August, 1988, replaced by a system based on Qmail and organized in a way similar to InterLink, but with a hub in Memphis, TN.

After the formal organization of InterLink, the host was moved to New York. Then the system began to expand both domestically and internationally. The first European and Australian systems were added in October 1988.

It spread from North America to England, to now include most European countries (indeed, there's a conference of conversations among the Euros, "just like they're chatting on the phone" Lee said.) Five boards have been admitted from South Africa, but the two from Saudi Arabia are gone. Having lost their phones in the recent unpleasantness, the boards there have not been able to hook up again.

"We're always growing, but slowing. Quality, not quantity is what we're after," Lee said. "We have always used a system of moderated (we say hosted) conferences. Newsweek said of us that we are an oasis of civility in the maelstrom that is e-mail. We're not family oriented, nor do we have a political position. But we insist on civility: no profanity, and keep the personal attacks to a minimum."

"There's a large group in Switzerland, I don't understand why," Lee said. "Seems to be some law that every fifth house has to have a BBS." And they are very active.

"The beauty of echo mail is that in 48 hours a file posted in the US can be all over North America. But we communicate only through the words. You don't know if I'm short or tall, black or white. All you can see is the ASCII," Lee said. Which makes the civility all the more imperative.

ILink is choosy and has an application process. After meeting the software and hardware requirements, the prospective member is checked out by an anonymous committee, to see whether the tone and quality of the board will meet ILink's standards.

"A network enhances a BBS, that's a given," Lee said. "The question for us is, will this board enhance the overall network? After all the t's are crossed and the i's are dotted, that's the question they [the committee] asks."

They look for new ideas, honest voices, and above all, civility.

Topics range from software support to learning programming, installing PC hardware, discussing politics, graphics, law, medicine, jokes, books, audio and video; anything you'd care to discuss. The most popular conferences ("omitting of course, my own, the Mozart Conference," Lee said) are Opinion, Politics, Religions, and the Buy/Sell conferences. The Eurochat is pulling up fast in popularity.

Each board is required to carry at least 15 conferences to qualify. Some carry them all. Some of the software specialty conferences are supported by software authors, such as Quarter Deck in the Multi-Tasking conference, John Friel in the QMODEM conference, and Sparky Herring in Qmail.

Indeed, InterLink deals exclusively in conference mail. Conferences are special message areas dedicated to a specific topic of conversation (accessible with the "J" command in PCBoard). In these message exchanges, you can listen in and start conversations with expert, beginning, and in-between users and professionals.

So if you are struggling with installing some software or can't get your hardware to cooperate, or maybe if you have some free time and want to get away from work for a few minutes, you can call an InterLink board and use the conferences.

There, you may read messages from (or post messages to) a professional hardware or software person who knows precisely the answer you seek. You can get a real lawyer's or doctor's opinion of some legal or medical issue you have been wondering about, with a lot of kibitzing thrown in. ILink was designed to help you get advice on a knotty programming problem or just spend a few minutes goofing off.

When you send an ILink message, turnaround is generally 1 to 2 days. This time varies depending on which system the message was placed, the message's destination, when the caller posted a reply, and when the last mail run was made on both boards involved. In some cases, callers that left a message in, say, Toronto, have received a reply from NY the very same day, but that's really just luck.

When the mail runs is at the discretion of your sysop: you should leave a message to that person if you have questions about when and where the mail goes from your local BBS. In InterLink, the regional SR system is ready to take his/her call at any moment; it is a mail-on-demand system. As a practical matter, most sysops call in the evening, or on a script during their boards' daily "events" after midnight when the board is taken down for housekeeping tasks. This makes sense because phone rates are much cheaper then.

How do I use InterLink?

Every InterLink board is required to use PCBoard software, so the commands you use will be the same across the network. You type J to join (read and write messages to) a conference. Generally, a list of the conferences available on this particular BBS will be displayed. To write a message, the command is Enter. (See FIGS. 18-1 and 18-2.)

Some conferences are strictly local, and some can be echoed across the network. Every time you type a message in an InterLink conference, you are asked if you want to "echo" this message. If you choose to echo it, your message will be sent out to all other participating InterLink systems and affiliates.

There are a few tips you should remember when using the conferences. First, lurk a while. Read the threads, catch up on what's being discussed and by whom. After a few days, send a message to "ALL" introducing yourself and your interest in this topic.

If you echo a message, make sure it's precise and to the point. Thousands of people read your message and want to spend their precious BBS online time downloading pertinent messages.

To make your message clear, you should make it a general practice to quote a *small* part of the previous message to which you are replying. Many of the offline readers we have covered in these BBS chapters will do this for you automatically. This

```
╔═════════════════════[ PUBLISHERS' PARADISE ]══════════════════════╗
║╠═[ Mail ]══════════════════[ System Commands ]══════════════[ File Commands]═╣
║[E]nter a msg                                              [U]pload to BBS    ║
║[K]ill a msg        [A]bandon Conference    [M]ode (colors)   [D]ownload a file║
║[Q]uick scan        [B]ulletins             [O]perator page!! [F]ile directories║
║[R]ead a msg        [C]omment to SysOp      [P]age length     [L]ocate a file  ║
║[Y]our mail         [G]ood-Bye (logoff)     [U]iew settings   [Z]ippy file scan║
║[NEWS] display      [HO]tkeys on/off        [W]rite user info [N]ew files list ║
║[QMAIL] QMAIL!      [J]oin a Conference     [X]pert on/off    [T]ransfer types ║
╚═════════════════════════════════════════════════════════════════════════════╝
ProDoor Commands:   [FU] View ZIPfile    [J N] New messages      [?] Help!
                    [SC] Toggle Conf Scan [ S ] Script Questionaire
(8 used, 19 left) [Main Board] Command?
```

18-1

Generally, if you type J, you will be shown which conferences you can Join on this board.

```
█ To: MICHAEL CHARNESS                                ┌─Insert Mode ──┐
  From: LIBBI CROWE                    Read: NO       │(Ctrl-Z)=Help  │
  Subj: DEMONSTRATIONS                                └─(Escape)=Exit─┘


────────────────────────────────────────────────────────────────────────
This is a demonstration of how to enter a message manually to the ILink
network.

Thank you for your time and attention.
```

18-2

Entering and replying on PCBoard are one-keystroke commands.

```
(13 used, 14 left)
A)bort, C)ont, D)el, E)dit, I)ns, L)ist, O)rig, P)rot, Q)uote, S)ave, U)isual
Message Entry Command?
```

practice reminds the regular users what was said, helps the new people understand where this thread has been going, and sets up your reply. On ILink, if you have something to say that is of strictly local interest, do NOT flip the "echo" flag. That way, it will be visible to callers who read the mail on your local BBS but keeps down superfluous national mail traffic (and your sysop's bills!) Ignoring this rule on ILink has consequences, as we will see.

Now all of this describes the manual way to do your ILink mailing, but really, the simpler way is to use the Qmail door, and an offline mail reader. (See FIG. 18-3.)

When you call up this program, the PCBoard software steps aside and the Qmail program steps in. Choosing C for configure, you select the conferences you are interested in, and whether you want ALL messages there or ONLY the ones to you. (See FIG. 18-4.)

The program, when you ask it, will compact your messages into a compression program of your choice, download it with the protocol of your choice, and sign off when done, if you say so.

As most BBS sysops set a time limit on your connection, this allows you to call the BBS later and upload your answers, using the same steps, and still have time to download a file or two. All your reading and replying will be done while you are not connected to the BBS, freeing up your phone and the sysop's.

```
Current autostart sequence is: DZ;Y;UZ;G

              (------------)
ENTER new sequence:

(17 min. left) QConfig Command? Q
```

```
┌──────────────────────┐
│ ██                   │
│ ██   Mail Door        │    Main System Menu
│ ██      3.00          │
│ █                     │
├──────────────────────┤
│  CLS    Clears your screen                        │
│  HELP   Help with system commands                 │
│  C      Configure the Qmail Door                  │
│  D[p]   Download messages (optional protocol)     │
│  G      Logoff and disconnect from PCBoard        │
│  M      Toggle graphics mode                      │
│  O      Chat with the sysop                       │
│  Q      Quit Qmail Door and return to PCBoard     │
│  U[p]   Upload replies (optional protocol)        │
│  X      Expert mode toggle                        │
└──────────────────────────────────────────────────┘

(16 min. left) Qmail Command?
```

18-3

Qmail and an offline reader are the best way to read mail on ILink.

Name	Last Read	High Msg	Flags	Name	Last Read	High Msg	Flags
0. Main Board	1,371	1,371	X	14. Win.Apps	0	379	
1. FONTS	0	496		15. Sharware	0	2,113	
2. FORSALE	238	238	X	16. C-Lang	0	2,165	
3. Corel	0	336		17. Consumers	0	222	
4. Hardware	0	6,891		18. MAC	0	463	
5. DeskTop	0	1,041		19. Amiga	0	422	
6. Graphics	0	509		20. Buy-Sell	0	14,191	
7. Writers	4,200	4,327	X	21. Gaming	0	2,745	
8. WordPerf	0	1,247		22. StarTrek	0	3,846	
9. MS-Word	0	232		23. QMail	0	1,630	
10. DOS-Tips	0	1,700		24. USR-Modem	0	1,401	
11. Tech	0	3,342		26. NetUsers	430	435	X
12. HardDisk	0	1,342		27. TeleComm	0	1,540	
13. Windows	0	8,331		28. Telix	0	404	

```
Flags: [X]=Selected  [Y]=YOUR messages only  [Q]=QNet status  [S]=Sysop status

Enter conference number to select or ALL (ENTER to see more) or QUIT?
```

18-4

Choosing your preferences among the ILink conferences on your local BBS.

Sysop Michael Charness, Publisher's Paradise

Michael Charness, typeface designer and aerospace engineer, is not only sysop of Publisher's Paradise but also host of two conferences on the ILink network—DeskTop and Corel. His company, which sponsors the board, is an official Beta test site for XEROX/Ventura, Borland International, Ares Software, Altsys, Atech, MicroSoft, and Corel. Charness' typeface designs, under the Font Pro label, are everywhere.

An ILink user for years, Mike was a Beta tester for "the grandfather of all Off-line Reader/Responder/Mail-Doors: QWKMAIL (now 'Qmail') v1.0.," when he was living in Los Angeles and using Sleepy Hollow BBS. "I came to Alabama about four years ago [1988], and I went into withdrawal," Charness said. "There was no ILink board here. As a matter of fact, there were no networks running PCBoard, which happens to be my favorite software as a user, as well as a sysop. So I started the BBS primarily to be a carrier for the local area as well as get it myself." Not a hub, Publisher's Paradise (launched March 19, 1990), is a node on ILink. A moderate size board, Paradise covers 35 of the 150 conferences on ILink, most of them having to do with desktop publishing and related subjects such as writing, product support and ILink business and news. Traffic in messages about 300K per day.

"The best part of being on ILink is what makes it, in my mind, different from some of the other networks. It is very structured and professionally moderated. When you have a series of messages with subjects you are pretty well assured that there is no idle chatter, that the messages have some discussion really on that topic. The moderators actually get training, and as a result, the moderators do a very good job. Politely, but they have teeth as well. If someone does not follow the rules, they will get a temporary suspension on their home board for 30 days, just in that conference. The suspension can go to 90 days or be permanent. It is a very professionally run network, although there are some very casual and fun topics on it."

Asked what is worst about being on ILink, Charness said, "Nothing really bad. Having to follow some of the politics in administration of the network." These discussions will be found in the discussion conferences the sysops will see. "To keep something professionally run internationally, you will have that kind of politics, and disagreements. And in something this big, it sometimes takes a while for those things to be resolved." At the end of 1992, the biggest rhubarb was all the time and hoops involved in becoming an ILink sysop. Because of the length of time it takes for review and decision, some geographical areas who really wanted ILink could not get ILink service. The discussion, and resulting politics, centered on the logistics of streamlining the process without sacrificing the professionalism and control.

The local response to ILink connection has been good, Charness said. "When we opened up, no one had seen Qmail before. It's just been phenomenally positive. People have been buying high-speed modems just to be able to get larger message packets. Other local boards have asked 'How do I join ILink', because I don't carry all the conferences, and they'd like me to serve as a hub for them for the conferences I do carry. People who find out-of state long-distance calling is cheaper call here. Others who don't have a local ILink connection call long-distance here to get the mail.

"Publishers' Paradise BBS is three years old now and gets calls from all over the world. In fact, a full third of our calls come from out of state. Before we added the second line in mid 1991, utilization of the BBS was over 80% during the hours from 6 a.m. to midnight, and even the wee hours in between were getting heavier." In the last six months, Charness has had 2100 different people call, about 50% of them from his home county.

"Many of our users have contributed financially towards my running of the BBS to help out for phone charges, electricity, hardware upgrades, maintenance, access to special files, etc., and both they and I feel that they ought to be allowed special privileges and make it easier to get on the BBS. Contributors automatically have access to our second high-speed HST 14.4 D/S 'subscriber only' phone line.

"I don't want to lock out budding computer users who just can't get it together on their budget. Contribution is strictly voluntary. You still get access even if you choose to just take what you get at no charge. No pressure . . .," he said. He considers his BBS a public service.

Charness sees himself in different roles as a moderator. "When we don't have any work to do [such as disciplining a user], we call ourselves conference hosts. When we have work to do, we call ourselves moderators: 'you have been moderated.'

"Everybody sees every message, which I think is really good and healthy. There's a tremendous variety of topics to choose from. When somebody asks for one conference, I post a public message about it. And if at least five people vote to have it, we'll try it."

Interest and traffic in local conferences keep him busy, and his local COREL Draw conference became so active and useful, he took the message base and went from there to become ILink's COREL conference.

A host must maintain order in his conference. Flaming is never allowed; one must always discuss the argument, never the person. Off-topic discussions might spring up, and they will be gently nudged over to the appropriate conference. The all-purpose, no-particular topic gabfest is ChitChat. Charness carried it for a while, but it was so huge that, when no one used it, he dropped it.

Other than that, he said it's "really not much more work than regular BBS." It takes hours to get it set up, but now that it's set up, the BBS can do the mail chores automatically. His computer calls Pennsylvania every morning at 3:15, sends up the new mail and gets down new mail, and then inserts it into the proper message base.

"When I get up in the morning, the first thing I do is come in the computer room and see if the mail has run. And if it hasn't, I feel obligated to do a manual mail run. Because I have an amazing number of people, first thing when they get up in the morning is call in here and get their morning dose of ILink.

"One of the guys called from Grosse Point Woods, Michigan, used to call at 5:45 every morning. Somebody else started calling in at what he considered his slot. He just blew a gasket. That was HIS time, and he wanted to get the mail!" Charness said.

"I feel a lot more obligated and tied to the BBS than when running just a local message base. People are dependent on me, just like the postal service, to run the mail," he said, "but that also gives a lot more sense of fulfillment.

"It's always amusing when some board is setting up or changing configuration; you will get messages posted to the wrong conferences. You will see a series of messages going on about DeskTop Publishing, or Windows, or WordPerfect, and right in the middle you'll get a discussion of 'Is Jesus the Messiah?' And, strangely enough, for whatever reason, it's the Religion conference that seems to move in mysterious ways," Charness said.

Buy-Sell became so busy that ILink tried to split it into one strictly for computer stuff and one for anything else. An example of ILink's structure with flexibility, to Charness, is that after trying this for a while, the administration took a vote over the network and remerged them. Buy-Sell is still the most active conference.

"They are constantly trying to find ways to better serve the members," he said. ILink's traffic does not fluctuate seasonally, in Charness' experience. Any variation in the volume of messages means there's some problem with the mail.

What does it take to be a sysop?

Tips for the new user

Asked what tips a new user should know, Charness said, "For any BBS network, get a good offline mail reader. My favorite is the first one I used, Qmail, the latest version being DeLuxe-2, by Sparky Herring. He's a friend of mine and I like to support him, as he started the whole thing. But there's lots of them out there based on Qmail, and WinQuick for Windows is another good one."

He also suggests downloading the ILGUIDE file, required to be on any ILink BBS, and quoted in this chapter. It contains "Users' Etiquette Guide to ILink," which describes ILink's definitions of civility, and a short glossary of common ILink network terms.

He also suggests making good use of ILink Info, a conference with answers to general questions on the network itself and required to be carried by all ILink BBS. Another is called MOD&USER, where you can discuss things with a moderator about differences you might have with him/her. Other files show all the ILINK boards, the ILTREE will show how all those boards are connected, and those can be interesting.

"Just remember this is a public forum, and all kinds of people use it: Professionals, high schoolers, young kids, casual users. Courtesy is not just important," Charness said, "on ILink, courtesy is mandated. If you can have such a thing as ethics in a computer network, ILink has it. That's not for everybody, and other networks serve other interests."

19 New Parents Network
Bulletin boards for baby

E-mail FidoNet address 1:300/31
U.S. Mail P.O. Box 44226
Tucson, AZ 85733-4226
Phone (602) 326-9345 [BBS]
(602) 327-1451 [voice]
(602) 881-8474 [fax]
Hours 24 hours a day
Basic rate No online fee, except long distance call. Supports up to 9600 baud
Notes Three components: a BBS in Tucson is the central hub of a Fido-based network of 30 BBSs in the US and Canada; a database and forum on DELPHI; and a licensed software package at hospitals, libraries and social service sites.

When Karen Storek Lange had her first baby, she studied everything she could get her hands on. Trouble was, it was difficult to find materials. And she found that books, magazines and brochures still might not cover everything a new parent needs to know, or that it might be covered but so well hidden the new parent might not find it.

Her baby was several months old before she found out that ipecac syrup should be in every household with babies and toddlers. It can save a life, if you know about it.

"I was finding out about information on a hit-or-miss basis . . . there was no national central distribution point of information, so I decided to create one!" Lange said.

Not one to leave a problem alone, Lange put together a packet of information for new parents and distributed copies at Tucson hospitals. The response, back in 1988, was tremendously positive. The demand became great, and she looked for another way to disseminate it.

So she founded the New Parents Network, a nonprofit organization. New Parents Network led to NPNet as a national information service to all people and agencies concerned with parenting and relies solely on grants, contributions, corporate

Conceiving an idea . . .

. . . & getting triplets!

underwriting support, and revenue from its site licensing program. Information on the networks ranges from car seat and toy recalls, to poisonous plants, to support groups for parents.

New Parents Network disseminates its gathered parenting files through a BBS network, a Delphi forum and message base, and a software program called New Parents Network on Disk.

"We're a non-profit corporation created to collect and disseminate a databank of information," Lange said. "We grew from a single BBS to a network. We invite all social service agencies, government agencies, and support groups to submit text files of what they do, where they are, and any information they have to share."

Lange is also proud that the New Parents Network was nominated by U.S. Robotics, Inc. for a 1992 Computerworld Smithsonian Award, given to organizations that are using computer technology for the betterment of mankind.

"We didn't win, but even being nominated was an honor," she said.

NPNet staff

All three components are being run by Lange, who is paid staff, and several dedicated volunteers. The office and BBS are in her home. "I can't wait to get an office," she said. "Right now, it's being run out of my house, and it's out of control! This home office is taking over."

Karen is a 33-year-old mother of two. Before she started the network, she was not very computer literate, only using WordPerfect from time to time. Now she knows more than she'd like about BBS software. She gives great credit to three computer consultants who helped her create the network of 30 BBS in 16 states and Canada. These BBS have a FidoNet structure, but their net is separate and autonomous from FidoNet itself.

"My assistant sysop is William Logan. He is a computer consultant, and he specializes in viruses. He is a licensed MacAffee agent. Two other volunteer staffers are John Fucci and Jeff White. They helped design the net and they're the pulse behind it. I can't wait to get them on paid staff," she said.

The best part of begetting her triple creations, though, has been using the latest technology to help people with one of the world's oldest problems: babies don't come with owner's manuals.

But it has had its downside. Lange is quick to say she loves the work and believes in the mission of NPNet. But long days do get old, and sometimes lonely.

"There are very few female sysops out there," she said. "It's been a real experience for me." Not all has been positive: she said she has had some harassing notes, and 99–100% of them are from men.

"Some really blow my mind. Sometimes I laugh, sometimes I cry, but then I just get back to business. My business is this BBS and the NPNet. This is my job, in my home office. I work 12 hours a day sometimes, 7 days a week."

Becoming an NPNet sysop

To become a sysop on the NPNet of BBS, one must first download the file NP_NET.ZIP from the main board. There's a form to fill out and policies to agree to. The policies are firm: NPNet is a public service. No commercial advertising is allowed unless approved by NPN Headquarters; NPNet information should not be on boards with sexually-oriented material.

"We don't want our material on any board that might offend our users," Lange said. "I'd say about 80% of the boards out there have some pornography on them. I don't have a stand on that one way or another, but I just don't want NPNet on those boards."

All NPNet material is copyrighted; no annoying or abusive language is allowed, and certainly no obscenity. NPNet material must be on a board open to the general public, and there must never be a charge for a BBS user to access NPNet files.

The headquarters require a New Parents Network sysop to have an IBM-compatible computer with DOS 2.0 or above, and operate a BBS capable of FidoNet standards. In addition, the sysop must have a front end mailer that is capable of network mail, echo mail conferences, and file transfer capabilities. NPNet is a separate and autonomous network, and any FidoNet board is compatible.

Each BBS is required to have the NPNet Public Forum and the NPNet NPN Sysop Support Forum, a private forum for the sysops.

The BBS began when, in May 1991, Lange was given a used IBM computer and modem. By November, the economics and Spanish baccalaureate had conquered the labyrinth of putting together a BBS. Putting her information online, she found, was the key to becoming a truly national resource. This created NPNet, the nation's only centralized computer data bank designed to link all agencies involved with children and parenting.

The Headquarters BBS

Dialing (602) 232 6934, you log onto the BBS, the heart of NPNet. The opening screen tells you you're in the right place. (See FIG. 19-1.)

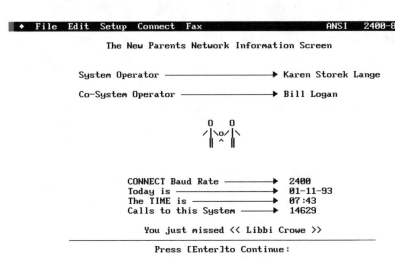

19-1
NPN's opening screen shows you the emphasis of the place. The BBS software is Remote Access.

"Eventually we will have graphics files," Lange said, "but right now we have ANSI support, though it is not required, and text files.

"The most important thing for the new user is to first download 300_31.ZIP. That filename is our node address. It is updated continually and is the master files list. Do that first, read it offline, and decide what you might need," she said. "You must have PKZIP to read it, however, and you can download that offline from our BBS, too."

The over 300 files (15,624,849 bytes) on the Headquarters New Parents Network BBS can be found on any of the 30 BBSs on the NPNet. The major headings are

Child care
Commercial services
Crisis & help information
Disorders, diseases, & disabilities
General parenting information
General safety & poison control
Government programs
Health & nutrition
Media, television, & publications
New files
New parents network information
Other parenting resource organizations
Prenatal & childbirth information
Product recall information
Support groups & newsletters

Under the main headings are several subheadings. Files on some of these main subject headings are national, and some on the same subject headings are from some of the states in the NPNet: Arizona, California, Virginia, and Illinois, among them. These files are all included in the licensed software and on the Delphi forum too.

Bulletins

The bulletins are important, too. Bulletin 1, Lange says, is one of the most important things for a user to remember:

"None of the information contained on the National New Parents Network BBS or distributed through NPNet in the form of bulletins, files, messages, etc., should be used as a substitute for a doctor's advice. NPN functions solely as a central distribution point of parenting information, not as a medical adviser," it says, and Lange will emphatically remind you occasionally.

Also, "all information contained as New Parents Network files or bulletins has been copyrighted by each respective social service organization or commercial entity and CANNOT be duplicated (with the exception of electronic mail transferring) without the express written consent of both New Parents Network and respective social service."

Files on NPNet include specifics on product recalls from car seats to high chairs to toys, general safety, child care, support groups, disabilities, as well as government programs and crisis information. All social services, support groups and government agencies that help parents or children are invited to have a file description on NPNet at no cost.

But it doesn't stop there. NPNet has computer programs, including games for infants, math adventures, spelling games, geography games, and more. You'll find a file to help you name the baby, as well as files on health problems you might not have heard about. Whether you need to inoculate your computer or your baby from viruses, the files cover most areas a new parent with a new modem might need.

"We support up to 9600 baud, but we have only one line," Lange said. "Set your parameters to 8-N-1. ANSI is supported but not required.

"We also have a list of the BBS across the country that are on our net. It's in the bulletin menu. Choose the option NPNets in Other States." (See FIG. 19-2.)

```
┌──────────┐                    0   0
│ Bulletin │                   / \ \0/ / \
│ Menu     │                  ‖   │  ^  │  ‖
└──────────┘                      ‖     ‖

                                   NEW
                                 PARENTS
                                 NETWORK
─────────────────────────────────────────────────────────────────
[1] Read This First!      [8]  NPNets in other states  [15] (unused)
[2] New Parents Net Info  [9]  Darwin's US BBS List     [16] (unused)
[3] Donors to NPNet       [10] Rules of the System      [17] (unused)
[4] Bulletin Sponsorship  [11] Listing your Agency      [18] (unused)
[5] NPNet Site Licensing  [12] New User Guide           [19] (unused)
[6] Reading Files Online  [13] FidoNews                 [20] (unused)
[7] Telecomputing Terms   [14] (unused)                 [21] (unused)
─────────────────────────────────────────────────────────────────
New Parents Network    Tucson, Arizona      Voice: (602) 327-1451
FidoNet: 1:300/31      NPNet: 79:300/31     BBS:   (602) 326-9345
─────────────────────────────────────────────────────────────────

File to view (Enter=quit):
```

19-2
From the Bulletin menu, you can find NPNet BBS in other states.

There are two mail doors—MakeQWK and RA Offline Mail. Most people use MakeQWK, but the two are very similar. Again, have PKUNZIP on hand to read the messages later. The message base is small, although some good conversations are to be found. There are several FidoNet conferences. (See. FIG. 19-3.)

```
F1=Help                 Cedar Island Link           5:36  F10=Menu


Message Areas: ----------

  1  * User to User              2  * NPN Public Forum
  8    LOCAL - Security         14    Software Support
 25  * McAfee Support           27  * Laptop
 28  * Attention Deficit Disorder 29 * US and World News
 30  * Child Abuse              31  * Comp. Users and Social Science
 32  * Dads                     33  * HomeSchool
 34  * Missing Child            35  * Parents
 36  * Please stop Abuse now    37  * Problem Child
 38  * PCtools                  39  * Word Perfect
 47  * Telemate Support         49  * Disability issues echo

Select area:
```

19-3
The message base is small but concentrated on issues important to families. Only the NPNet Public Forum is strictly NPNet. The rest are FidoNet Forums. The Mothers' and Dads' forums were discontinued in January 1993.

The top of the main menu has a helpful file, "Where to find our parenting files." To sum it up: To find the parenting files, go to any Files Menu (type in F at the main menu or message menu). Once at any Files Menu, type in A for Area Change. It is here that you will see the categorization of files. All social services, support groups, and government agencies that assist parents or children can have a file on the network. These files have been categorized into either national or state-by-state menus. Once the BBS receives one file from a specific state, that state's menu will be activated.

Once you have chosen a category (i.e., National) at that Files Menu, type in F for Files List. At the following prompt, type in L for List area. Now you can easily scroll through the list of files for that category. Follow the bar at the bottom of the screen as a guide.

Reading a "zipped" file online

If you want to read a file while online, go to any Files Menu and type in Z for Zipster. Enter the full name of the file (i.e., BLECHE.ZIP) and hit Enter. Next type in P for Process, and hit Enter again. Type in R for Read, and the file will open for you to review.

The sysops suggest that you have your capture feature on at all times so that you can read all information that has passed across your screen after you have logged off.

Logging off is as simple as typing G. When you see this screen, you know you're about to get a NO CARRIER: (See FIG. 19-4.)

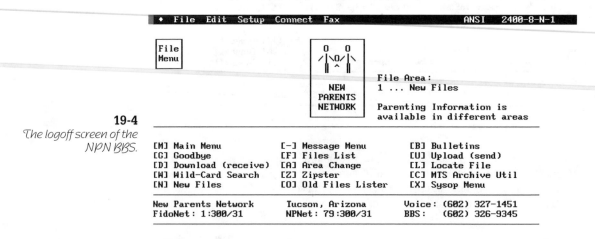

19-4
The logoff screen of the NPN BBS.

```
 ♦  File  Edit  Setup  Connect  Fax                    ANSI   2400-8-N-1

File
Menu                       O   O
                         /|\O/|\          File Area:
                            ||  ^ ||       1 ... New Files
                          NEW
                         PARENTS         Parenting Information is
                         NETWORK         available in different areas


[M] Main Menu          [-] Message Menu      [B] Bulletins
[G] Goodbye            [F] Files List        [U] Upload (send)
[D] Download (receive) [A] Area Change       [L] Locate File
[W] Wild-Card Search   [Z] Zipster          [C] MTS Archive Util
[N] New Files          [O] Old Files Lister  [X] Sysop Menu

New Parents Network     Tucson, Arizona      Voice: (602) 327-1451
FidoNet: 1:300/31       NPNet: 79:300/31     BBS:   (602) 326-9345


            20 Minutes Remaining - Select Command:
```

DELPHI'S connection

Lange's efforts have been noted in stories on television and in publications such as *The Wall Street Journal*, *Parent Post*, *U.S. News and World Report*, and the *New York Times*. But it was the four-line splash in *USA Today's* Tip Off box that got DELPHI'S attention. "DELPHI contacted me and wanted to know if we wanted to have NPN on DELPHI" Lange said. "In August of 1992, we went online there. I call them daily, upload a new file there as soon as I get it. We also have a forum there of DELPHI users, messages, and so on. All the text files we have on the BBS are on DELPHI."

In most cities, DELPHI is a locally available online service that costs $10 a month for four evening or weekend hours, more during the day. See Chapter 11.

NPN software

Lange speaks with special pride of the New Parents Network's (NPN) first version of software as a further extension of its national information system NPNet. Now hospitals, universities, public libraries, etc., can set up dedicated computer sites and provide NPN Software to their employees and the population they serve.

While the New Parents Network distributes these educational parenting files through its computer bulletin board system (BBS) network and through the international commercial network DELPHI, Lange hopes to reach even more parents with New Parents Network Software. "NPN Software is a powerful tool for institutions to educate the general population that might not have access to a computer and modem," she said, pointing out that unless one lived in Tucson to receive the printed packets she began with, a modem was the only way to enter NPNet.

Her first client, Tucson Medical Center, a member of the nonprofit Voluntary Hospitals of America, is setting up dedicated computers throughout the hospital and installing NPN Software. The data on these computers will be updated bimonthly, she said, so the latest information will be available to parents as soon as they have the baby.

"Through these computer sites, TMC is able to reach all socio-economic levels of the population with vital parenting information," she said. Using a touch screen program, developed with the help of Tucson Medical Center, this original program includes computers with NPN Software that are available for maternity patients and their families, right in the maternity ward. All a parent has to do is walk over, select the needed subject, and print it out on the nearby jet printers. All maternity patients will leave the hospital with a New Parents Network brochure detailing how the parent can keep in touch with NPN for further information once they are home. Additionally, nursing stations throughout the hospital and special computer stations in lobbies will also carry the software, reaching employees and hospital visitors. She hopes to soon have it in libraries and other public service sites.

"New Parents Network is a centralized point to gather and disseminate information of great importance to our nation's parents," said Lange. "Parenting is one of the most challenging experiences in life, and without education and access to simple information, we will continue to see the kinds of crises that frequently headline the news. New Parents Network provides an organized link that responds quickly and clearly to parenting needs and concerns. NPNet's evolutionary character is unique because the more it is used, the more complete it will become."

New Parents Network urges all social services, support groups and government agencies that assist parents and children to have a complete description of their services on NPNet free of charge. Lange hopes having the licensed software in many sites will not only reach more parents but also help gather more localized information for the data bank.

The future

Lange has three major goals for the future of her organization: "I'd like to see a BBS with a toll-free number in each state with NPNet information on it," Lange said. "But more importantly, I'd like to see all hospitals nationwide have the licensed software. And I'd like to take the information gathered by NPNet by electronic means turned into a series of publications for maternity patients: a national directory and state editions." More immediately she hopes to have several toll-free lines to the headquarters BBS.

But right now, just as it is, NPNet is something no new parent should be without.

20 RIME rings the world

E-mail	*runninga* [RIME mail net]
U.S. Mail	6901 Whittier Blvd.
	Bethesda, MD 20817
Phone	(301) 229-7574 [fax]
Modem	Your local RIME BBS's
Hours	Your Local Rime BBS's
Basic rates	$75 to become a RIME BBS. Otherwise your local BBS's charges.
Notes	A decidedly non-techie, highly personal mail echo. And proud of it.

"We are RelayNet International Message Exchange, or Relay or RelayNet," says Bonnie Anthony. "We started this because my brother in New York and I wanted to communicate electronically. We had both just gotten a PC and modems, and so we got PCBMAIL and tried to make it work." That was 1988, when her family, friends and patients were all beginning to get into computers and modems. Now RIME is something of an institution.

Now at nearly 1000 BBSs around the world ("Croatia, Russia, Japan, Brazil, the Caribbean, Africa, Canada, the US . . .," rattles off Anthony) they have nearly 400 conferences and move about 5 megabytes of mail a day.

Some sample conferences:

Name	Electronic Freedom Foundation (EEF)
Number	357
Description	A bridged conference with the Internet. Discussions center around how they are a watchdog in Congress for laws as they pertain to CyberSpace.
Host	Jim Wenzel Node ID ->GRAPEVINE #318

Name	Advertising
Number	361
Description	This conference will examine and critique all forms of advertising: TV, radio, magazine and other print media (i. e., billboards). All areas

of this industry will be explored: agencies (practices and ethics); mechanics (how ads are done); effectiveness; enjoyment by consumer (versus the irritation factor), favorite ads, etc.

Host   Kelly Keniston Node ID ->OLDTOWN #203

Name   TECHNO-ETHICS (TechEthc)
Number   382
Description   Discussions on the ethical and legal implications of new and soon to be developed technologies.
Host   Bart Lidofsky Node ID ->RUNNINGB #3

Name   BOSTON COMPUTER SOCIETY (BCS)
Number   387
Description   The BCS is a large international organization with over 22,000 members. The BCS is dedicated to helping users advance in their knowledge of the use of computers. It provides over 70 meetings per month and has user groups set up for specific computer systems as well as for certain purposes within the field of computers. This conference is 'bridged' with FIDO through EAGLE Site 8.
Host   Robert Gorill "BRIDGED CONFERENCE"

Who's who

RIME is proud of their organization, which to date is still mainly volunteer. The people who keep it running as of December 1992 are as follows:

Steering committee

Bonnie Anthony	RUNNINGA	Rex Hankins	IBMNET
Howard Belasco	RUNNINGB	J. Thomas Howell	MORE
Mike Glenn	PARTY		

Conference related

Rick Kingslan	OMAHANET	Marketing Coordinator (PR)
Patrick Lee	RUNNINGB	Statistician
James Wall	DREAM	Conference Manager
Penny Plant	BOREALIS	Conference Moderator
Lana Fox	MODEMZNE	COMMON

The cooperation and dedication of this group is also evident in their conference rules.

Beside the usual injunctions against flaming—profane or not—advertising is allowed only in the appropriate conference: BBS operators can advertise their boards in BBS AD and anything for sale can be posted to FORSALE. ANSI fans have their own conference, but one cannot post ANSI graphics in any other conference. (ANSI graphics are pictures, menus, colored letters and so forth. They use up MANY more bytes than ASCII—just plain old letters.)

Signatures are limited to two lines and ASCII characters, too. We've seen before how signatures, while cute, should be short and to the point. A common practice among many net users is to copy a message from one conference, or even one net, to another, if it seems interesting and pertinent. At first glance, this seems harmless. But it is strictly verboten on RIME unless you have permission of the originator of the message. Further, anyone who posts the private transmissions meant for the administration to the general users' purview might wind up RIMEless.

If you have a gripe or difference of opinion over rules or the administration of them, you must use the NETADMIN or USERS conferences for this. The rules state that you are to approach the person with a private message, politely expressing the problem, and work it out from there. Things might eventually be taken to the top (the people mentioned earlier) or even to Bonnie. Things are quite serious by that point, so try to avoid that.

Some RIME history

Until August of 1992, they used PCRELAY (at one time, Anthony said that "PCB ECHO software wasn't available, they had 20 boards and were very exclusive. We're not like that.") and now use and sell POSTLINK. Along the way they tried to separate the mail community from the software, going from being called PCRELAY to RelayNet to RIME (Relay International Mail Exchange).

"Of the small networks, we're the biggest," she says. "We're certainly not as big as the Internet, but we're the biggest of the small ones. Also, we've been around the longest. We've never split, or disintegrated. Of course I'm prejudiced, but I consider us the prime network, too."

Hobbyists are the emphasis on RIME. Online Alcoholics Anonymous meetings, Survivors of Incest, and Relationships are typical conferences. There are product conferences, too, representing everything from Norton to IBM to modem manufacturers. But relationships and people are the main point, Anthony says.

Which conferences you can get depends upon the sysop's choice. But for the average small, mom-and-pop board, usually if two or three regular users say they want a conference, it can be added.

"We run the gamut. We're not strictly technical, although we have that, of course. But we're for someone who uses a BBS as a means of communication, of reaching out. And it's such a blind medium. No one knows if you are blind, or fat, or decrepit. All you are are your words on the screen. We're not here to support a product, although that happens; it's just a side effect."

A psychologist by trade, with five children, Anthony runs RIME as a hobby/passion. Her oldest son, who was about 13 when RIME began, helped a lot with the network, spending a whole summer learning to program in Turbo Pascal to develop software for it. The other children are hired by Anthony when workload demands it, "and they love the money."

How it runs

"We are an open network," Anthony says. "We'll take anyone who pays the small fee. You have to run the POSTLINK software, that's a requirement (it's the second generation of PCRELAY). And you have to pay $75 for that. That represents a commitment even if you're a teenager, and we have some young sysops; for $75 you have made a commitment to RIME."

The sysops, who include a few females, decide how many and which conferences to carry, although RIME requests certain generic ones are carried by all. The conferences chosen help determine the flavor of the board, she points out. Some are strictly for people recovering from various mental and emotional ills; they might opt only for the conferences that deal with recovery, ignoring the technical, chatty, or product-oriented ones.

"Some take them all, while some take 10, and that's ok with us," Anthony says.

The following is the file given to RIME sysops:

A brief word on RELAYNET:

1) over 350 ACTIVE conferences available—broad range of topics (active on our network means if you take all our own conferences, 4.5 megabytes of new quality mail available daily!) Others claim activity and quality—we provide it!

2) only two required conferences—COMMON conference, which provides a link between every board in the network and a small announcement-only conference—RIMENEWS

3) all conferences available to every node—each node selects those conferences that interest him/her in order to maintain own BBS "flavor"

4) powerful software, auto-configurable for conferences, add and subtract with ease, sysop flexibility, real routed mail, file sends, file requests

5) over 975 active boards—including Canada, Saudi Arabia, Norway, Denmark, Portugal, Spain, Holland, England, Japan, Sweden, Yugoslavia, Taiwan, New Zealand, Brazil, Mexico, Croatia, Yugoslavia, France, and Russia, to name a few.

6) friendly group of sysops, working together to produce an outstanding network

7) your board maintains it own internal structure, no need to conform to a network-wide structure

8) interactions with other networks—including MediaNet, MetroLink. In the main however, we support our own conferences with our own usership. Watch your user base increase when they discover the potential of International communications with active message bases and outstanding discussions.

9) not limited to PCBoard, network includes QBBS, RBBS, WildCat, EIS, GAP, SpitFire, TBBS, Remote Access, Tritel among others—many author supported—almost any system is welcomed.

10) We allow you to remain a member of any other network of your choosing

11) for information on joining, call:

- the Running Board * Bethesda, MD, (301) 229-5342/5623 (dual standards)
- the Running Board * New York City, NY, (212) 654-1349
- or any board listed in our RelayNet list!!!

The sales pitch is not all fluff, as we'll see later, when we talk to a RIME sysop.

The RIME is very controlled. It's a three-tiered system, with Anthony's as the top. This gives the mail handling a rapid turnaround, of which she is proud.

"I watch my system like a hawk. October 10, in fact, and I remember because it was my daughter's birthday, I came home to find my server dead as a doornail. Someone on the network loaned me a $2000 hard drive, someone else on the net came over to help. We had the system back up in 36 hours. That's all from volunteer work. That's what we're all about."

It's all fun and pleasure for her, she said, "except the phone bills. It's an expensive hobby."

"We're friendly, and certainly cheaper than the commercial nets. For the individual we offer much . . . personal relationships. We might not have MicroSoft but we have real people. You become part of a community," Anthony says.

As an example, during the Gulf War, when mail could not get through to Saudi Arabia, boards all over RIME banded together to get messages through. Using faxes, BBS systems, printers and footwork, families of troops were able to send letters to their loved ones in Saudi Arabia; the soldiers could send back 25 words. This was at a time when the US couldn't find room on the transports for personal mail. This was done by volunteers, for as long as it was needed.

"That's what we're all about," says Anthony.

A sample RIME BBS

Power Windows! BBS, run by Cyrus Cathey of Huntsville, Alabama, has been a RIME hub since August of 1992. Sitting in a hi-tech town, Cathey chose RIME for its personality. After running a BBS for two and a half years, he felt RIME would fill a gap in the local online community.

Figure 20-1 shows some of Cathey's choices for RIME conferences.

```
Conferences available:

   0) Power Windows Hoopla-(LO)    1) Comments to SysOp----(LO)
   2) WindNoise News-------(LO)    3) Alias Conference-----(LO)
   4) PC-HELP--------------(LO)    5) Modems & Commo-------(LO)
   6) Windows--------------(LO)    7) OS/2-----------------(LO)
   8) Windows NT-----------(LO)    9) BBS Users in Training!
  11) Ultimate Gamers------(LO)   12) MIDI Maestro---------(LO)
  13) The Hangar-----------(LO)   14) Religion ------------(LO)
  15) Computer Flea Market-(LO)   16) Tennessee Valley News(LO)
  17) Power Win Contributor(LO)   21) Common-Net Messages--(RI)
  22) Newusers------------(RI)    23) Relay Users----------(RI)
  24) Rime News-----------(RI)    25) Buy & Sell-----------(RI)
  26) Ansi Codes----------(RI)    27) Astrology------------(RI)
  28) Audio---------------(RI)    29) BBS Issues-----------(RI)
  30) Beer!---------------(RI)    31) CD Rom--------------(RI)
  32) Communications------(RI)    33) C Language----------(RI)
  34) Boating-------------(RI)    35) ASP Support --------(RI)
  36) Deadhead------------(RI)    37) Desqview------------(RI)
  38) DOS-----------------(RI)    39) Data Protection-----(RI)
  40) Engineering---------(RI)    41) Entertainment-------(RI)
  42) Electronic Freedom!--(RI)   43) Financial-----------(RI)
-Pause- [C]ontinue, [N]onStop, [S]top? [C]
```

20-1
Like most BBS sysops, Cathey will add the conferences his regular users say that they want.

"I feel the reason BBS were started was the exchange of information among people of similar interest. Not really for files, because the files just support the things talked about in the messages. I wanted a good e-mail network or offer. There were already FIDO and ILINK nodes here, but no RIME," Cathey said.

FIDO being anarchistic, and ILINK being very technical, Cathey felt there was room for some human interest e-mail.

"In my opinion, RIME and ILINK are the best BBS nets available. RIME is more personal, very people-oriented. ILINK is more technologically oriented. The messages on RIME are about people. It has many, many, many conferences that deal with nothing but social issues, human interest issues.

"The people are wonders. In communication with RIME people, I have found a tremendous outpouring of support you just don't find with ILINK."

Which leads to the only negative things Cathey could bring himself to say about RIME. As the network was changing over from RELAY to the current software (POSTLINK), at first it was an option, and the two mail systems were running parallel. Of course, some BBS sysops were clinging to the tried and true (and paid for!) and weren't getting on the bandwagon fast enough. So finally a drop dead date was established to get the new program or be off the mail distribution.

Which would have been fine, except the new program didn't work very well. And this was the very time frame during which Cathey was trying to set up his RIME hub.

"I had called Bonnie's bulletin board just to find out about RIME, and she jumped on in chat mode. I asked her how to become a hub, and she said she had none in North Alabama, why didn't I just download the software package now and mail her the registration fee later? This is after 8 months of trying to get ILINK to even talk to me. So I did. But we had a lot of problems."

Deluged with complaints, Anthony had to set up some volunteers around the country to consult with the hub sysops on getting the new system running. Lana Fox spent eight hours on the phone with Cathey one day until the program was working. This has been typical of RIME's way, Cathey said: Hold your hand and work until it's done.

Cathey noted something else as this was progressing: on other nets, when the e-mail is not getting through, the messages to the local sysop tend to be along the lines of "Why the hell aren't the messages getting through? I'm waiting for a reply on X conference! Are you going to get the mail or not?!"

But on RIME, the messages were of genuine concern, he said. "That's the kind of thing you find here: 'What's wrong, and how can I help?'"

The new user should definitely introduce herself in the NEWUSERS conference, where greetings from old RIME hands and tips on getting the most out of RIME will rebound.

Mailing on RIME

They will tell you first to download RIMEMAN.ZIP from your local BBS and read it. It's full of useful tips, the rules of the RIME, and the important skill of routing messages.

Messages on RIME can be marked "private," so that only the recipient need download it. But be aware that the sysops, the conference moderators and the other RIME administrators can read any mail on the net at will.

Similarly, to save on everyone's phone bill, RIME has a system of routing messages to only the recipient's board, not across the international net.

You should send a routed note in reply to someone, when that reply wouldn't interest everyone else in the world.

To do that, first look at the END of the message you want to reply to. It will look something like this:

   * PostLink(tm) v1.04 AJJJR (#5011) : RelayNet(tm) Hub

PostLink(tm) v1.04 tells you this is a message from RIME. AJJJR and 5011 are the id codes you need to send the message on a particular route. The AJJJR is called the id code and the 5011 is the site number. Using a dash and a greater than sign ->, you can use either of these to route the message to just that board. If your sysop allows private messages, it can also be made private.

So, using what ever method you usually do, REPLY to the message. The *first characters* of that reply should be:

```
->5011
```

or they could be:

```
->AJJJR
```

Then skip a line or put in a few spaces and start your message. Put no characters in front of the ->. Then, the boards and people not concerned with this message won't spend a second downloading your message.

It's all part of trying to control, politely, what is going on.

Standing guard

In that spirit, all RIME BBS get the RIME TIMES, an online newsletter about goings on in the online network world (sometimes called CyberSpace). A recent issue had an excellent article citing several cases of BBS in general and "hackers" in particular being portrayed as scum. From reading these books, articles, and in one astounding case, a press release from a major software company, one would think that CyberSpace makes the Wild West look like Queen Victoria's court.

But rather than moan about it, RIME TIMES had several practical tips for sysops and users to help improve the image of BBS and hackers, who are generally just people trying to make software work for people instead of the other way around. The suggestions, by Curt Akin in his "Frankly, Curt" column, included

- Don't let negative articles go unanswered. Write letters or make phone calls to editors and tell the positive side of BBS.
- Don't let the "nasty" stuff go by, either. Report people who leave counterfeit messages. Report those who pirate software on their boards.

In the same issue was a touching story: after sending messages to a point of becoming online friends, two RIME users met in person. A few more months of messages back and forth followed, 4400 miles apart, and gradually they began to notice they had fallen in love. The article does not mention on which conference they met and fell in love, but they got married in December 1992 (F2F!)

That's RIME: A very personal network.

Appendices
Being there

We discover some adventures journeying electronically, and some things that make it easier.

Appendix A   *Around the world in 80 minutes.* " Phileas Fogg" journey recreated with systems you've read about.

Appendix B   *Electronic Frontier Foundation.* Not a service or BBS, but text fields, discussions, and messages available on many systems, large and small.

Appendix C   *Your first trip on the Internet.*

Around the world in 80 minutes

PC-Computing, Oct 1992 v5 n10 p200(7)
By Michy Peshota

It was an ordinary day on the BBS when I made the innocent remark that was to set in motion the electronic journey of a lifetime. "There isn't a country on the map you can't send electronic mail to," I said.

"That's wrong. Global connectivity is a wash," proclaimed a closet Luddite. "I can hardly e-mail my mom on Sundays without a long-distance network jam signal croaking in my modem."

"I've heard that there are places where they don't even have fiberoptic phone lines yet," a Yankee elitist sniffed.

"That's right!" exclaimed another in the next message. "In some countries, you can't even get a long-distance fiberoptic calling card."

Soon everyone was placing bets. As often happens on computer bulletin boards, not everyone was sure what they were betting on or even what the bickering was about in the first place, but before long the situation became clear: There was a wager on as to whether I could, with the help of my faithful modem Passepartout, forge a unique e-mail link with every major location visited by Jules Verne's intrepid globe-trotter " Phileas Fogg" in *Around the World in Eighty Days*. My modem and I had just 80 minutes to do it. We were allowed to use only one phone line, and long-distance calls were forbidden, although we could place as many local calls as we wished.

There was an easy way to do this: We could have dialed any of the major e-mail services such as Sprint Mail, MCI Mail, or ATTMail—all of which can be accessed in virtually any country in the world—and with a single command dispatched memos to all those ports. But that would have been dull, like riding a Greyhound Scenicruiser all the way across the country without ever getting out. So we chose more exotic routes—FidoNet to Hong Kong, Internet to Calcutta, USENET to San Francisco—using a different means of communication to each locale.

The stakes were high. Were we to succeed, skeptics would be forced to concede that the world is contracting into a smaller electronic place—that it is as easy to hobnob with Indian princes via e-mail each morning as it is to wrangle with one's boss over the office LAN. Were we to fail, we would be known forever on our favorite BBS as Big Talkers with Limited Connectivity.

Passepartout & I reach the City of Light

My guide and companion in my travels, Passepartout, had entered my life by way of a mail-order catalog. At first I'd lacked confidence in the light, plastic box that came to me in a Ziploc bag without the benefit of a warranty card. I'd grown up in a time when one trusted only leaden appliances, ornamented with chrome and rubber feet, that shared the same ancestry as a boat anchor. I came from a place where one never set out on a road trip driving anything lighter than a Buick. This modem looked like it would be the first thing to melt were lightning to strike my desk. But despite its resemblance to a cheap dime store recipe-card file, Passepartout soon proved itself capable of agile and unexpected feats like error-checking computer data on the windiest phone lines and holding a phone connection while the dog sat on top of it. Our journey would test its powers to the limit.

Our first stop was Paris, and we arrived in good form on MCI Mail. There we found ourselves surrounded by the bustle of grand public computer networks with elegant names, all built around lofty dreams. ARISTOTE, for example, is a research network designed specifically to facilitate the daily hobnobbing of French telecommunications experimenters and gurus. ARISTOTE is both French for Aristotle and an acronym for the Association of Information Networks in a Completely Open and Very Elaborate System. Who but the French would so fearlessly weave Very Elaborate into a computer acronym?

As with food and fashion, the French networking vision is bold, one step ahead of the times. Paris was a hub in one of the world's first computer networks— CYCLADES (named for a ringlike archipelago in the Aegean), which was linked by CIGALE, a packet network named after cicadas and their orchestras of chirps. CYCLADES had links to foreign physics labs nearly 20 years ago, when computer communication was as novel a pursuit as hot-air ballooning.

Back in the early eighties, before most people had even heard of the word *modem*, the French government was passing out free terminals to its citizens to replace their phone books. With the terminals, the French could connect to Minitel, a video text service and a forerunner to Prodigy. Since then, Minitel has blossomed into the world's biggest commercial online service, with an estimated four million users, more than all such services in the United States combined. The French have plans to expand Minitel around the globe, even into the United States.

On MCI, we posted a message to Lambert Mayer, an international public relations consultant and e-mail bon vivant who connects to MCI Mail several times a day from his Paris office via TRANSPAC, the French computer packet network. He also connects to CompuServe. He told us of wild CompuServe user parties in Paris, and we yearned to stay. But we had to proceed to Italy, to the small ferry town of Brindisi, located in the heel of the boot.

There we sent a note, on MCI, to Manuel Fernandez, a physics student at the University of Lecce, which is about 20 miles from Brindisi, who goes by the log-on *nom de plume* "Terminator." Through the physics department, Manuel taps numerous international e-mail networks through the network of the Italian National Institute for Nuclear Physics. Our message to him bounced from MCI to Internet to INFNET, the physics network.

We also wrote to Carlo Rizzo, a recent graduate in electrical engineering who lives in York, England, but maintains an INFNET e-mail box in Lecce, where he grew up. He accesses the mailbox daily through a tortuous international computer network route for reasons we could only ascribe to homesickness.

Down the Mediterranean, the next stop on " Phileas Fogg's" original itinerary—Suez— posed a problem: We could not hunt down an e-mail correspondent there. But we did find one in nearby Cairo—a harried American writer teaching at American University, who could only drop a quick note on her way to summer in Europe. Her message traveled by way of the Egyptian Science and Technology Network—the sole e-mail network there, which links the universities—on to BITNET, through Princeton, on to Internet, and then to us on MCI Mail. It took several messages to reach her, and she me. There are a few BBS in Egypt, enough for at least one American BBS Fido-like message network, SmartNet, to extend there.

In *Around the World in Eighty Days*, " Phileas Fogg's" trans-India trek was interrupted when the railroad tracks ended without warning in the middle of a forest—he was forced to purchase an elephant to get to the point where the tracks resumed. We had anticipated similar trouble in reaching Bombay, the next stop on our itinerary: According to the reports we'd heard, phone connections there sound worse than a walkie-talkie at a rock concert. Our Bombay pen pal, Peter Walker, says it takes him an hour of successive tries to phone his wife and tell her that he'll be late for dinner.

Eastward, ho!

While phone service in parts of India is primitive and patchy (it takes six months to two years to get a phone there), the situation is improving, especially in cities like Bombay. Half the phone exchanges there are modern digital ones. A new fiber cable links Bombay with Delhi, and digital microwave connects a number of other Indian cities. Although computer bulletin boards are as sparse in this technologically barren land as alkaline batteries and modern cars, tens of thousands of PCs and modems have been sold in India in recent years.

Peter, an Australian banker who is working on setting up a network to link Indian banks, dials CompuServe several times a week through international long-distance lines. There's nothing like Telnet or Tymnet in India to ease his bill. When he was first transferred to Bombay, he couldn't get phone connections clean enough to allow him to communicate with CompuServe until a friend pulled strings and got him a spot on one of the city's new digital exchanges. Now most of his calls to CompuServe go through. I sent him a message through CompuServe, and it was just like mailing a postcard to a friend down the street (although it took him two tries over static-filled phone lines to pick it up).

Writing from Bombay, a gracious and erudite computer enthusiast who signs his messages S. Ramani and works at India's National Centre for Software Technology introduced us to a coffee klatch of modem users all the way across the country in

Calcutta. All were denizens of India's budding Education and Research Network, which was conceived three years ago by the Centre for Software Technology. The network links 4000 Indian computer users on 80 campuses throughout India and ties into UUNET in Falls Church, Virginia, via a 9600-bit-per-second leased line.

Curiously, none of the correspondents identified themselves by any name other than "Postmaster," and none divulged anything about themselves other than the places where they worked—places with futuristic names like Nodal Centre for Knowledge-Based Computing or Variable Energy Cyclotron Centre, all of which portend great things to come technology-wise for India. Their messages wound their way from Calcutta over ERnet, via a network host computer called Shakti—that's Indian for "peace"—over UUNET to the United States, on to Internet, and finally to me on MCI Mail. It usually took two or three attempts to get a message back to them.

I was confident that our next stop, Hong Kong, would be the easiest place to e-mail. After all, the eastern trade mecca teems with brilliant, state-of-the-art BBS. There are hundreds of them, each decorated with lavish, often animated screens featuring skyscrapers replete with blinking lights, all boasting top-speed modems and more call-in lines than a charity telethon. But none of my requests for conversation mailed over either the international BBS network FidoNet or Internet netted a single response from the boards—not even from the one where the sysop referred to himself on the greeting screen as "Your BBS Friend."

I sent more messages but received no replies. Time was running out. In desperation, I sent an emotional plea for help to my "BBS Friend." Finally, one of my dispatches landed in the hands of Samson Luk, coordinator of FidoNet in Hong Kong and Macao.

Samson explained the silence that greeted me in his city. "Ninety-five percent of the sysops in Hong Kong are teenagers," he said, "and you will find they are not mature enough to communicate with others." He described the world of Hong Kong BBS as anarchic and rife with bickering, software piracy, and more teenage intrigue than an old Disney movie. "In order to manage such a mess," he said, "I need to enforce FidoNet Policy in a straight and relentless manner." I didn't know what FidoNet Policy was, but I hoped not to learn firsthand.

Samson was an otherwise affable, 30-year-old system security analyst whose street address included the quaintly apt lines "Data Security Division, Happy Valley." His great ambition was to establish a FidoNet-Internet marriage in Hong Kong. While Internet reaches to Hong Kong, the link is owned by the universities, and they refuse to provide feeds to other organizations like FidoNet. In order for a FidoNet BBS user in Hong Kong to send e-mail to a pal in a Hong Kong university, he or she must route the message through Fido offices in Portland, Oregon. An anarchic world, indeed. Luk's other quixotic dream is to one day extend FidoNet into mainland China. I sent him messages through a local Fido BBS over FidoNet to Hong Kong, and also from MCI Mail over Internet, then through FidoNet overseas.

A study in contrasts

Passepartout and I were eager to reach Shanghai. It seemed the most remote and mysterious of our destinations—after a harrowing voyage to this port, " Phileas Fogg" himself had not so much as set foot on shore. We didn't know much about modeming in China, but we feared the government might have erected a barrier between computer users there and in the outside world. Our contact was a graphic designer named Welkins Yang who works for a Far East franchise of Alpha-Graphics. We conversed with him via Connect, the American online service that his employer relies on to keep its American, Shanghai, Beijing, and Hong Kong offices in touch with one another.

Welkins' messages traveled to us from his office in Shanghai, over CHINAPAC, the two-year-old government-owned computer-packet network; through a satellite link to Tymnet, the American packet network; on to Connect in Cupertino, California. A reserved young man, Welkins' main ambition in life is to have enough time and "quietness" to read and study—an example the Hong Kong BBS operators would do well to emulate.

Welkins could not tell us if there were any BBS in China, and no one else we contacted there could provide any information, either. Circumstances make it unlikely: Phone service is poor, and few Chinese citizens own phones, probably because it costs the average person at least two years' income to install one. (Even those who can afford a phone or have an employer who will subsidize one may spend years haggling with the Chinese government.)

It's not against the law in China to own a PC or modem, but few Chinese have those, either: A PC costs four years' income, while a modem cost one years'. At this point, there are no regulations against dialing out with a modem; but since the Tiananmen Square uprising, when Chinese students deluged the world with faxes, authorities have cracked down on fax ownership, requiring citizens to register fax machines and pay extra fees to own one. We heard rumors of laws against connecting modems to phone lines in cities like Beijing.

A couple of struggling academic networks exist, but lack of government funding has curtailed their growth. Accounts on these networks cost an emperor's ransom—a month's subscription to one Chinese research network runs what a college professor earns in a year. A few Chinese universities enjoy a tenuous tie to Internet through a 2400-bps satellite link to a computer in Germany, but since users are billed staggering fees for any e-mail they receive, the Chinese prefer to keep their Internet addresses secret from the rest of the world. Chinese citizens do not have access to USENET or any other international message systems on which they can communicate freely with the outside world.

Large American companies operating in China have far less trouble than Chinese citizens gaining access to global e-mail nets, but costs are high, and they do occasionally find themselves smuggling in telecommunications gear. One can't help but wonder what will happen to those gaudy Hong Kong BBS once that city becomes part of China.

Across the East China Sea to Yokohama, we found electronic life more relaxed and immeasurably more cosmopolitan. Via the American online service GEnie, we conversed in ASCII with Janusz Buda, a university English teacher living in southern suburbs of the Tokyo-Yokohama metro sprawl. "As I write, the neighborhood announcement system has just finished playing the daily five o'clock time-for-kids-to-go-home melody," said Janusz, making Yokohama sound a bit like Mayberry R.F.D., were an efficiency expert to get hold of it. General Electric's GEnie is a menu option on the Japanese commercial online service PC-VAN, which Janusz connects to for a pricey $42.52 per hour.

Commercial online services are prevalent in Yokohama. In addition to PC-VAN, Janusz has access to Nifty-Serve, a jumbo Japanese service that's affiliated with

CompuServe; Nikkei MIX, a service with links to Byte's BIX; and a plethora of bulletin boards. (Lambert, over in Paris, told us that the first time he visited Japan, he sent messages to a group of Japanese CompuServe users whom he had never met. He was later greeted by ten of them at his hotel, some bearing gifts.)

From Yokohama, we skipped to San Francisco on USENET, the helter-skelter academic network where potential Nobel laureates fritter away their professional careers niggling about dog-training or Star Trek, like freshmen in a campus pub. In the public newsgroup devoted to boomerang use and appreciation, we corresponded with William Rodarmor, a university alumni magazine editor who had recently celebrated his 50th birthday by bungee jumping. Our greetings to him ricocheted off a local BBS onto USENET and across the country to The Well, the hip San Francisco electronic salon owned by The Whole Earth Catalog people.

After that, we hopped to New York on SmartNet. A BBS network similar to FidoNet, but smaller and emphasizing computer support, SmartNet links BBS as far away as Thailand and Argentina with the help of private leased phone lines and the communications resources of foreign offices of corporate patrons like Hayes Microcomputer and Quarterdeck Office Systems. We penned a memo to Larry Rosen, a service manager for educational computer networks in Long Island, who dials up several local BBS and checks for mail each morning. Our message bounced to him from a local SmartNet BBS to a SmartNet BBS in New York.

Our final port of call was " Phileas Fogg's" starting point and final destination, London, which we reached via another BBS network, ILink. ILink began as a FidoNet competitor five years ago and now connects about 250 BBS from Yugoslavia to Spain. From ILink's hub in New York, we dispatched a message across the Atlantic. There it was picked up on The Candy Shack BBS by Pete Hall, a technician at British Telecom. Pete haunts British boards and the London CompuServe node the way other Londoners frequent pubs—to make friends and chat. He reports, though, that modems are far less common in London than in the United States because local phone calls there cost so much more.

Back home

The hands of my synchronized Windows icon clock and Mickey Mouse watch simultaneously touched midnight. It had taken exactly 80 minutes to rattle off e-mail messages to correspondents in the major locations visited by Verne's footsore " Phileas Fogg" We had won!

A rough calculation of the online costs involved brought the bill to just under $20—most of that spent on dispatches mailed to indifferent teenyboppers on Hong Kong BBS. Most of the pen pals had received and replied to their electronic messages by that afternoon, although e-mail to India and Egypt took several days to reach its destination, as did messages wired over the BBS networks. In a few cases, I received no replies for several days.

Passepartout's modem-ready light blinked off in fatigue, and I settled back in my chair. Unlike Verne's hero, we had not rescued any Indian princesses or been chased by warring Apaches. Just as well, I thought, for the warranty on my PC motherboard had expired long ago. But I had learned many new ways to communicate with friends in Bombay and Cairo, and—as we'd proved—that kind of information never fails to come in handy in this day and age.

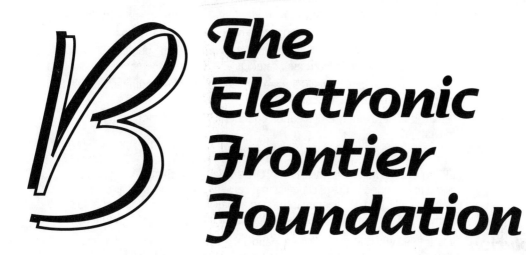

The Electronic Frontier Foundation

E-mail	*info@eff.org*
U.S. Mail	155 Second St.
	Cambridge, MA 02141
Phone	(617) 864-0665 [voice]
Basic Rate	$40.00 per year
Notes	Not a service or BBS, but text and messages available on the WELL, CompuServe, and other services.

We must all get along in this new place, called the underground, the frontier, the network. This is new territory, and some rules will have to be written, others rewritten. Some will remain unwritten and unenforceable except that if you violate them, no one in the virtuous part of the virtual society will speak to you. Yet we do not have to flounder about: we can organize, prioritize, and bring logic and cool reason to the process. And to that end, the Electronic Frontier Foundation was founded.

"The casual modem user should know our phone number [(617) 864-0665] and the name Mike Godwin (our staff counsel) in case of trouble. Although we only take on cases that promise to set legal precedent, Mike can do two things for you. First, we have a Cooperating Counsel Network, which is a group of attorneys familiar with and willing to take on cases involving computer crime and intellectual property. Secondly, if you already have an attorney, Mike can work with her and inform her of pertinent cases and information," according to Rita Rouvalis, an EFF staff member.

The staff at the main office includes:

Mitchell Kapor, the President and cofounder of the organization. His function is to supply know-how and organizational ability, as well as answer volumes of e-mail to the EFF. (Mitch is the founder of Lotus Development Corp.)

Mike Godwin, the EFF staff counsel, counsels people from all over the country on the nature of the law and its still unsettled relation to electronic travellers.

Rita Rouvalis is the associate editor. Her job includes diverse online publications, disparate discussion groups on the Internet, and incessant telephone calls.

Regina Blaney is the office manager. She handles the memberships.

Hae-Young Rieh Hwang—the librarian—keeps track of the perpetual stream of documents (paper and electronic), catalogs and arranges them.

Helen Rose and Chris Davis EFF's are the steadfast system administrators and despots of Internet Relay Chat.

Gerard Van der Leun is EFF's editor, communications director, and general roustabout.

EFF also has a brand-new Washington office.

EFF's paper newsletter is the EFFECTOR, and is free of charge. You only need to be asked to be added to the mailing list to receive it. EEFector Online is distributed only electronically. You can acquire it through e-mail if you are on the Internet in some fashion, FTP it from their archives, or download it from various BBS around the world.

EFF's evolution

It was 1990 when Mitchell D. Kapor and John Perry Barlow noticed a very disturbing legal situation and decided to begin the EFF to help rectify the wrong. Kapor (who founded Lotus) and Barlow (Grateful Dead lyricist and former cattle rancher/cowboy) saw a glaring example of how little some law enforcement authorities understand the technology and reality of the electronic underground.

Further, they saw a conflict between those who see information as free and those who see it as a commodity; between the need for access and the physical limitations of the Internet; between what the public knew about telecomputing and what they need to know. Laws (by nature local beasts) might not be able to cover all aspects of the international Internet, but it's a place to start. Though the First Amendment does not help the Chinese or the French, it can and must be upheld here. You won't be able to keep the politicians out anyway, and where they go, the police must follow. They saw that cooperation among the lawmakers, law enforcers, and the citizens of the virtual society would be the only answer.

What brought this to their attention was the case of Steve Jackson Games. The owner and namesake found himself the target of a Secret Service operation that seized all his company's assets and property. The case might have been funny as a movie; as reality, it was as bizarre as it was frightening. At first, Jackson had no idea why he was being raided.

Then, the Secret Service said they were impounding the company's computers and records because Jackson was about to publish a game that would have promoted hacking. Then, in court, they said it was REALLY because Jackson had published on the company's bulletin board system a highly secret, sensitive document about 911.

Steve Jackson Games has filed suit, with the help of EFF, against the US Secret Service. It is still in the filing stage and has yet to go to court.

But at the beginning of all this, seeing Jackson's plight got Barlow and Kapor moving. With seed money from their own pockets and from those of a few good friends in the computer industry, EFF was planted at the WELL, and within a year had its own Internet address (eff.org). They gave grants to help Jackson and others with defense costs (which were astronomical for a small businessman) and filed briefs pointing out the First and Fourth Amendment issues.

The EFF's position can be summed up this way: The Secret Service said they were preventing publication of something. According to the First Amendment, that's not supposed to happen except in extremely dangerous circumstances, proven in court before a judge. That step was overlooked. Further, while the search warrant was for one thing, their true intention was to stop publication of some "sensitive" 911 system information. The Fourth Amendment was violated at that point. Finally, the whole point was supposed to be that the government was cracking down on computer crime, but no crime had been proven. Cracking up a business is what they almost did—all from misunderstanding the nature of computers, computer crime, and the electronic underground.

At about this same time Craig Neirdorf, a 20-year-old college student was indicted for publishing in his newsletter a document about . . . 911. The truth was that, rather than being private and sensitive, that document was available—*legally*—for less than $20. EFF came to his aid with *amicus curiae*[1]. Again, the court costs were and still are high, and EFF members have volunteered their help. Craig is now an EFF staff member.

From the very beginning, the EFF has been firm about people who steal, defraud or damage information and services by computer: they are forthrightly against it. Yet, in some cases, when the government brings such charges, neither intent to damage nor genuine hurt are criteria used in the prosecution. These are essential, according to the EFF.

"I regard unauthorized entry into computer systems as wrong and deserving of punishment," Kapor wrote in EFF's first newsletter, December 10, 1990. [Look on the Well or CompuServe's EFFSIG Forum or EFF's own archives for this. It is necessary and important reading for those traveling the electronic pathways.] "People who break into computer systems and cause harm should be held accountable for their actions. We need to make appropriate distinctions in the legal code among various forms of computer crime based on such factors as intent and the degree of actual damage." Today, in addition to defending victims of the government's ignorance, the EFF is

- Sponsoring conferences and seminars for law, government and computer professionals on computer freedom and privacy.
- Speaking at various groups on EFF and its mission.
- Giving grants in aid to Computer Professionals for Social Responsibility for education efforts.
- Lobbying at the state and national level for open access to the Internet computer networks; affordable ISDN for every home; and rational and fair laws concerning computer crime.
- Maintaining a document library with all the EFF news releases and position statements. You can access it via anonymous FTP from *eff.org*. Mail *ftphelp@eff.org* with any questions on how to access it.
- Operating an active conference on the WELL, and a forum on CompuServe (EFFSIG).

• • • • • • • • •

[1]Latin for "friend of the court," *amicus curiae* is when a person or organization not involved in a case sends useful, pertinent information to the court. *Amicus curiae* briefs are usually submitted when the case involves matters of wide public interest.

- Hoping you will join them. Membership is $20 for students and $40 for other people. Their snail mail address is listed at the top of the appendix, and their phone numbers are (617) 864-0665 [voice] and (617) 864-0866 [fax]. They never sell their membership list and will not share your name with other nonprofit organizations unless you tell them in writing it's OK with you.

If there's a Scarlet Pimpernel for the Electronic Traveller, the EFF is it. Get to know them.

Your first trip on the Internet

E-mail *NSFNET-info@merit.edu*
U.S. Mail Merit
901 Hubbard, Pod G
Ann Arbor, MI 48109-2016
Phone (313) 936-3000 [voice]

A good place to start learning your way around the Internet is to send your first message to the Network Information Center (NIC). If you send a message that says "help" to *nsfnet-info@merit.edu*, the spires server will answer. This is provided by Merit, which we'll cover later.

Part of what the server will send you is this:

Your message has been received by the Merit-NSFNET information server. You can use this server to retrieve documents and other information from the Merit-NSFNET Information Services machine. Requested information will be sent to you by electronic mail.

Command syntax:

Commands followed by options in square "[ ]" brackets indicate that an option may be supplied but is not required. In such a case, the command alone will result in a "default" set of information being returned.

Where a command is followed by an option in angle "< >" brackets, an option must be supplied in order for your request to be filled.

The currently available commands are:

    INDEX:

    INDEX [directory-name]

This command will, in its base form, send you a list of the directories to which you have access. If you are interested in the index for a specific directory you can request it by including the directory name as a parameter. The command:

    INDEX LINKLTTR

will result in the index for the "LINKLTTR" directory being sent to you. The lines below are a partial listing from that directory.

The Link Letter (text only version)

LINKLTTR.880401 (Vol. 1, no. 1, 1 Apr 1988)
LINKLTTR.880415 (Vol. 1, no. 2, 15 Apr 1988)
LINKLTTR.880430 (Vol. 1, no. 3, 30 Apr 1988)
LINKLTTR.880513 (Vol. 1, no. 4, 13 May 1988)
LINKLTTR.880527 (Vol. 1, no. 5, 27 May 1988)
LINKLTTR.880610 (Vol. 1, no. 6, 10 Jun 1988)

SEND:

SEND <file.name>

The SEND command can be used to request a specific document. The name of the document, as it appears in the index, needs to be included in this command. The "directory" name should not be part of your request. Based on the index listing above, you would use the command:

SEND LINKLTTR.880527

to have the May 27, 1988, Link Letter sent to you. Some files, due to their length (over 1000 lines) or format (binary), are not available via electronic mail. If you request such a file, you will receive a message indicating that the file cannot be sent by mail, along with information on the use of FTP to retrieve it.

TOPIC:

To retrieve information on a specific subject, you can use the TOPIC command. This command, in the form:

TOPIC <subject> [subject] . . .

will return articles, from the "Link Letter" and other sources, on the subjects specified. For instance, the command: TOPIC grasp spires will retrieve the "Link Letter" articles on GRASP and SPIRES.

"Merit, in partnership with ANS, IBM, MCI, and the State of Michigan, has a contract with NSF [National Science Foundation] to provide backbone services to NSFNET, including user services support to the regional networks," explained one Merit administrator. "Our contract will expire at the end of October, 1992. Since the plans for 'what next?' have not been finalized, we have been given an extension for up to 18 months. (You can find more about the extension by using anonymous FTP to *nic.merit.edu* to retrieve the file /nsfnet/news.releases/nsfnet.project. development.plan. Also available on *nic.merit.edu*, in the directory /cise/recompete, is the just released 'NSF Implementation Plan for Interagency Interim NREN.')"

"Through the Merit/NSFNET project, we provide speakers to give overviews of NSFNET and the Internet, as well as offer seminars on these topics. We produce a newsletter, the Link Letter. We maintain an anonymous FTP archive of materials of general interest on the machine *nic.merit.edu* (also known as *nis.nsf.net*). We have a mail-query-server providing e-mail access to much of this information (send to *nis-info@nis.nsf.net* or, for bitnet, *nis-info@merit*, with no subject, and "help" as the text)," she added. "We have put together an interactive instructional guide to the Internet which runs on a color Macintosh computer. This 'Cruise of the Internet' is available for downloading from *nic.merit.edu*. We make an effort to keep abreast of new developments that make the Internet better accessible and usable by more people . . . not just the 'techies.'"

The NSF Network Service Center is operated by BBN Systems and Technologies (617/873-3400 or *nnsc@nnsc.nsf.net*). The contract from NSF to provide "end-user services" to NSFNET is operating on an extension. Bids are being considered even as this book goes to press. Regardless of who wins this bid, Merit expects to provide these services throughout the extension of the present contract.

Glossary

Some of these terms appear in the text; others are here simply because I know you are going to run across them in your travels along the electronic underground, and wonder "What on earth these people are talking about?" Soon you'll be able to use these terms like a native!

.ARJ   A file's extension denoting it is compressed, using the ARJ format. *See* zip.

arc   A slang term from the copyrighted compression software ARCE. *See* zip.

archie   An archive server program on many Internet systems. It helps you find what's in the archive, under what directory and name. You telnet to the nearest archie server like this—

```
telnet archie.sura.net
```

—and then issue the command to look for a program:

```
prog<topic>
```

When you have a list of programs in that topic, you can request the server to FTP the file to you.

From Scott Yanoff, I have a list of some archie mail servers:

Archie

telnet archie.mcgill.ca or 132.206.2.3 (Can./USA)

telnet archie.funet.fi or 128.214.6.100 (Finland/Europe)

telnet archie.au or 128.184.1.4 (Aussie/NZ)

telnet cs.huji.ac.il or 132.65.6.5 (Israel)

telnet archie.doc.ic.ac.uk or 146.169.3.7 (UK/Europe)

telnet archie.sura.net or 128.167.254.179

telnet archie.unl.edu (Login: archie, pasword: archie1)

telnet archie.ans.net or 147.225.1.2 (North America)

offers: Internet anonymous FTP database. (Login: archie)

Archie mail servers

```
mail archie@<INSERT ONE OF ABOVE ADDRESSES HERE>
```

Subject: help

Offers: alternative Archie access to those w/o FTP or telnet.

ARPA   Advanced Research Projects Agency. Now called DARPA, it is the U.S. government agency that funded the ARPANET, the Plymouth Rock of the electronic underground.

ARPANET   The Internet in its first life. It was a packet switching network, very cutting edge in the early 1970s. It was decommissioned in 1990.

ASCII   The letters of the word are an acronym for American Standard Code for Information Interchange, but hardly anyone remembers that anymore. In normal usage, it means a format for storing files that saves nothing but the letters of the alphabet and punctuation marks—text, not graphics, pictures, or programs. A file stored in ASCII (or, as some lazy typists write it, ascii) has no control characters, no print instructions, nothing you couldn't type with a 1950 Royal typewriter. (Except each digit has its own ASCII code; the capital O and lowercase l are definitely different from the numbers zero and one in ASCII.) Why this matters is covered in the entries for e-mail and FTP.

ASCII download   When you instruct your computer to capture the letters of a text file as they go across the wire (and, incidentally, your screen). If the file is not in ASCII, this won't work.

asynchronous   The most common telecommunications mode. The data stream starts and stops at irregular intervals. Data travels one character at a time at a designated speed. Start bits are sent at the beginning and stop bits at the end of each data word to give some order to the stream. This is always the communications strategy used when a PC is communicating with another PC, a BBS, or online service. Contrasts with synchronous.

backbone   The *main* connection of a network. All sites connected to an intermediate system on the backbone can connect to each other. They also can set up private traffic with each other and bypass the backbone for better cost, performance, or security; but being part of the backbone gives them all a standard protocol to go by. *See* CIX.

baud   A unit of speed in data transmission, named after J.M.E. Baudot (who invented the multiplex code for telegraphs). It is expressed in terms of the number of events (changes of state) that take place in one second. In certain cases, one baud is equal to transmitting one bit per second, but because of the nature of asynchronous communication, that equation does not always hold true.

BBS   A bulletin board system. Most often, one person running a program called something like PCBoard or WildCat, which allows you to get and receive messages, get and receive files, and read news, bulletins, and other information.

BITNET   Because It's Time NETwork. An academic computer network based originally on IBM mainframe systems interconnected via leased 9600 bps lines. BITNET merged with CSNET, The Computer+Science Network (another academic computer network) to form CREN.

block [of data]   A group of bits, bytes, or records treated as a unit for storage, retrieval, or transmission. Typically a communications program will have a display as you send or receive telling you how many blocks have been transmitted, and how many bytes that comes to.

bps   Bits per second. A measure of how fast the data is streaming down the wire. Not exactly the same as baud rate. The difference, however, only matters to an engineer. In the old days, baud rate and bps rate referred to two very different things. Baud rate was the number of signals sent over a phone line in a second, while bits-per-second referred to the number of computer bits sent over the line. At modem speeds below 2400 bps, a baud and bit are very close in value, hence the two terms have blurred in meaning over the years. In popular parlance, baud rate and bps rate have come to mean the same thing—bits per second.

broadband   The ability of a network to carry many different network carriers on a single cable. It is a goal in some places, reality in others. ISDN is one broadband technology.

broadcast   A packet delivery system where a copy of a given packet is given to all hosts attached to the network. Example: Ethernet.

bulletin board system   1. a computer system set up to answer phone calls and respond to remote commands for exchanging messages and files; typically the system is based upon one machine with one operator. Many BBS are run by and for hobbyists and are free of charge to the users. Others are major commercial ventures with subscription fees and a network of microcomputers. Most play host to tight-knit, if clamorous communities of friends. When you log on to a BBS, deport yourself as if you were walking into the BBS owner's living room. With the development of mail echo systems such as FIDO, the line between networks such as the Internet and bulletin board systems is becoming blurry. 2. Rarely: a forum on an internet.

chat   When two or more people logged into a remote system can type messages to each other in realtime. Much less efficient than a telephone conversation, more confusing than a CB radio, and sometimes tending to language appropriate in a frat house, it is nevertheless popular. Some online services use chat to let users communicate with computer industry big shots.

CIX   The Commercial Internet Exchange (CIX) Association was formed in February 1991 by several commercial networks with access to the Internet mail backbone; the purpose was to allow their subscribers to have Internet-type connectivity without the non-commercial traffic rules. The CIX members are connected to the Internet backbone but can communicate with each other without traversing the Internet. Subscribing to a CIX member gives you private mail, Internet news access, and communication with people on other CIX systems. This is an example of the privatization of the internets.

crc   Cyclic redundancy check, a method of verifying that what was sent by your computer was received correctly by another computer, and vice versa. Some modem programs have this, some don't; some give you a choice. It slows things down, but makes your data a little safer from line noise and other transmission gremlins.

It works this way . . .

In a block of data, the first bit of the first byte is added to the second bit of the second byte, and so on, until a check character is computed. That is tagged along to the tail of the data block in communications. It is a crude form of error-checking. When the block is received by the PC at the other end of the communications link, the PC recalculates the whole mess to determine if the block has been transmitted accurately. Some error-checking protocols like Xmodem-CRC use this form of data checking, and they are considered more reliable than protocols, like old-fashioned Xmodem, that merely perform a checksum on the blocks (i.e., add the bits together).

CREN   The Corporation for Research and Educational Networking. CREN's address is: CREN Information Center; Suite 600; 1112 Sixteenth Street NW; Washington DC 20036; (202)872-4200. You must contact them before using the BITNET/CSNET system.

CSNET   Computer+Science Network. A large computer network, mostly in the U.S. but with international connections. CSNET sites include universities, research labs, and some commercial companies. Now merged with BITNET to form CREN.

cyberspace A term coined by William Gibson to describe his fictional computer systems implanted in characters' brains to give them instantaneous connection of all senses to a remote site. Often used loosely and improperly to refer to the online virtual communities as a whole. It's improper because Gibson made it up (and thus has copyright to it) and because Gibson's version involves all five senses in a gestalt indistinguishable from physical reality; early 1990s online communities involve only sight and sound, at most.

daemon (mail) This is part of the e-mail system that checks to make sure your e-mail is ok, and that it was delivered without errors. If there are errors, it will send you a message about it.

DDN Defense Data Network, made up of MILNET and other networks used by the DOD and its contractors. Not as dull as it sounds, but one of those networks where you have to prove you need it to get on. Some parts are classified.

DECnet A trademarked network system by Digital Equipment Corporation. Also, DEC's own archive system, from which you can request some Internet archive files. Set up a file of UNIX commands to request the file and mail it to *ftpmail@decwrl.dec.com*. Be patient; this is a busy archive.

domain Part of an Internet address, describing where in the hierarchy the message is going to or coming from. Examples of domains are .org for organizations and .com for commercial connections.

door A program for accessing some feature such as games or e-mail on a BBS quickly and efficiently.

download Receive electronically.

EARN European Academic Research Network. A network using BITNET technology connecting universities and research labs in Europe.

echo mail *See* mail echo

e-mail A message you send or receive electronically. This can include messages on a BBS, Internet, or online service; some people consider pagers, fax messages, voice mail and even cellular telephone services to be e-mail, too. Customarily, however, e-mail must be ASCII characters, not sound or a word processing format or a program. (Note: some services allow you to append an ASCII file to a non-ASCII file as you would a Post-It note to a diskette, and send them together. This uses a form of FTP with e-mail, but this happens in the dark to you.) No paper, ink or stamps are necessary to send such a message. Costs can be hidden, however, in subscription fees, taxes, university overhead, BBS sysop fees, or other funding sources. It ain't free.

error-checking protocol   A scheme for sending computer files in binary form (as opposed to ASCII) in which both sending and receiving computers perform calculations on the data to check that it has arrived intact.

etiquette   A set of rules dictating polite behavior in a society, often neglected out of ignorance because the rules might vary slightly from society to society. However, using a modem does not preclude using etiquette. To learn the proper online manners, politely request this file:

From: spaf@cs.purdue.edu

Newsgroups: news.announce.newusers,news.answers

Followup-to: news.newusers.questions

Archive-name: usenet-primer/part1

Original-author: chuq@apple.COM (Chuq Von Rospach)

Last-change: Date Month Year by spaf@cs.purdue.edu (Gene Spafford)

flame   1. verb: Writing a vigorous opinion and/or criticism of something or someone, ordinarily as a thoughtless, blistering statement shot off in fit of pique, and posted as an electronic message for all to see. It's sometimes ok to flame an idea, but flaming persons is tacky. 2. noun: A series of flaming messages. In the worst sense, an online temper tantrum. "I do not allow flames on this system," a sysop might say, "so get off my board!"

forum   Also referred to as a newsgroup (on USENET), a SIG (special interest group), and, occasionally, (on the Internet) a bulletin board, this is a public discussion group where experts and other members post messages to each other about a certain topic. Just as the Latin word means "open market space," this is the market for ideas. Business, legal, societal, even religious issues are aired in forums. It is proper etiquette to write only about the forum's topic; failure to do so might get you flamed. Some forums (SIGS, bulletin boards) have a members-only policy before you may post messages; in other cases you cannot even read the messages posted there without clearing it with the sysop.

fred   The interface and the login to the PSI White Pages, currently the only cross-network directory to Internet users.

front-end software   A program written and designed specifically to help you sign onto and use a certain online service. Many of them have graphical interfaces, simplified menus, extra help screens you can read offline, and other features. Some can be used as general-purpose communications software, as well.

ftp or **FTP**   1. noun: file transfer protocol, the Internet standard for how to get files from one computer to another. 2. verb: the act of transferring a file from somewhere else to yourself, or vice versa.

FTP is different from e-mail in that FTP can handle non-ASCII characters, so programs and compressed files can travel this way. That means viruses can, too.

furry   One example of a role-playing fantasy group. It's more than a game, it's sort of a lifestyle. See a description in the Internet chapter. If you can telnet, go to *128.2.254.22323*.

gateway   1. The earliest Internet term for what is now called IP router (or just router). Now, "gateway" and "application gateway" refer to programs which translate from one native format to another. Examples include X.400 to/from RFC 822 electronic mail gateways. 2. a way to connect to a database or network through a first database or network. CIS has a gateway to DIALOG. A bulletin board system may have a gateway (or door) to the FIDO network.

gigs   Sysop shorthand for gigabytes.

gigabyte   A billion bytes.

glossary   In this book, a list of tricky, technical, or foreign terms found in the electronic underground, with the author's definitions or translations, in an alphabetical listing. As the definitions are very opinionated in this glossary, they are to be taken with a grain of salt. For a serious, technical glossary, request RF1208, "A Glossary of Networking Terms" by Jacobsen and Lynch; or RF1118, "The Hitchhiker's Guide to the Internet" by E. Krol; or RF1206, "Answers to Commonly-Asked New Internet User Questions" by Malkin, et. al, from any major Internet or USENET archive site.

handle   Your nickname on a particular system. This can be philosophically meaningful or meaningless; it can be easier to type than your real name, or harder. While some people use it to protect their privacy, it is often a way to hide behind the modem, and some sysops do not allow them.

host   Someone nice enough to let you use his machine for access to an internet. To be a purist about it, the actual machine is the host, and it is the main computer of a system or network. But some person or persons will be doing the programming and flipping the switches to make the machine work.

For BBS, this is the system and sysop that send your mail echo on to its destination(s). For internet systems, it is the backbone, or the place to which or through which you telnet or FTP. The use of the word host implies you are a guest. Remember that.

HSLINK   A modem protocol which is high-speed, bidirectional, and has batch file transfer with full-streaming-error-correction. Each side of the link is allowed to provide a list of files to be sent. Files will be sent in *both* directions until both sides of the link are satisfied. Written by Samuel H. Smith, and released in 1991, it's challenging to learn, but a major advance in modem protocols. It is a shareware program.

ID   Your identity on that particular system. This could be your real name, an acronym of your name, a totally fictitious handle, or a string of letters and numbers assigned to you by the sysop.

Internet   With a capital I. The latest incarnation of the original ARPANET. It is partially funded with tax dollars, partially supported by computer industry giants (in the form of equipment and labor), partially supported by research and educational organizations. It has strict rules about what can go over the system, and in some cases, who can use parts of it. It is the largest internet in the world and includes the big national backbone nets (such as DDN, NSFNET and CREN) and various regional and local campus networks all over the world. To be "on" the Internet, you must have TCP/IP connectivity (i.e., be able to telnet to—or ping—other systems). Networks with only e-mail connection are not precisely "on" the Internet, but to the casual user that's connected enough.

internet   With a lowercase i. Any collection of two or more networks interconnected by routers that allow them to function as a single, large virtual network. This can be as small as one company, middling as a state-wide educational internet, or international as EARN.

Internet Society   This users' group for the Internet was formed in August 1991, an outgrowth of the old Internet Activities Board (IAB). Its goal is to be a source of information and assistance to researchers on the Internet, continue discussing and refining OSI and TCP/IP, and help the various agencies and bodies who actually run the Internet.

interrupt   Transferring the control of the computer from one program to another. In hardware, the interrupt, like a whiney child, demands the CPU's attention turn to some device or program. The computer, like a harried mother, is interrupt-driven. Your peripherals each have an assigned interrupt: the video card, the modem, the printer, the keyboard, the mouse, etc. The computer has a system of prioritizing interrupts, however, occasionally these ostensibly inanimate objects have an annoying tendency to fight over interrupts with results quite maddening to the user.

IRQ   All I know is that if your COM is 4, your IRQ has to be 3, and vice versa. Why is beyond me: I think it's a guy thing, like power tools.

ISDN   Integrated Services Digital Network. A set of standards for data transmission, it will eventually allow us to send and receive signals and data from our telephone, computer, fax, television, and electronic mail over our phone lines. It will require digitized telephone service from your local phone company, a digital telephone instrument at your house, and an adapter to run all these on one line, and simultaneously at that. It's being tested in certain cities (Huntsville, AL is one) right now.

JANET   Joint Academic Network, in the United Kingdom. In the US, it is accessible by e-mail via BITNET.

JUNET   Japan's UNIX Network. As with JANET, you exchange e-mail with JUNET via BITNET.

Kermit   A modem protocol that varies the size of the blocks and checks for errors in transmission. It is a standard protocol included with many communications programs.

knowbot   An Internet server program from the CREN to look up the e-mail address of some people on some networks. Knowbot's address is *netaddress@nri.reston.va.us*. Send a message with the name of the person whose Internet address you would like to know as the first line (with no leading spaces at all). If you happen to also know the service that person uses, or the country, or the organization, you can add:

Person's Name

service mcimail

country US

org AAA

Notice that the service is in lowercase and the organization is in uppercase; that matters to the knowbot. For a list of knowbot commands, send an e-mail message with a question mark on the first line. Knowbot will mail you a help file. *See* whois.

login   The process of identifying yourself to a remote computer, and being granted access. This will involve your ID, your password, and possibly your credit card number.

mail echo   A BBS feature for your electronic messages. If you put the "echo" flag on a message, the text will be forwarded to at least one other BBS, perhaps thousands worldwide. The flag designates the interest groups and mail echo network to receive the message. On the Alabama Echo, for instance, you could aim a message at discussions about legal issues, hiking, photography and others; you could even send it to a combination, if it is a legal issue concerning photography, for example. Be careful, however, to echo the message only to the groups who would be truly interested, or you will be flamed by the group sysops (also called moderators) for being "off-topic!"

manners   Deportment in reference to polite conventions; remembering the needs and feelings of others. The use of a modem does not excuse the lack of good manners. For a satiric look at the results of forgetting one's manners, look for the file

"Emily Postnews Answers Your Questions on Netiquette"

Original-author: brad@looking.on.ca (Brad Templeton)

Archive-name: emily-postnews/part1

Last-change: Day Month Yr by brad@looking.on.ca (Brad Templeton)

Any system or archive worth its salt has a copy to download.

martian   The facetious term for a packet that turns up accidentally on the wrong network because of spurious routing entries. Also used when the packet has a totally fictional Internet address. It happens.

menu   A display of a set of commands for the program you are running from which you can choose at the moment. In menu mode, valid choices for a command to enter are presented to you, sometimes with optional subcommands. In command mode, you are presented with a prompt and have to remember the correct keystrokes yourself. As Judy Heim says, "The selection of choices presented to you by the remote system is often as expensive and worded as inscrutably as those on the menu of the local Chez Le Michel."

NEARNET   A regional internet, which is being considered for a connection to BIX.

newsgroup   A forum on the USENET.

network   1. in hardware: any set of electronic components connected in a way to allow them to work together for specific functions. This can include a set of computers directly connected by wires; or your computer, connected to telephone lines to other computers; or a combination of many other components and circuitry. Also described as a hierarchical distributed system. 2. people and their machines that communicate with each other at discrete but fairly regular intervals to exchange information, e-mail and data files.

NREN   National Research and Education Network. Funded by VP Albert Gore's High Performance Computing Act of 1991, this will be a high-performance computer research and development network, targeted for completion in 1996. It will, according to its proponents, be 30 times faster than the NSFNET, using ISDN and fiberoptics to connect even the most rural locations and smallest elementary schools to the major universities and research centers in the U.S.

NSF   National Science Foundation. Federally funded, its many goals include forming a national internet comparable to the interstate highway system: accessible to everyone, funded by local, state and federal taxes, and built according to certain specifications. Sponsors of the NSFNET, they definitely have other fish to fry as well.

NSFNET   National Science Foundation NETwork. A collection of local, regional, and mid-level networks in the U.S. tied together by a high-speed backbone. NSFNET provides scientists access to a number of supercomputers across the country such as ASN, the Alabama Supercomputer Network. To some, this is the Internet cake, and all the other networks are just frosting. However, it may be superseded by the NREN.

NYSERnet   New York State Educational Resource network, a statewide internet.

offline   The state of not being connected to a network, online service, BBS or any other computer. The best time to be reading and composing e-mail if your front-end software or mail door supports it.

online   The opposite of offline; the state of being connected to a network, online service, BBS or any other computer. Often costs you dollars each minute.

online service   A for-profit enterprise offering chat, a database or set of databases, e-mail, gateways to other services, forums, information storage and retrieval, and other services, or any combination of these, for which the users are billed. As they offer the chance to interact with other users both real-time and with e-mail, they are often called "networks," but this is as much in the human, social sense, as the computer hardware sense. Examples include Prodigy, America Online, CompuServe and GEnie. Some are not connected to anything but their own subscribers (like Prodigy); some have Internet e-mail connections (like AOL); some have gateways to other services (As CIS does to ZiffNet).

OSI   Open Systems Interconnection. The set of communication standards that competes with TCP/IP to be THE standard.

packet   A group of data a communication program bundles together according to its protocol for the most efficient shipping across the line.

packet switching network   How you dial faraway online services with a local number. The data going to and from your computer or terminal is divided into "packets," each of which is sent by the most efficient route at that split second. This all happens "in the dark" to you; but it might interest you to know that when you are "on" America Online, you are really talking to a packet-switching network, such as Tymnet, which is talking to AOL, which is talking to the network, which is talking to you. X.25 is a standard for packet-switching networks, and is sometimes used as a synonym. "I have access to an X.25 network" is a specific way of saying "I have access to a packet switching network."

parallel port   A connection from your computer to a peripheral where the data is sent in groups of 7 or 8 bits simultaneously down several wires of a cable. Many printers and modems have parallel ports.

password   A set of letters, symbols and/or numbers that identifies you as the authorized person to use your account on a BBS, an internet, or an online service. As this special set of characters should be known only to you, it is best not to use a word that can be found in the dictionary, or any permutation of your name or a relative's name. An example of a good password would be A/PR23IL$—"April" with numerals and symbols mixed in.

ping   A lovely little onomatopoeia. An acronym for Packet INternet Groper (note the male adolescent tinge), it's an echo of sonar technology. Just as a submarine sends out a "ping" to get an echo from any ships around it, you send out a signal to a computer to see whether it answers, and how. It is used as a verb: "Ping the host, maybe it's up now."

protocol   1. a standard format for exchanging data. 2. a set of rules to follow for an internet, which can be as delicate and intricate as diplomatic protocol. 3. an error-checking method.

remote   Not where you are. Perhaps, far away. If you're connected by some communication line to the company computer, which happens to be down the hall from your terminal, your connection is "remote." Ditto if the main computer happens to be across the continent, or over the ocean. Ditto if you are using your microcomputer to run another computer, wherever it is.

RFC   Request For Comments. A collection of documents, stretching back to 1969, which contain the Internet suite of protocols, Internet standards, and many historical and informational papers relating to the Internet. All Internet standards are written up as RFCs, because they are developed by first asking the technocrats on the Internet to submit by e-mail their wisdom and opinions on the subject. However, not all (in fact very few) RFCs describe Internet standards; some are much more interesting.

rlogin   The UNIX command for remote login. Strictly, this is a specific program service offered by Berkeley UNIX for running someone else's computer from your own at a different site; as a practical matter, the Berkeley version has many imitators. When it is active, it seems your computer and the remote one are directly connected. It is comparable to TCP/IP's telnet.

rotate 13   A way to make sure a message is read only by those who are willing to work at it. The message is transcribed into a simple substitution code:

A B C D E F G H I J K L M

N O P Q R S T U V W X Y Z

Thus the word "question" in rotate 13 becomes "dhrfgvba". UNIX has a command to do this automatically. It is used to protect the punch line of a joke, the end of a book or movie in a review, or possibly offensive material. Such an encoded message will have Rotate 13 or R13 in its header.

router   A system that decides which way a packet will get from sender to receiver. It uses a routing protocol to get information on network system traffic at the moment, and an algorithm to choose the best route. A router is useful but not infallible. *See* martian.

serial port   A connection from your computer to a peripheral where the data will be sent one bit at a time down the wire. Often, a mouse will connect to a serial port.

server   A computer that distributes its resources, such as printers and files, with other computers on the network. Those machines using the resources are "clients."

SIG   Special Interest Group. *See* forum.

site   A specific place in a domain. eff.org is the site of the Electronic Frontier Foundation in the organization domain.

smileys   Little faces drawn with punctuation marks so people can tell:

when you're joking :-)

when you're unhappy :-(

when you're disgusted :-P

or just confused :-\

(Tilt your head to the left to get the full effect.) Also, abbreviations for stage directions to your messages such as <<g>> or <<grin>> for a smile or

<gd&r> for "grin, duck, and run." There are smiley dialects in different sites across the underground. Poke around in the libraries to see if someone has uploaded a dictionary of smileys for that system.

snail mail   Messages sent on paper through a physical distribution system, e.g., United States Postal Service or a parcel service. Used to distinguish from e-mail.

stuffit   A slang term from the copyrighted compression software for MacIntosh computers. *See* zip.

synchronous   A mode of sending data where the blocks are sent at set, regular intervals. Unlike asynchronous, it does not require start and stop bits.

sysop   The System Operator, one who administrates a network or forum or BBS. Not exactly a policeman, but as Tony Lockwood puts it, "the 300-pound gorilla." What the sysop says goes as far as that particular system is concerned.

TCP/IP   The name of the standard protocols allowing all the different systems of the Internet to communicate with each other. OSI is a different standard. The protocol standard wars continue. Read "The Simple Book" by Marshall T. Rose.

telnet   The virtual terminal protocol in the Internet suite of protocols. It is comparable to the UNIX rlogin. It allows users of one host to act as normal terminal users of another host. It is, incidentally, one way viruses are deposited on unsuspecting systems. For this reason, few online services allow real telnet (or rlogin) commands. You must have permission and know what you are doing to use this.

THEnet   The Texas Higher Education Network, an example of a statewide internet. It uses more than one protocol. THEnet connects most major academic and research institutions in Texas, as well as some institutions in Mexico. It is attached to and accessible by the Internet.

thread   A series of messages on the same subject, constituting a discussion among two or more people. It's okay to add to a thread, just be sure to introduce yourself first; it's just like joining in a conversation.

UNIX   AT&T's trademarked set of communications protocols and utility programs for computers. Also, a way of life for certain programmers.

upload   To send electronically. *See* download. (I have never understood why the computer nerds felt compelled to invent new words for "send" and "receive," as those words not only existed but also are easily comprehended. Oh. I guess that's the reason!)

USENET   A set of discussion and news e-mail on the Internet. It's supposed to be a network for sending and receiving useful information. Some of it actually is. UNIX is the societal norm on the USENET, and many messages need UNIX programs such as uuencode and uudecode to be read.

UUCP   The UNIX program UNIX-to-UNIX Copy Program. Used extensively in the USENET. Trademark of AT&T.

whois   An Internet server program to query a database of people and sites on a particular part of the network. Another such program is knowbot.xmodem: one of the very first modem protocols for individual users (as opposed to the Internet). Written by Ward Christensen, it sends the data in blocks of 128 bytes. The original version let errors slip through and was very slow. Then CRC was added, and it got a little faster and more accurate. It's reliable, established, and a classic. XMODEM-CRC should be your choice when sending a file over especially bad phone lines. Almost any communications program you get will have an xmodem option.

X standards   OSI data communication standards for different network functions. X.500 is the OSI standard for directories; X.25 is a packet switching network standard used by public networks like SprintNet and Tymnet; X.400 is a message handling system.

ymodem   Chuck Forsberg's successor protocol to Ward Christensen's xmodem. It sends data in blocks of 1024 bytes. It's faster than xmodem, and a standard inclusion in many communications programs.

zip   A slang term for compressing a file, making it take up less room on a disk and take less time to send or receive over a modem. From the copyrighted software PKZIP and PKUNZIP.

zmodem   A modem protocol, it is Chuck Forsberg's one-up on ymodem. It adjusts the size of the blocks and the error checking to how well your modem and the line are handling the data stream. If the phone line is noisy, however, it's no faster than xmodem or ymodem. It will also check the size of the file and abort the transfer if you don't have enough disk space. It's included in many newer communications programs.

Index

Glossbrenner's Guide to Shareware for Small Businesses
—Alfred Glossbrenner

Now, in as little time as one hour, you can use a personal computer to keep track of your customers, ride herd on your inventory, and run your business with a degree of control you may have only dreamed about. This valuable book/disk package clears away the misconceptions surrounding today's computer jargon and products, offers solid advice on how to select IBM-compatible hardware, and reviews and recommends dozens of today's hottest shareware programs—all at the lowest possible prices! 432 pages, 64 illustrations, 5.25" disk. Book No. 4059, $27.95 paperback, $37.95 hardcover

Memory Management and Multitasking Beyond 640K
—Lenny Bailes and John Mueller, Foreword by John C. Dvorak

Extend or expand your memory options for your IBM PC or compatible with this in depth guide to breaking the 640K barrier. Even if you can't afford expensive memory expansions, the authors will show you a variety of ways to get the most bang for your buck out of applications and operating systems software. 456 pages, 140 illustrations, 5.25" disk. Book No. 4069, $29.95 paperback, $39.95 hardcover

Norton pcAnywhere™: The Complete Communications Guide
—Jack Nimersheim

Avoid the headaches associated with learning a new software package with this quick-start guide to pcANYWHERE™. You'll configure pcANYWHERE and customize it for computers or networks you regularly communicate with . . . learn to send and receive data and take remote control of a computer . . . and automate your on-line activities to streamline access and response—saving you money when accessing such services as CompuServe, GEnie, and Delphi. 320 pages, 137 illustrations. Book No. 4175, $19.95 paperback, $29.95 hardcover

Norton Desktop® for Windows® 2.0: An Illustrated Tutorial—
Richard Evans

"Evans tells the reader virtually everything necessary to use the Norton Utilities . . . Recommended."
*—**Computer Shopper** on a* previous edition

This example-packed guide gives you step-by-step, illustrated instructions for using each Norton Desktop library—including valuable troubleshooting advice and solutions to common problems. Evans, whose previous books on the Norton Utilities have sold more than 50,000 copies, not only shows you how to optimize the Norton Desktop Utilities, he also demonstrates the use of Norton Disk Doctor and Norton Backup. 240 pages, 109 illustrations. Book No. 4208, $19.95 paperback, $29.95 hardcover

80386/80486 Assembly Language Programming—Penn Brumm and Don Brumm

A sheer masterpiece and a thorough reference . . . worth every penny."
—Computing

Spending too much time writing assembly language code? Why reinvent the wheel when two of the industry's leading assembly language experts have compiled and documented the most complete set of fully tested, ready-to-use 80386/80486 programs and routines available? Penn and Don Brumm have put together this convenient, time-saving handbook that will give you the type of reusable, error-free code you need to develop reliable, high-powered applications for today's state-of-the-art PCs. 592 pages, 203 illustrations. Book No. 4217, $29.95 paperback, $39.95 hardcover

DR. Batch File's Ultimate Collection
—Ronny Richardson

Boost productivity, enhance DOS performance, and save hundreds of unnecessary keystrokes with this practical library of programs—no programming skills required. Assembled here and on the FREE 3.5" companion disk are over 120 of the most useful batch files available for creating and using keyboard macros, saving and reusing command lines, tracking down viruses in COMMAND.COM, and much more. 440 pages, 146 illustrations, 3.5" disk. Book No. 4220, $29.95 paperback, $39.95 hardcover

Builder Lite: Developing Dynamic Batch Files—Ronny Richardson

With this software and Richardson's accompanying user's manual, even beginners will be able to build and test sophisticated batch files in as little as 10 minutes. Richardson's step-by-step tutorial demonstrates how to write batch files that manipulate displays, create menus, make calculations, customize system files, and perform looping operations. This isn't a demo package, either. Builder Lite was developed by Doug Amaral of hyperkinetix, inc., especially for this book. 368 pages, 61 illustrations, 3.5" disk. Book No. 4248, $32.95 paperback, $44.95 hardcover

Bit-Mapped Graphics—2nd Edition
—Steve Rimmer

Create intricate graphics and more with the ready-to-run code in this bestseller. Featuring complete, easily portable source code in C and assembly language, this desktop guide demonstrates the mechanics of working with bit-mapped graphics in different formats and on a wide variety of computer hardware. Widely regarded as the bible of graphics programmers, this book is a valuable source of ready-to-use program code and easy-to-follow explanations for one of the most complex and poorly documented areas of software development. 496 pages, 117 illustrations. Book No. 4266, $26.95 paperback, $38.95 hardcover

Build Your Own486/486SX and Save a Bundle—2nd Edition—
Aubrey Pilgrim

This hands-on guide makes it possible for you to build your own state-of-the-art, 100% IBM-compatible PC for about one-third of the retail cost or less with little more than a few parts, a screwdriver, and a pair of pliers. So don't shell out huge sums of money for a PC at your local retail outlet. This book will allow you to enjoy the speed and power of a 486—and still put food on the table. 256 pages, 58 illustrations. Book No. 4270, $19.95 paperback, $29.95 hardcover

Networking With LANtastic®
—Michael S. Montgomery

With this instructive book you'll have an easy-to-read alternative to the program documentation—a comprehensive guide to setting up and running an efficient, high-performance LANtastic network. The author describes proven techniques for sharing files, printing, and using peripherals. Focusing on ways to configure LANtastic to meet specific needs and ensure maximum productivity, he shows you how to plan and design networks, install LANtastic software, use program functions and menus, and more. 632 pages, 199 illustrations. Book No. 4273, $22.95 paperback, $34.95 hardcover

Mac Online!: Making the Connection—Carla Rose

Get to know the Macintosh telecommunications scene with this comprehensive online primer. Carla Rose, well-known columnist for *Portable Computing*, makes Mac telecommunications simpler, more productive, and more enjoyable for all users. You'll explore modems and cables, commercial and shareware telecommunications software, online services, bulletin boards and BBS networks. E-mail, and more. 448 pages, 100 illustrations. Book No. 4296, $24.95 paperback only

LAN Performance Optimization
—Martin A.W. Nemzow

Resolve your most stubborn network performance problems with this practical resource for LAN managers and consultants. This book/disk package will help you locate and eliminate bottlenecks in local area networks quickly. The diagnostic tools provided are equally effective with Banyan Vines, Novell Netware, UB Access One, Unix, Sun, NFS, IBM LAN Server, Microsoft LAN Manager, Ethernet, Token Ring, and FDDI network operating systems. 230 pages, 90 illustrations, 5.25" disk. Book No. 4310, $29.95 paperback only

Prices Subject to Change Without Notice.

Look for These and Other TAB Books at Your Local Bookstore

To Order Call Toll Free 1-800-822-8158
(24-hour telephone service available.)

or write to TAB Books, Blue Ridge Summit, PA 17294-0840.

Title	Product No.	Quantity	Price

☐ Check or money order made payable to TAB Books

Charge my ☐ VISA ☐ MasterCard ☐ American Express

Acct. No. _____ Exp. _____

Signature: _____

Name: _____

Address: _____

City: _____

State: _____ Zip: _____

Subtotal	$	_____
Postage and Handling ($3.00 in U.S., $5.00 outside U.S.)	$	_____
Add applicable state and local sales tax	$	_____
TOTAL	$	_____

TAB Books catalog free with purchase; otherwise send $1.00 in check or money order and receive $1.00 credit on your next purchase.

Orders outside U.S. must pay with international money in U.S. dollars drawn on a U.S. bank.

TAB Guarantee: If for any reason you are not satisfied with the book(s) you order, simply return it (them) within 15 days and receive a full refund.

BC

YES! I want to try EZ-E-Mail electronic mail service. Send my free software!

Name _____
(Please print.)

Company _____

Address _____

City _____ State _____ Zip _____

Please indicate the diskette format you need.

☐ 3.5" diskette
☐ 5.25" diskette
☐ Mac Version
☐ PC Version

Have you used other electronic mail services? ☐ yes ☐ no

If yes, please indicate which ones:

_____

_____

I understand I'm under no obligation. If I decide not to subscribe to EZ-E-Mail electronic mail service, I owe nothing.

Detach and mail

Compare!

EZ-E-Mail offers many cost-effective features.

▲ There is no charge for EZ-E-Mail software — ever!

▲ You pay only a **fixed monthly fee**. There are no message-unit fees or extra charges for sending the same message to multiple addresses.

▲ Each account can have **multiple users** at no additional charge.

▲ You compose messages **before** you connect to the service to minimize telephone charges.

▲ You can select **offhours delivery** to take advantage of low-cost offhours telephone rates.

john@anywhere NH1 com

EZ-E-Mail is simple to use.

▲ Pulldown menus guide you through every EZ-E-Mail function.

▲ Use your favorite text editor. There's no need to learn another editor.

▲ Full documentation and online help are included. Online help can be accessed from the main menu bar, or press F1 at any time to display information related to the selected item.

▲ Telephone technical support is available between 8 AM and 5 PM Eastern Time.

See for yourself. Send for your FREE SOFTWARE today.